Memories of a Cuban Kitchen

Mary Urrutia Randelman and Joan Schwartz

Color photography by David Bishop

Macmillan • USA

Memories of a Cuban Kitchen

MACMILLAN
A Simon & Schuster Macmillan Company
1633 Broadway
New York, NY 10019

Library of Congress Cataloging-in-Publication Data

Randelman, Mary Urrutia.
    Memories of a Cuban kitchen / Mary Urrutia Randelman and Joan
Schwartz : photography by David Bishop.
        p.   cm.
    ISBN 0-02-860998-0 (pbk edition)
    1. Cookery, Cuban.   2. Cookery—Cuba.   I. Schwartz, Joan.   II. Title.
TX716.C8R36   1992
641.597291—dc20   92-23633   CIP

10 9 8 7 6 5 4 3 2 1

Printed in the United States of America

To my mother and grandmother

Contents

Acknowledgments

Many are the people who made this book possible. They are all intertwined in the history of Cuba, my life, my family, and my friends during the course of this century. They brought together their experiences and recollections for this book. Many, many thanks are due to all of them.

To Jeff Degen, whose relentless efforts led me to Jane Dystel; to Jane Dystel, my terrific and energetic agent who believed in the project from the start and guided me at every turn; to Joan Schwartz, who enthusiastically compiled hours of tapes and notes about Cuba and heard my voice from proposal to final manuscript; to Pam Hoenig, our editor at Macmillan, for her insight and encouragement; to Justin Schwartz for his dedication to the project. Special thanks go to the University of Miami, Special Collections, especially to Esperanza de Varona, who searched through the treasures of Cuban history looking for background material.

To my loving family: my grandmother (Mama Nena), whose fresh recollections of the past generations, told in detail large and small, were the invaluable foundation of this book; Hilda Mas

(Titi), whose confections fulfilled the fantasies of my childhood; Dr. Ildefonso Mas (Tio Ilde) for his beautiful photographs; Carmen Sampedro Mas (Tia Mani), whose beautifully handwritten recipe books were a pleasure to read and translate; and José Sampedro (Pepe), for his memorable stories.

To those relatives and friends who opened up their homes and hearts to me, offering recipes, recollections, and anecdotes: Gladys Besu (Chicha); Roberto Besu; Luis Fernandez; Miguel, Yolanda, Yoyo, and Chiqui Balais; Olga Martinez-Montiel; Gustavo and Aurora Lopez-Muñoz; Guillermo Fernandez; Maria del Carmen Echevarria (Rosalie's granddaughter); and Rosa Arocha Ferrán.

To my friends, whose encouragement and criticism were indispensable during our many testings: Geraldine Serbe, my knowledgeable and unofficial assistant; Harold Streitman, for his reviews and inspiration; Billie Taylor, who sees the possibilities in all things; Michael Nichols, the dearest and best; Lee Bobker and Nona Bleetstein, for the belief that you can do anything you set your mind to.

To my wonderful brothers and sisters: Tony, Ralph, Mary Helen, Annie, and Cali, who are all passionate cooks and who shared their specialties with me. Most of all I am so glad we got to share this life together! Thanks to my cousins: Drs. Ilde, Cecilia, and Ralph Mas, and Carmen Iturralde, who contribute to the joy of our families.

To my beloved grandmother (Abuela Ina); my kind and gentle grandfather (Abuelo Mas); my splendid aunt (Tia Yeya); and to Rosalie (Rosalie Galves). Memories of them lived with me throughout my writing of this book.

To my wonderful in-laws, Roslyn and Milton Randelman, who understood the magic and laughter of Havana; and to my stepchildren, Craig and Nicole, who think I am the best cook in the world.

To my loving mother, whose liberating presence and unconditional love gave us the freedom to grow and express ourselves. To this book, she added her admirable passion for food and life, which is her unique spirit.

Most of all, to my wonderful husband, Hal, who with one hand stirs the soup and with the other, holds my heart and all my love.

Introduction

Lo que bien se quiso nunca se olvida.
That which you greatly loved never is forgotten.

Cuba, the magical island where I was born, was a paradise—a place of dazzling light, tropical breezes, and starry nights. After I left, I searched for the same magic all over the world, and, to my delight, I found hints of it everywhere—in a garden in Paris, on a boulevard in Barcelona, in the aroma of chestnuts on New York's Fifth Avenue. I know now that the magic lives in me. It is my love for Cuba, never to be forgotten, deep and indescribable.

The last time I saw Havana I was ten years old. In my child's perception, it possessed a kind of mythic beauty, with its broad, tree-lined avenues and grand turn-of-the-century buildings and monuments standing brilliant in the sunlight. Its air was clear and bright, smelling of the sea. Its sounds were joyful, a mixture of automobile horns, trolley-car bells, the calls of lottery vendors and snack vendors, the clink of coffee cups in the sidewalk cafés, and the music of street bands.

I spent all my childhood summers there in perfect freedom, released from my boarding school. Aunt Titi, my mother's young, unmarried sister, filled her Jeep with laughing nieces and nephews and conveyed us from one end of the city to the other. Titi loved Havana almost the way we children did. She delighted in taking me with her to shop for shoes at the "California," in the center of the busiest shopping area, where she bought stylish pumps and I was outfitted with summer sandals—and where the salesman rewarded my good behavior with San Bernardo ice cream. I accompanied her to the couturier for her many fittings of stylish party dresses and to El Encanto and Fin del Siglo, the elegant department stores. Then we would stop for a "mile-long hot dog" at a shop called Coney Island, across the street from CMQ, Havana's main television network.

Our drives would take us through the center of town, where we were surrounded by the beauty of ornate cathedrals and grand monuments and plazas. Our favorite was *la fuente de la India* where, just a stone's throw from the colossal capitol building, Neptune sat with his dolphins, surrounded by spray that seemed to crystallize in the sunlight. The avenues were dotted with statues of heroes and patriots: José Martí, Máximo Gómez, and Christopher Columbus stood larger then life in bronze and stone. Architectural gems lined the boulevards, the National Theater being one of the most elegant and extraordinary.

Havana's most famous boulevard was the Malecón, a broad, modern ribbon winding parallel with the ocean, along which you could stroll, watching the street vendors by day and the lovers by night. In the early part of the century it had been mostly residential, but later on offices and hotels were built there, many in the Bauhaus style that became so popular in 1950s' Havana.

El Prado, another famous street, was reminiscent of a European boulevard, enormously wide and beautifully designed, with an allée of trees, old street lamps, and benches. The symmetrical buildings were neoclassical beauties, possessing an elegance and order reminiscent of French architecture, with grand stone pillars and balustrades encrusted with relief work. El Prado had been a residential area in the mid-1800s, but when I was a child, it was filled with shops and restaurants.

Many excellent restaurants dotted the city, serving foods that ranged from Spanish to Italian to French: La Zaragozana was famous for the shellfish prepared by its Spanish chef; El Monsignor, near the Hotel Nacional, where Angelito, the charming maître d', made sure his regulars got the best tables while they enjoyed the romantic music of violins, was popular with tourists as well as Cubans; La Plaza de la Catedral was filled with Hollywood stars and international glitterati; La Reguladora, popular with the tobacco brokers, was the place my grandfather would meet his friends for lunch and stay on, deep in conversation, until ten at night; El Frascati, in the Prado, was known for its Italian antipasto and its Cuban *yemas en Marsala,* a dessert rich with custard and Marsala wine; El Carmelo, in the Vedado section, was convenient to the Riviera Theater and the Sociedad pro Arte, the home of musicals, opera, symphony orchestras, and ballet. And there were many others, including Havana 1800, La Roca, El Pacifico, El Miami, El Paris, El Jardin, and Centro Vasco, later reborn in Miami, menu and all.

For children, one of the greatest attractions was the humbler F. W. Woolworth's, which had come to Havana in the early 1920s, settling into a block-long store nestled among the old buildings on Havana's busiest and noisiest corner. Cubans always referred to it as the *tencen,* Havana slang for ten-cent store. I enjoyed going there for lunch and shopping for American Ginny dolls.

Every Havana restaurant had its special aroma, and Woolworth's lunch counter was perfumed by toasted white bread. Waitresses served us chicken salad sandwiches on "American bread," followed by gooey banana splits. The lunch counter was always jam-packed when Titi or my mother arrived with the children after a morning of shopping, but the long row of patrons, shuffling noisily, managed to rise and move down a seat or two to accommodate us. It was a routine we all expected, for Cubans would never be impolite to a woman with children.

The most popular gathering places of all were the lively outdoor cafés near the capitol, where people stopped for snacks or lingered over strong Cuban coffee or cocktails as the bright afternoon sun began to set, providing Havana's most stunning visual effect. The magnificent sunsets never disappointed, with their fiery changing colors and, finally, the gently fading light, signaling that evening had come and soon the city would burst into fantastic color. Luminous fountains that flowed crystal clear all day magically splashed red, yellow, blue, and orange under colored lights at night. Now was the time for the adults to shine, while we children stayed at home watching American television shows.

Havana's nightlife was lively, with private parties, restaurants, and nightclubs. As for music, Havana moved to the ardent Afro-Cuban beat which, when fused with jazz, resulted in the magic of Dizzy Gillespie, and was also made famous by Hollywood personalities such as Xavier Cugat and Carmen Miranda (neither of them Cuban). Celia Cruz, a young black beauty (today called "the queen of salsa"), was a popular singer in the 1940s.

Havana's residential neighborhoods were absolutely beautiful, reminiscent of those near the Borghese Gardens in Rome, the Bois de Bologne in Paris, and the Serrano in Madrid. The University of Havana School of Architecture had followed the teaching of the School of Beaux Arts in Paris for nearly a century, and the results were ornate mansions mixed with what came to be known as neo-colonial houses. Later, sleek modern homes in the Bauhaus style were added to the scene. Birthday parties and frequent visits to relatives would take us to all the city's neighborhoods, such as El Vedado, Miramar, and Kohly.

A common sight in all these neighborhoods was *el Caballero de París* (the Gentleman from Paris), a long-haired, bearded eccentric dressed in a flowing robe. No one knew who he really was or where he had come from, although it was rumored that he had once been a divinity student at the university, but it was common knowledge that he wandered the streets constantly. Our unfounded fear of this man was comical, as we fled from the gardens and crouched on the floor of the car whenever he came near. Anyone who was a child in Havana in the early 1950s remembers him with a grin.

All children think their parents are wondrous, and my brothers, sisters, and I were no different. Our mother was and still is delightful and bright and our father possesses great charm and wit. Their lives in Cuba were filled with joy and vitality and their schedules were filled with activities. My father was active in local politics in the province of Pinar del Río, and my mother taught English to underprivileged children and kept busy with her family. Their circle of friends was large, creating constant movement, but I knew when Mom was near by the scent of Shalimar in the air. And we children were busy as well, darting between school in Pinar del Río and vacations in Havana.

Quite unexpectedly for me, one of the stops on our active schedule one summer was the American Embassy in Havana. As my grandmother's chauffeur dropped us off at its door, I asked, "Why are all these people standing in line?" My grandmother replied softly, "They are getting papers to go to the United States and we must get ours, too." I smiled at the prospect of a great adventure, not knowing it would alter drastically the course of our lives.

Accompanied by Aunt Titi and Grandmother Ina, we children arrived in Miami on the S.S. *Florida* in June 1958. Our parents had preceded us by several months, and our new home was ready for us. Our parents and aunt, who knew the city well from previous trips, took us to the movies, to Pickin' Chicken, which featured American fried chicken in baskets and drinks with little paper parasols, and to the miniature golf course that adjoined it. It seemed like a delightful vacation and quite temporary, until I entered my new school and reality set in.

My mother says that of all the children, I complained the most. I hated the window screens that made our house seem like a prison. I hated my room, which was normal by anyone's standards. I pleaded to be taken back to Cuba, where, I said, dollhouses were bigger than my new room. But Mom gently told me that we could not return to our home. "Never look back," she said. "Sometimes a broken toy can't be put together again." Then she usually delivered a speech on character building, to which I was tearfully oblivious.

The first day of school was my first experience with fear. I couldn't communicate with my schoolmates or understand my teachers, and I looked different from everyone else. While I wore a proper schoolgirl plaid dress, the other girls bounced around in puffy skirts buoyed by crinolines. I was shod in cordovan saddle shoes and neat socks and the other girls were bare-legged in low-vamped shoes, the creases between their toes showing like décolletage.

At lunchtime I was accompanied into the cafeteria by a kind soul named Judy who had two-toned hair—blond with visible black roots. As we moved our lunch trays along the counter, a uniformed woman wearing a hair net dropped a glob of white, pasty substance on my plate and covered it with a ladleful of thick, brown liquid. I recognized neither. I knew fish was being served because I could smell it, but I had never seen a square fish like the one she next tossed onto my plate. Curiously, I examined the leafy green balls she dished out—I had never been close to brussels sprouts, either. The only recognizable food on my tray was Jell-O, which, along with chocolate cake, became my lunch.

That afternoon I walked home from school with my brothers, carefully following the route we had walked with Mom the previous week, during our rehearsal for school. Mom was now a saleswoman at Burdine's department store, and couldn't pick us up in the afternoons. When we arrived home, we found a note announcing that she would have to work late, along with a box of Uncle Ben's rice and Mom's directions, in Spanish, for preparing it. Now we were the cooks!

Our dinner was very successful, and in a short while we proudly became Mom's prep chefs. She taught us to slice onions and peppers for *sofrito*, to marinate snappers in olive oil and lime juice, and to make meat loaf—Cuban style, of course. As our duties also included picking up bread and milk at the grocery store, we started buying the American products that we recognized from television commercials. For a while, it seemed that Mom had created culinary monsters, for we began preparing macaroni and cheese, stuffings, and pancakes from packaged mixes. Happily, this was just a stage in our adjustment to America, and we soon returned wholeheartedly to the Cuban dishes we loved.

We all made it over the hump, Mom was right. I found friends, Ralph made the Little League team, Tony was on every school committee, and my little sisters, Mary Helen and Annie, soon forgot all their Spanish. Most important, the family was together, with the sad exception of my grandfather, who had not been allowed to emigrate. Miami was different from Cuba, but the emotions were like old times.

As children in prosperous, postwar Cuba, we had inhabited a very special world. We had lived a joyous, hopeful, and privileged life, but there was a price to be paid for our privilege. People who left Cuba with me tell many tales of hardship, separation from loved ones, and difficult adjustment to a strange new place. Hardest to bear, by far, was the loss of our country. Had I remained in Cuba longer than the first ten years of my life, no doubt I would have had a political point of view, but I left with a child's perceptions and memories, and I treasure them.

My youngest brother, Calixto, was born in Miami and I always tell him how much I wish he had known Cuba with us. I try to paint a picture of our life for him, so he will understand our deep feeling of country. These stories and recipes are written for Cali, and for my young nieces, nephews, and cousins who have never seen Cuba. For them and for other Cuban-American children, I hope to keep the traditions of Cuban life and food alive.

Our personal wealth is our memories. We, as Cubans, are endowed with riches to have experienced the real and inexplicable — the fantasy of Cuba.

La memoria es la dueña del tiempo.
Memory is the guardian of time.
CREOLE SAYING

Mary Urrutia Randelman
New York City, 1992

Cuban Cooking

Cuban food provides me with a constant reminder and a true picture of the country I left in 1958. Cuba's diverse culture is a fascinating mixture of Old-World grandeur and Caribbean color, and the dishes I prepare and serve reflect these qualities.

This book offers an introduction to a rich and varied cuisine. The dishes that appear in each category—appetizers and snacks; soups and stews; meats and poultry; fish and shellfish; rice, beans, and eggs; salads and vegetables; desserts; and drinks—best represent everyday Cuban cooking, although because of space limitations, not every one of the many Cuban recipes I love could be included. Consider this collection to be just a sampling of a huge national treasure.

The Cuban style of cooking commonly called Creole, or *comidas criollas*, is an amalgam of tropical and European elements. It is based on the white sweet potatoes, squash, corn, and yuca that had been cultivated by early Taino and Siboney Indian inhabitants and later were adopted by the African slaves; on Spanish saffron, rice, beans, and *sofritos* (simmered sauces) combining garlic, onion, pepper, and tomato; on Indian and Chinese culinary contributions; and, finally, on the fish, meats, vegetables, and herbs native to our island.

Cream and béchamel sauces, pilafs, and dishes prepared *a la Milanesa* entered the cuisine as adaptations of their European counterparts, but today they too are considered Cuban food. And American cooking of the 1950s was a major influence, one that hangs on tenaciously.

In the 1950s, Cuban housewives wanted to cook like American housewives, and so they embraced canned vegetables and fruits (in this land of fertile farmland), processed cheeses (when the best homemade cheeses came from our dairies and kitchens), and newly invented recipes (with classics all around them). Canning became an important Cuban industry at that time, so our own canned products were easily available, in addition to American imports. Ana Dolores Gómez was a famous Cuban cooking teacher and television personality (her program was called *La Cocina Frigidaire*—Frigidaire Cuisine) on whom many women of my mother's generation relied. Reading her voluminous lecture notes and recipes today, I feel transported to an earlier world of women's magazines and family cookbooks, where mayonnaise, aspics, gelatin molds, canned fruit cocktail, and canned vegetables were celebrated. The processed cheese concoctions that appeared on American television commercials during that decade were popular in Cuba as well.

But overall, Cuban cooking is a peasant cuisine that is fairly unconcerned with niceties of measurement, order, and timing. Simple techniques and ingredients, such as tangy lime juice or sour orange juice marinades and fragrant *sofritos*, appear throughout and a cook can improvise, guided by the tastes and textures of the foods themselves.

Fritters, puffs, and croquettes are quickly and simply fried over high heat (lard is the traditional medium, but I substitute olive or vegetable oil). Soups and stews simmer in *sofrito* together with soaked dried beans, fresh plantains, corn, squash, fish, or meat. Meats and poultry are marinated in citrus juice and then are braised or roasted until very tender and falling off the bone—except for burning, it is hard to ruin them. In fact, anything less than over-cooking often is insufficient, since our dishes are marked by rich flavors that take a lot of cooking time to blend and mellow. Red snapper receives a citrus marinade and then is baked, while other fish is marinated and then grilled, or fried quickly in olive oil. Rice combined with beans, chicken, fish, or shellfish is simmered with *sofrito*. Cornmeal is mixed or layered with mixtures of *sofrito* and crabmeat, chicken, or pork. Eggs are stirred with *sofrito*, ham, chorizo, or plantains and quickly cooked into chunky omelettes. Salads are rarely leafy; either they are based on simple avocado or they consist of chicken, seafood, or fruit mixed with mayonnaise. Plantains, white sweet potatoes, okra, and squash are the most common fresh vegetables, and pimientos and canned peas are ubiq-uitous as garnishes. Spices are added to all foods according to taste since Cuban dishes, although highly seasoned, are not spicy. But every Cuban restaurant places a bottle of Tabasco sauce on your table, in case you want to make adjustments. Although Havana's pastry shops offered elegant French-style desserts, at home we pre-pared flans and puddings, as well as sweets based upon sweet potato, orange, coconut, banana, or guava. These were sugar-rich but otherwise simple. And our famous daiquiri, a quick shake of Bacardi rum, lime juice, and sugar, was the cocktail of choice.

These facts notwithstanding, I have provided fairly detailed in-structions for preparing the dishes of my childhood. This is to give non-Cubans and others who are meeting these dishes for the first time an idea of how the foods will look, feel, smell, and taste each step of the way. Once the new cooks have become acquainted with the repertoire (and it won't take long), they may confidently rely on their own good judgment in the kitchen.

The latest generation of talented young chefs in and around the Cuban-American community does just that. Experimenting with our traditional cornmeal, *picadillo*, red snapper, and desserts, imaginatively preparing our healthful, flavorful root vegetables, grilling plantains on the barbecue instead of boiling or frying them, these cooks are creating a new Cuban cuisine that flows logically from its source. And they are proving that true classics can lend themselves to innovation.

Glossary of Cuban Ingredients

Aji Cachucha, **Rocatillo, or Scotch Bonnet Pepper:** Small, round, green, red, or yellow hot pepper, very strongly flavored.

Aji Picante, **Hot Pepper:** Any small, hot home-grown pepper that many Cubans substitute, to taste, for *aji cachucha;* usually *pequin* or tabasco.

Avocado: Large, green-fleshed, pear-shaped fruit with a buttery texture, used in Cuban salads.

Bacalaito: Small codfish fritter, made with desalted codfish.

Bacalao, **Salt Cod:** Salt-preserved dried fish often used in Cuban recipes. To desalt and cook cod, follow these steps:

1. One day in advance of serving, rinse the salt cod under cold running water. Break it into large chunks, place in a bowl, and cover with cold water.

2. Change the water several times until it is no longer salty. This process should take 24 hours.

3. Drain the fish, place it in a small saucepan, cover with fresh water, and bring to a boil over medium-high heat. Lower the heat to low and simmer 5 minutes. Drain and cool the fish, remove any skin and bones, and flake. It is now ready for your favorite recipe or it can be frozen for later use.

Banana:

RED CUBAN — small, fat, and purplish red, its flavor is richer and its texture creamier than that of the yellow banana.

CHICADITA, LADY FINGER — a sweet, miniature yellow banana.

Beans, Dried Black: Cuban staple, often combined with white rice to make *Moros y Cristianos.*

Beans, Dried Red: Cuban staple, often combined with white rice to make *Congrí.*

To prepare dried beans, follow these steps.

1. Rinse the beans in cold water, pick over, and soak overnight in cold water to cover by 1½ to 2 inches. The next day check that the water is still covering the beans by 1½ to 2 inches, and add more water if needed. Do not add salt.

2. Pour the beans into a large saucepan and bring to a boil over high heat. Reduce the heat to low and cook, uncovered, until tender, about 2 hours. One cup dried beans will yield approximately 2½ cups prepared beans. See individual recipes for more specific instructions.

Depending on their quality and freshness, beans will vary in the amount of cooking time needed and the amount of liquid they will absorb. Check them while cooking and add more water or stock if necessary.

Bijol: Condiment used to give rice a yellow color, containing cornflour, ground cumin, and food colorings. It is often substituted for the more expensive saffron.

***Boniato,* Cuban White Sweet Potato:**   Often sold in Florida as Florida yam, it has thick, brown skin and white, mealy flesh and tastes like a combination of the white potato and the American sweet potato. It can be boiled, fried, pureed, or made into *boniatillo* (sweet potato paste), a sweet dessert.

Bread, Cuban: An oblong or round crusty bread similar to French and Italian breads, but with a coarser texture. See page 44 for the recipe.

***Calabaza*, Pumpkin:**   Also known as West Indian pumpkin. A large, round squash (not a gourd) with firm, orange flesh and a sweet flavor, it is added to soups and stews, boiled and served as a vegetable with garlic sauce, or made into a custard. It is sold in precut chunks at Hispanic markets. Butternut and Hubbard squash are good substitutes.

Capers: Pungent buds of the caper plant, packed in brine, used to season chicken and beef dishes. Spanish capers are the plumpest and best-tasting.

Cazuela: A heavy, round cast-aluminum casserole used for frying, stewing, and boiling. It ranges in size from very small (just large enough to hold two croquettes) to very large (used to make rice for twenty). Available at Hispanic markets.

Cazuelitas* or *Cazuelitas de Barro: Small, round, glazed earthenware casserole of Spanish origin, used for individual baked egg or rice dishes. Available as "individual Iberian bowls" at the Williams-Sonoma shops or through the Williams-Sonoma *A Catalog for Cooks*.

Chorizo: Smoked pork sausage, highly seasoned with garlic and paprika, Spanish in origin. It is available in small (2-inch), medium (4- to 5-inch), and large (7- to 8-inch) sizes and comes canned in lard, dried, or plastic-wrapped. It is often prepared with rice, beans, or eggs, or served alone as an appetizer. Any spicy garlic sausage, while not exactly the same as chorizo, may be substituted.

Coconut: Fruit of the coconut palm, with a hard, brown shell and white, edible meat surrounding a liquid center. Both the meat and the "milk" can be used in desserts and drinks. Preshredded coconut meat can be purchased at supermarkets or Hispanic markets.

Cracker Meal: Fine meal sold at Hispanic markets or made from crushed saltine crackers and used for breading. Thirty-six to 38 single crackers, crushed in a food processor, yield 1 cup cracker meal.

Cumin: A pungent seed used whole or ground in Cuban cooking.

Empanada: Fried or baked pastry turnover, stuffed with chicken, meat, or fish.

Escabeche: Pickled or marinated dish, such as swordfish *escabeche.* Food is first cooked and then marinated in oil and vinegar.

Fruta Bomba, **Papaya:** Fruit with yellow-orange flesh and skin and black seeds. When ripe, it is soft to the touch. It is eaten out of hand or used in desserts, salads, ice cream, milk shakes, or other drinks.

Guava: A green, oval fruit with sweet, pink flesh. When ripe, it is soft to the touch. It is eaten out of hand or used for jellies and preserves, and also is made into syrup, pureed marmalade, drinks, and ice cream.
GUAVA PASTE — a sweet preserve used in desserts and pastries, is sold in 13-, 16-, and 18-ounce loaves in Hispanic markets.

***Harina de Maiz,* Cornmeal:** Ground kernels of dried corn. Cuban cornmeal, which can be found at Hispanic markets, is more finely ground than American, but when it is unavailable, regular ground cornmeal can be used. In Cuban recipes, cornmeal is boiled and then eaten as a porridge, baked, or combined with fish, meat, or chicken. It is important to start cornmeal cooking in cold water, not boiling water. It should then be brought to a boil, whisking frequently to prevent sticking. To prepare cornmeal, follow these steps:

1. In a medium-size, nonstick saucepan, combine cornmeal with cold water in a ratio of 1 to 6, whisking to blend. Bring to a boil over medium-high heat, whisking constantly until thickened.

2. Cover and simmer over low heat 15 to 20 minutes, until thickened.

***Jamón,* Ham:** The ham most often used in Cuban recipes is a steak called *jamón de cocina* (cooking ham), sold in chunks at Hispanic markets. Regular ham steak can be substituted.

***Limón,* Lime:** The primary citrus fruit in Cuban cuisine. Lime juice is used for marinating meat, fish, and poultry, and for flavoring in many Cuban recipes. Cubans often refer to limes as "lemons" in casual English.

***Malanga, Yautía,* Taro:** A root with white flesh and brown skin which turns slightly gray when boiled. Its flavor resembles that of the white potato and it is used in the same way. It is boiled, deep fried, or added to soups. *Malanga amarilla* is a yellow-fleshed variety.

Mango: A large yellow, orange, or red fruit with a sweet, peachlike flavor. When ripe it has brown spots and is soft to the touch. It is eaten out of hand or used in drinks, ice cream, sorbet, salads, mousses, marmalade, and chutney.

Ñame, Tropical Yam: A large tuber that sometimes can reach a weight of a hundred pounds, with thick skin and white, yellow, or red flesh that is slightly sweet. It is used in *Ajiaco Criollo* (Cuban Creole Stew).

Okra: Vegetable with green, beanlike pods with gummy consistency, used in soups and stews. Frozen okra may be substituted for fresh. When buying fresh, be sure to buy the smallest unblemished pods.

Orange, Sour: The seville orange, a bitter citrus fruit whose juice is used in marinades. When sour orange juice is not available, substitute half sweet orange juice, mixed with one-quarter fresh lime juice and one-quarter lemon juice. Seville oranges are available at Hispanic markets.

Oregano: Aromatic herb used dried, usually ground.

Pimientón, Paprika: Sweet-to-spicy ground pod of a red pepper. Spanish in origin, used to flavor sauces and chicken and meat dishes. Spanish paprika, used in Cuban dishes, is mild in flavor.

Plátano, Plantain: A relative of the banana, which it resembles, although its flesh is thicker and its fruit is larger and not as sweet. Plantains can be prepared when green, ripe, or very ripe. They are technically fruits, but are used as vegetables in Cuban cuisine.

GREEN PLANTAINS — are unripe and very hard. They are usually sliced into slivers and deep fried to make *mariquitas* (plantain chips) fried twice to make *tostones* (twice-fried green plantains), and boiled and added to soups and stews.
To peel green plantains:

1. Cut off both tips and cut in half crosswise.

2. Make four lengthwise slits, making sure the knife goes through the flesh.

3. Peel off each section of skin.

YELLOW PLANTAINS — usually having some dark spots, are medium-ripe and semisoft and are used for soups and stews, or boiled and eaten as a vegetable.

BLACK OR DARK BROWN PLANTAINS — are fully ripe and very soft. Baked with butter, sugar, nutmeg, and wine, they become *plátanos a la tentación* (baked sweet plantains). Fried, they are called simply *plátanos maduros fritos*. They also can be served cut into chunks, boiled in their skins, and served as a vegetable or side dish.

Rum: An aged liquor made from the molasses that comes from sugarcane. Bacardi rum originated in Cuba and is the most popular brand among Cubans. It is labeled light — for the lightest blend — through dark, reserve, añejo, and black — the richest blend.

Saffron: Yellow-orange spice used to give color and flavor to rice dishes. The dried stigma of the saffron crocus, it is very expensive, but is used sparingly.

Sherry: A fortified Spanish wine that ranges from dry to sweet, with a nutlike flavor. The finest extra-dry sherry, such as La Ina, is my choice for fish dishes and desserts, while any good quality dry sherry or cooking sherry can be used for all other dishes.

Sofrito: Sauté of onions, tomatoes, pepper, garlic, herbs, and spices, used as the basis of many Creole dishes.

Tasajo, **Salt-dried Beef:**   Preserved beef that must be desalted before it is cooked. To prepare *tasajo,* follow these steps.

1. Cut the beef in half, place it in a nonreactive bowl with water to cover, and soak it overnight, changing the water several times.

The beef does not have to be refrigerated while soaking.

2. The next day, drain the beef and discard the soaking water. Place the beef in a large saucepan with fresh cold water to cover and 1 bay leaf, bring to a boil over high heat, then reduce the heat to low and cook, covered, until tender, 1 to 1½ hours (some cuts of *tasajo* are drier than others and will take longer to cook). Remove the meat from the saucepan and allow it to cool at room temperature. Two dishes using *tasajo* are *Tasajo a la Cubana* (Stir-fried Dried Beef) and *Aporreado de Tasajo* (Salt-dried Beef Stew).

Tocino, **Slab Bacon:**   Smoked bacon sold unsliced and used for seasoning.

Tomatoes: Originally, fresh tomatoes were used in Cuban cooking, but in the 1950s canned or prepared tomato sauces became popular as a basic ingredient of many Cuban dishes. Today, good-quality canned plum tomatoes, crushed tomatoes, or tomato sauce are most often used.

Yuca, **Cassava:**   A root vegetable with starchy flesh and a bland, potato-like flavor. It can be boiled, added to soups, made into fritters or croquettes, or fried as chips or chunks.

Travels with Titi: Appetizers and Snacks

Every summer, as soon as school was out, we left Puerta de Golpe for Havana, where we were swept into rounds of social events under the direction of our Aunt Titi. Our days were filled with birthday parties, swimming, roller skating, and dates with Titi's friends at the yacht club to watch regattas and tennis and swim tournaments.

My mother's beautiful young sister delighted in showering attention on me and on my brothers Ralph and Tony. In her new yellow convertible, she drove us all over Havana and to events at the Havana Yacht Club, the Miramar Yacht Club, and the Vedado Tennis Club. Laughing with delight, we sped along the broad avenues with the car's top down and Titi's long scarf flying in the breeze à la Grace Kelly in *To Catch a Thief*. Titi always seemed more American than Cuban, dressed in Bermuda shorts, casual cotton shirt, and sunglasses purchased on her many trips to the United States.

Titi concerned herself with my wardrobe as well as with her own, and before each day's outing, she saw to it that I had enough clothing packed to last a week. I was given bathing suits for before and after lunch, a lunch outfit, an afternoon outfit, and a pristine little dress to carry me through an afternoon party. Although she left dressing duties to the nannies, she always did my hair, combing it as I stood obediently still in front of her dressing table. She pulled my blond hair into a neat ponytail, stroking it perfectly into place and securing it with an elastic band pulled so tight that my eyes looked slanted. She then sprayed any wisp that dared to poke out of this arrangement and finally covered my whole head with a coat of hairspray, turning my hair a shade darker because of the lacquer. Coiffure completed, I scurried to the car to begin an active day.

The Havana Yacht Club was my favorite playground — even the approach, a long, wide boulevard bathed in salty sea air, was glorious. Our drive to the entrance took us right through the club's stately marble gates, where we were greeted by Felix the doorman, deeply tanned and resplendent in white livery. He knew everyone by name, from the white-haired patriarchs to the sun-bronzed children running noisily in all directions. Felix ushered us into an extraordinary tropical garden of pink oleander, bright red cannas, and long, yellow rocket flowers.

Havana Yacht Club. Reprinted with permission of the Richter Library of the University of Miami.

*My godmother Rosita Arocha with friends on the staircase of
the Havana Yacht Club in the early 1950s.*

Set in the middle of this vibrant foliage, the palatial white stone
clubhouse, with its wide, breezy verandas, overlooked the sea. It
was a grand, impressive edifice. Transpose the Paris Ritz to a
broad, sun-swept beach and you will have an idea of what the
Havana Yacht Club was.

Perhaps it was the ocean air, or even our happy mood, but we
children found the food at the yacht club incomparable. After a
morning of swimming and practicing diving from the high board,
we waited for the adults to begin lunch in the dining room. Then we
bounded into the snack bar, where a "proper lunch" was not required. We were greeted by the irresistible aroma of freshly fried
potato chips, hot, crisp, and generously heaped in napkin-lined
baskets. (According to club legend, when chips were introduced in
the 1930s they were served only at the men's bar. If a woman
wanted to enjoy some, she had to shout her order to the bartender
from a respectable distance.) Sitting at our table, we devoured
mountains of these salty, crackling gems while we considered our

menu options. Hot, fresh *mariquitas* (green plantain chips,) although second-best to the potato chips, were another welcome treat.

Alongside the chips were placed baskets of crisp croquettes *(croquetas)* filled with smoky creamed ham and splashed with lime juice. After gobbling as many mouthfuls as we could handle, we moved on to our main course: steaming, flaky chicken turnovers *(empanadas)*, or perhaps a perfectly grilled Cuban sandwich *(sandwich Cubano)*. We finished with ample scoops of freshly made coconut ice cream mounded high in half a coconut shell. The freedom of these unplanned meals—which were simply course after course of appetizers—added to our summer fun.

After lunch our parents required us to stay out of the water for two hours, but if we pestered Aunt Titi sufficiently and disrupted her canasta game, the law was waived. She shooed us away, making us promise to shield our fair skin from the sun so her indulgence wouldn't be discovered.

Lunch at the Havana Yacht Club in the early 1950s, Aunt Mani on the left.

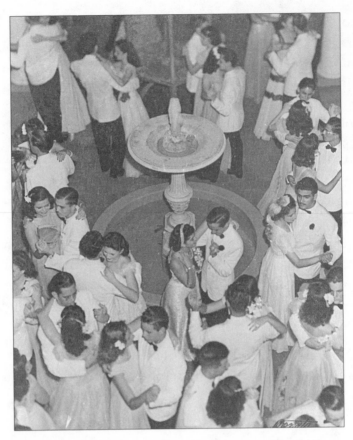

A formal dinner dance at the home of my Aunt Mani (Carmen Sampedro).

Late in the afternoon, we usually found ourselves at a birthday party, often as not for a child we didn't even know. Scores of cousins, as well as the nieces and nephews of Titi's friends, invited us to celebrate at their clubs or their homes. And a birthday party was not simply a matter of sharing some ice cream and cake; we were fed handsomely on all manner of finger foods and appetizers.

Bocaditos, or tiny mouthfuls, were the ubiquitous party food. These little sandwiches came in many varieties: chicken salad moistened with mayonnaise and dotted with chunks of hard-boiled eggs;

pink ham studded with pimientos; pimiento-stuffed green olives with cream cheese; salty ham with bland Swiss or muenster cheese; delicate asparagus with chicken; creamy shrimp or lobster salad; and even sliced cucumber and watercress—an homage to "American" canapés. They were cut into rounds, squares, triangles, or stars, and some more elaborate *bocaditos* were made to look like playing cards, with pimientos and olives providing their pictures and numbers. Ribbon sandwiches and pinwheel sandwiches were assembled in layers, frosted with cream cheese, and decorated with pimientos.

We also were offered quantities of croissant-shaped pastries filled with ground spicy sausage *(cangrejitos)* and small puff pastries *(pastelitos)* filled with savory meat hash *(picadillo)* or sweet guava paste *(guayaba)*. Stuffed with snacks, we still managed to consume an elaborate birthday cake and petit fours.

The adults had their own refreshments at these parties. To the abundant finger food they added cold-cut platters *(entremés)* consisting of sliced ham, loin of pork, cold meatloaf *(carne fria)*, chicken salad, or an elaborately molded fish pudding *(pudín de pescado)*.

MERIENDA *AND THE LAST EMPEROR*

Merienda, the Cuban afternoon tea, is a meal made up entirely of appetizers and desserts. Coming between lunch and late-evening dinner, it offers another opportunity for gathering together and sharing conversation and it becomes a social event in its own right. At my cousin Pepe's home in Havana, *merienda* was raised to an art form, and it is his version that I remember most clearly.

Pepe lived in the Vedado section of Havana, a quiet old neighborhood where classic mansions were guarded by wrought-iron gates and night watchmen. His parents' house had started with a single story, but as the family grew, so did their home—into a sprawling, two-story, twenty-five-room compound. The grounds were magnificent, with formal clipped hedges, a tennis court, and manicured topiaries.

My cousin José — Pepe — was the late-arriving, only male child in a family of five grown-up, doting sisters and their children. In the eyes of his worshipful father, Dr. Sampedro, he was heir to the throne. In fact, he was treated like a prince and that delighted all his cousins, because whenever we visited him, we became a part of his kingdom.

Afternoons with Pepe usually began in his courtyard, where all the cousins would play spirited games of tag and then, dipping our bare hands into the splashing fountain, try to catch the shimmering carp as they darted back and forth. When our *tatas* (nannies) felt we were getting too rambunctious, they led us to Pepe's room and we happily followed. Our cousin inhabited a museum of the best that F.A.O. Schwarz had to offer, grand and glorious toys selected by his father on frequent trips to New York City and augmented by telephone orders from Havana. Beneath the American college pennants that decorated his four walls, we played with an array of games, puppets, and vehicles and watched Spanish versions of "I

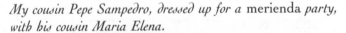

My cousin Pepe Sampedro, dressed up for a merienda *party, with his cousin Maria Elena.*

Pepe with his sister Mani and her baby, and a family group, at the afternoon house.

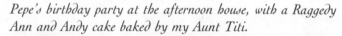

Pepe's birthday party at the afternoon house, with a Raggedy Ann and Andy cake baked by my Aunt Titi.

Love Lucy" and "Highway Patrol" on his state-of-the-art television set. The only oddities in this pleasure palace were Pepe's plastic Howdy Doody and Peter Pan dolls, which had been sterilized in boiling water by his zealous mother and deformed for life.

When we had had our fill of games, we were ushered downstairs to the formal dining room for *merienda*. Our little heads barely showed above the dark, polished dining table as we took our seats and politely turned to our host. Seated at the head of the long table, Pepe was in his glory, reaching into two huge Venetian, dolphin-footed bowls and passing out pinecone-shaped lollipops flavored with maraschino cherries *(pirulis)* and thin, crisp wafers dipped in chocolate *(Africanas)*.

Soon steaming trays began appearing from the kitchen, borne by a parade of indulgent maids and cooks, and Pepe and his court were served a variety of teatime treats. First came the tiny *croquetas,* fried croquettes filled with cream sauce and bits of smoky ham. As we sank our teeth into their perfectly crisp crusts, we had to breathe quickly through our mouths to expel the steam. Then came the *bocaditos,* many stuffed with Pepe's favorite asparagus paste. Often as not the parade of snacks ended gloriously with *cangrejitos* fetched by Agustin, the family's chauffeur, from El Carmelo, a popular Havana restaurant.

When we rose from the table after *merienda* the party was not yet over. Cousins, nannies, Pepe, and Agustin all piled into cars for a twenty-minute drive to the "afternoon house," a country house that Dr. Sampedro had built especially for his grandchildren and his young son, where costume parties were de rigueur.

As we drove through the gates protecting the house, the adult world was left behind. We entered a fairyland of gardens, fruit trees, rare orchids, a winding river, and a sparkling creek, where pony carts awaited our pleasure. We spent wonderful hours in that paradise, playing games, smashing toy-filled piñatas, climbing on the jungle gyms, and swinging high on the sturdy swings. None of us has ever forgotten this child's dream world created for us and our cousin to enjoy.

And how did Pepe fare in the real world? Along with us, the Sampedro family left Cuba and settled in Miami. I don't know how his confusion and his pain compared to mine, but his recovery is a story worthy of the magic kingdom. Pepe as a grown man is a totally generous and nurturing soul who reflects the kindness he was raised on. He is now a social worker and his life is devoted to helping handicapped children. I think he is still dipping into over-flowing bowls and sharing his lollipops and cookies.

CUBAN SNACKS IN THE UNITED STATES

Although we have all grown into adulthood and restraint, today we eat in America very much as we did in Cuba. Most Cubans will tell you that we have two food groups: party food—made up of snacks—and real food, complete meals built around fish, chicken, stews, and soups. We seem to consume more of the former, partly because our parties are not occasional, but ongoing. In the small Cuban communities in the United States, birthdays, weddings, an-niversaries, showers, and christenings, along with the regular cal-endar of holidays, are celebrated with great fervor. A Little League game, a dance recital, or a day of boating will bring out entire families and involve complicated menus. For these occasions large buffets consisting of appetizers are either prepared or store-bought.

Like Havana's bakeries before them, Miami's Cuban bakeries are famous for their finger foods, selling *croquetas, cangrejitos, pastelitos, empanadas,* and many variations of *bocaditos.* They also sell *bocadito* fillings *(pastas de bocadito)* so you can prepare your own "tiny mouth-fuls" at home.

Even when there are no parties, such foods are eaten throughout the day, much in the manner of American fast food. Folks in a hurry will stop by a kiosk and get a Cuban coffee and *croquetas* or *pastelitos de carne* or *guava. Frituras* (fritters) and *mariquitas* (chips) are con-sumed with cold beer at small stands where workers stop to drink and talk. A platter of *entremes* often serves as a quick lunch at a luncheonette and a Cuban sandwich is the fast food of choice in South Florida.

When I am far from Cuban shops and restaurants, I find it easy to prepare these foods at home, and they make ideal dinner-party appetizers, cocktail nibbles, and buffet platters. To American cooks, Cuban appetizers and snacks are a delightful introduction to the style of the Cuban kitchen.

Aceitunas Aliñadas

OLIVES IN OIL

This simple olive preparation was always on hand in our house to accompany cocktails. I keep a large jar of it available for the same purpose and also to add to salads for interesting taste and texture. You can vary the recipe by adding a bit of your favorite herb or spice or, for a little fire, one dried chili pepper.

You can easily double or triple this recipe and pack the olives in attractive jars for gift giving.

1½ cups unpitted green Spanish olives in brine, drained and rinsed
½ cup pure Spanish olive oil
2 tablespoons red wine vinegar
1 bay leaf, broken into pieces

1 clove garlic, unpeeled and crushed
Freshly ground black pepper to taste
Peel of 1 lemon, without the white pith, whole or in large pieces
½ teaspoon cumin seed, optional

Mix all the ingredients together in a nonreactive bowl, cover, and refrigerate at least 2 days. Bring to room temperature before serving. The olives will keep, refrigerated, for several weeks.

MAKES 1½ CUPS

Papitas del Yacht Club

YACHT CLUB POTATO CHIPS

More like manna than potato chips, these were the favorite of children and adults at the Havana Yacht Club. The chips were served hot and crisp from the kitchen, wrapped in snowy linen napkins. As my brother Tony and I sat in the snack bar, basket after basket passed into our hands and went quickly back to the chef for refills.

I have made only one change in the classic recipe: I fry the potatoes in peanut or vegetable oil, rather than the original lard.

4 large baking potatoes, peeled   *Salt to taste*
Peanut or vegetable oil for frying

1. Using a mandoline adjusted to the thinnest cutting width, slice the potatoes paper thin, and immediately place the slices in a large bowl filled with cold salted water.

2. In a deep fryer or a frying pan over medium-high heat, heat 2 to 3 inches of oil to 375° F, or until a slice of potato sizzles when it touches the oil. Drain the potato slices, pat them dry with paper towels, and fry a handful at a time, turning with a slotted spoon until brown and crisp. Do not fry too many chips at once, or the oil temperature will fall and the chips will be soggy rather than crisp. Drain on a paper-towel-lined platter, transfer to a serving bowl, sprinkle liberally with salt, and serve hot.

MAKES ABOUT 4 CUPS OF CHIPS

Mariquitas de Plátanos

GREEN PLANTAIN CHIPS

These tasty chips are the ubiquitous snack in the Caribbean and although they are now commercially packaged, there is no substitute for the original, homemade variety. The chef at Islas Canarias, a popular restaurant in Miami, gave me the secret for his marvelous plantain chips: The oil must be perfectly clean and the temperature hot enough so that the chips become golden when they are "just dunked."

2 large green plantains, peeled (see pages 9–10) and cut into paper-thin slices

Peanut or vegetable oil for deep frying
Salt to taste

1. Place the plantain slices in a bowl, cover them with cold water, and soak 30 minutes. (If you are frying right away, you do not need to soak in water.)

2. Drain the slices and pat dry with paper towels. In a frying pan or deep fryer over medium-high heat, heat 2 to 3 inches of oil to 375° F, or until a slice of plantain sizzles when it touches the oil, and fry the plantain chips a handful at a time, turning them with a slotted spoon until they are golden brown and crisp. Do not fry too many chips at once, or the oil temperature will fall and the chips will be soggy rather than crisp. Drain on a paper-towel-lined platter, transfer to a serving bowl, sprinkle with salt, and serve hot.

MAKES 2 TO 2 1/2 CUPS OF CHIPS

Mariquitas de Yuca

YUCA SHAVINGS

There seems to be no end to the uses clever Cuban cooks can find for yuca. The bland tuber lends itself to soups, stews, fritters, and these delicate, tasty snacks, which are perfect with cold drinks.

2 large yuca, peeled (see page 11)
Peanut or vegetable oil for frying

Salt to taste
½ cup Mojo Criollo (recipe follows) or juice of 1 lime

1. With a vegetable peeler, pare the yuca lengthwise to get long shavings, discarding the stringy core. Fill a large bowl with cold salted water and soak the shavings until ready to fry.

2. Preheat the oven to 250° F. Heat 2 to 3 inches of oil in a deep-fat fryer or frying pan to 375° F over medium-high heat, or until a yuca shaving sizzles when it touches the oil. Drain the yuca, pat dry with paper towels, being careful not to break the shavings, and fry 6 to 8 shavings at a time, turning them with a slotted spoon, until golden brown, and keep hot on a paper-towel-lined platter in the oven. Do not fry too many shavings at once, or the oil temperature will fall and the shavings will be soggy rather than crisp. Place in a serving bowl, sprinkle liberally with salt, and serve hot, accompanied by the *Mojo* for dipping or fresh lime juice for sprinkling.

MAKES 4 SERVINGS

Mojo Criollo

CREOLE GARLIC SAUCE

Mojo criollo is not for the faint hearted—it is a truly potent garlic sauce, although most of the variations served at American-Cuban restaurants are only poor imitations. *Mojo* is served with *Mariquitas de Yuca* (Yuca Shavings, see previous recipe), with most pork and chicken dishes, and with root vegetables. It is traditionally made with lard, but I prefer to substitute pure olive oil. This sauce can be made in advance and reheated as needed.

6 to 8 cloves garlic
1 teaspoon salt
1 medium-size onion, very thinly sliced

½ cup sour (Seville) orange juice or ¼ cup sweet orange juice and ⅛ cup each fresh lime and lemon juice
½ cup pure Spanish olive oil

1. Using a mortar and pestle or a food processor, crush the garlic with the salt to form a thick paste.

2. In a mixing bowl, combine the garlic paste, onion, and juice, and let the mixture sit at room temperature for 30 minutes or longer.

3. Minutes before you are ready to serve the *mojo*, heat the oil over medium-high heat in a medium-size pan until it is very hot, add the garlic mixture (do this quickly because it will splatter), stir, and serve immediately. To reheat, simmer over low heat until heated through, 6 to 8 minutes. The sauce keeps several weeks refrigerated.

MAKES 1 CUP

Frituras de Yuca

YUCA FRITTERS

Leftover yuca often became part of this tasty appetizer at home in Cuba and Miami. You can add minced fresh parsley, coriander, or ham to the basic recipe, and further spice it up with Mojo Vinegreta (garlic dip; the recipe follows).

If the salt and pepper called for seem excessive, remember that yuca has very little natural flavor, and that the finished fritters should be highly seasoned.

1 pound yuca, fresh or frozen (see page 11)
2 tablespoons pure Spanish olive oil
1/2 cup minced scallions, the white bulb and tender part of the green stem
2 cloves garlic, finely chopped
2 large eggs, lightly beaten
1 tablespoon finely chopped fresh parsley

1 to 2 teaspoons salt
1/2 to 1 teaspoon freshly ground black pepper
1/4 teaspoon baking powder
1 teaspoon minced fresh coriander (cilantro), optional
1/4 cup chopped ham, optional
Peanut or vegetable oil for deep frying
Mojo Vinegreta (see page 28)

1. If you use fresh yuca, peel and cut it into chunks, place it in a medium-size saucepan, cover with salted water, and boil over medium-high heat until tender but not mushy, about 30 minutes. Drain the yuca and remove the stringy center portion. If you use frozen yuca, cook it whole according to package directions, then cut it into chunks and remove the stringy core.

2. In a small skillet, heat the oil over low heat until fragrant, then cook the scallions and garlic, stirring, 3 to 5 minutes, until tender.

3. Place the remaining ingredients (except the oil and mojo vine-

greta) in a food processor fitted with a steel blade, and pulse on and off until smooth. Refrigerate the mixture, covered, for 30 minutes.

4. Preheat the oven to 250° F. Bring the mixture to room temperature. In a heavy-bottomed skillet or deep fryer over medium-high heat, heat 2 to 3 inches of oil to 375° F, or until a drop of batter sizzles when it touches the oil, and fry 1 tablespoon of batter. Taste for seasoning, adjust if necessary in the remaining batter, drop the mixture by tablespoonfuls into the hot oil, and fry the fritters until golden brown on all sides, turning with a slotted spoon. Do not fry too many fritters at once, or the oil temperature will fall and they will be soggy rather than crisp. Place the fritters on a paper-towel-lined platter in the oven until all have been cooked, and serve hot with the garlic dip.

MAKES 35 TO 40 FRITTERS

Mojo Vinegreta

GARLIC DIP

I developed this tangy vinaigrette, which incorporates the elements of *Mojo Criollo* (Creole Garlic Sauce, see page 26), the potent garlic sauce traditionally served with yuca, fried chicken, and many other Cuban foods. I like to use it as a light dip for fritters.

4 to 6 cloves garlic
1 teaspoon salt
⅓ cup sour orange juice (see page 9) or equal parts of fresh lime, lemon, and sweet orange juice, to make ⅓ cup

Salt and freshly ground black pepper to taste
1 cup pure Spanish olive oil

1. In a mortar, mash the garlic with the salt until a smooth paste is formed. In a food processor fitted with a steel blade, combine the

garlic paste, citrus juice, and salt and pepper. With the motor running, add the oil very slowly, processing until smooth. Remove any pieces that aren't processed. (Alternatively, the ingredients can be mashed together in a mortar.)

2. Cover and refrigerate, and bring to room temperature when ready to use. *Mojo Vinegreta* will keep about 1 week refrigerated.

MAKES 1 1/4 CUPS

Frituras de Carita
BLACK-EYED PEA FRITTERS

All-night soaking softens the black-eyed peas so that you can puree them for these fritters. Some cooks grind the softened peas in a meat grinder, but I find that a food processor does a fine job — just remember to process them until thoroughly smooth. This is a Creole recipe that appears in Cuban cooking manuals as far back as the 1850s.

Chinese-Cuban street vendors called these fritters *bollitos*, and their cries of *"Bollitos! Frituras!"* echoed through the streets and alleys of old Havana.

½ pound dried black-eyed peas, rinsed in cold water, picked over, and soaked overnight in cold water to cover, changing the water several times

4 cloves garlic, crushed

2 teaspoons salt

1 teaspoon freshly ground black pepper

4 to 6 tablespoons water

Peanut or vegetable oil for frying

Fresh lime juice to taste

1. When the peas have softened, remove their skins (just rub them off), soak an additional 30 minutes, drain, and rinse.

2. In a food processor fitted with a steel blade, process the peas, garlic, salt, and pepper. With the motor running, add the water through the feed tube and continue processing until the puree is smooth and thick.

3. Preheat the oven to 250° F. In a large, heavy-bottomed skillet or deep fryer over medium-high heat, heat 2 to 3 inches of oil to 375° F, or until a drop of batter sizzles when it touches the oil, and fry 1 tablespoon of batter until golden brown. Taste for seasoning and adjust if necessary in the remaining batter, then drop the mixture by tablespoonfuls into the hot oil, and fry the fritters until golden brown on all sides, turning with a slotted spoon. Do not fry too many at once, or the oil temperature will fall and they will be soggy rather than crisp. Place the fritters on a paper-towel-lined platter in the oven until all have been cooked, and serve hot, sprinkled with salt and lime juice.

MAKES 20 TO 24 FRITTERS

Frituras de Cangrejo
CRAB FRITTERS

La Reguladora restaurant in Havana was a gathering place for the tobacco brokers, where they met after concluding their deals with the growers and chatted, over drinks and dinner, far into the night. A big basket of these golden fritters always accompanied their drinks.

3 tablespoons salted butter
½ medium-size onion, finely chopped
1 clove garlic, finely chopped
¼ cup dry sherry

6 to 7 ounces cooked or canned crabmeat, picked over for cartilage and flaked
1 tablespoon finely chopped fresh parsley

1 cup all-purpose flour
1 teaspoon baking powder
1 teaspoon salt
1 teaspoon freshly ground black
  pepper

4 large eggs, lightly beaten
Peanut or vegetable oil for frying
Fresh lime juice to taste

1. In a large skillet over low heat, melt the butter. When it begins to foam, add the onion and garlic and cook, stirring, 3 to 5 minutes. Add the sherry, crabmeat, and parsley and cook, stirring, until the onion is tender, another 5 minutes.

2. In a large bowl, sift the flour together with the baking powder, salt, and pepper. Pour in the eggs and mix by hand until the batter is smooth. Add the onion-and-crab mixture and stir to blend. Refrigerate the batter, covered, at least 2 hours.

3. Preheat the oven to 250° F. In a large heavy-bottomed skillet or deep fryer over medium-high heat, heat 2 to 3 inches of oil to 375° F, or until a drop of batter sizzles when it touches the oil, and fry 1 tablespoon of batter until golden brown. Taste for seasoning and adjust if necessary in the remaining batter, then drop the mixture by tablespoonfuls into the hot oil, and fry the fritters until golden brown on all sides, turning with a slotted spoon. Do not fry too many at once, or the oil temperature will fall and they will be soggy rather than crisp. Place the fritters on a paper-towel-lined platter in the oven until all have been cooked, and serve hot, sprinkled with lime juice.

MAKES 20 TO 25 FRITTERS

Frituras de Garbanzo
CHICK-PEA FRITTERS

These simple fritters are wonderful to serve with cocktails or as a side dish with a vegetarian dinner. *Salsa de Aguacate* (smooth Avocado Sauce, the recipe follows) is my inspiration for the perfect complement to the crisp, spicy fritters.

½ pound dried chick-peas, rinsed in cold water, picked over, and left in water to cover overnight, or 3 cups drained canned chick-peas
2½ quarts water
2 tablespoons salted butter
2 cloves garlic, finely chopped
1½ teaspoons salt

Few dashes of Tabasco sauce
¼ teaspoon ground cumin
1 tablespoon minced fresh parsley
2 tablespoons all-purpose flour
¼ teaspoon baking powder
2 large eggs, lightly beaten
Peanut or vegetable oil for frying
Salsa de Aguacate (see page 33)

1. If using dried chick-peas, place them in a large stockpot with the water, and simmer, covered, over low heat for 2½ hours. Drain and set aside.

2. In a small skillet over low heat, melt the butter. When it begins to foam, add the garlic and cook, stirring, 3 to 4 minutes, until tender.

3. In a food processor fitted with a steel blade, puree the chick-peas, whether cooked or canned. Add the remaining ingredients (except the oil and salsa de aguacate) and process until the mixture is smooth. Correct the seasonings and refrigerate the mixture at least 1 hour.

4. Preheat the oven to 250° F. In a large, heavy-bottomed skillet or deep fryer over medium-high heat, heat 2 to 3 inches of oil to 375° F, or until a drop of batter sizzles when it touches the oil, and

fry 1 tablespoon of batter until golden brown. Taste for seasoning and adjust if necessary in the remaining batter, then drop the mixture by tablespoonfuls into the hot oil, and fry the fritters until golden brown on all sides, turning with a slotted spoon. Do not fry too many at once, or the oil temperature will fall and they will be soggy rather than crisp. Place the fritters on a paper-towel-lined platter in the oven until all have been cooked, and serve hot with the *salsa de aguacate*.

MAKES 24 FRITTERS

Salsa de Aguacate
AVOCADO SAUCE

Served as a dip, Avocado Sauce complements the Chick-pea Fritters, above. Served as a traditional sauce, it enhances delicate, poached fish (see *Pescado con Salsa de Aguacate* — Fish with Avocado Sauce, pages 170–71).

2 large, very ripe avocados,
   peeled and pitted (reserve
   one pit)
Juice of 1 lime
½ cup finely chopped
   pimiento-stuffed green olives

1 tablespoon brine-packed
   Spanish capers, drained
Salt and freshly ground black
   pepper to taste
6 tablespoons pure Spanish
   olive oil

Using a fork, in a nonreactive bowl, mash the avocados to a paste. Add the lime juice, olives, capers, salt, and pepper, blend well, and mix in the olive oil. Place an avocado pit in the sauce to keep it from darkening, and refrigerate until ready to serve.

MAKES 1½ TO 2 CUPS SAUCE

Bolitas de Bacalao y Papa

CODFISH AND POTATO PUFFS

These tasty fish puffs, a legacy from my paternal grandmother, Abuela Ina, are delicious sprinkled with fresh lime juice and served with cocktails.

1 pound dried salt cod (see page 4)

4 medium-size all-purpose potatoes, peeled and cubed

2 cloves garlic, crushed

1 tablespoon salted butter, softened

Salt to taste

Generous grindings of black pepper

2 large eggs, lightly beaten

2 tablespoons minced fresh parsley

1 cup cracker meal (see page 7) or very fine bread crumbs

Peanut or vegetable oil for frying

Fresh lime juice to taste

1. Drain the fish, place it in a small saucepan, cover with fresh water, and bring to a boil over medium-high heat. Reduce the heat to low, and simmer 5 minutes. Drain and cool the fish, remove any skin and bones, and flake.

2. In a medium-size saucepan over medium-high heat, cover the potatoes and garlic with salted water, bring to a boil, and cook until tender, 20 to 25 minutes, then drain.

3. Mash the potatoes, using a potato masher or fork, add the flaked fish, butter, salt, pepper, eggs, and parsley, and mix well. Refrigerate the mixture at least 30 minutes.

4. Sprinkle a light layer of cracker meal on a work surface. Taking a generous tablespoonful of the codfish mixture in the palm of your hand, form it into a ball about 1½ inches in diameter, and

roll it in the crumbs; repeat with all the codfish mixture, renewing the crumbs when necessary.

5. Preheat the oven to 250° F. In a large, heavy-bottomed skillet or deep fryer over medium-high heat, heat 2 to 3 inches of oil to 375° F, or until a drop of batter sizzles when it touches the oil, and fry the puffs until golden brown on all sides, turning with a slotted spoon. Do not fry too many at once or the oil temperature will fall and they will be soggy rather than crisp. Place the puffs on a paper-towel-lined platter in the oven until all have been cooked, and serve hot, sprinkled with lime juice.

MAKES 25 TO 30 PUFFS

Bolitas de Papa y Camarones

POTATO AND SHRIMP PUFFS

Although these crisp nibbles were traditionally formed into cylindrical croquettes in our kitchen, my sister Annie prefers to shape them into round puffs and to add coriander to the original recipe. They are the perfect foil to sweet drinks, such as the *Puesta de Sol* (Havana Sunset, pages 323–24) and the Havana Yacht Club Cocktail (page 320).

1 pound all-purpose potatoes,
   peeled and cubed
1 large egg yolk
1 tablespoon salted butter, at
   room temperature
1 teaspoon salt
½ teaspoon freshly ground black
   pepper
2 tablespoons finely minced onion
2 tablespoons finely minced fresh
   parsley or 1 tablespoon finely
   minced fresh coriander
   (cilantro)

1½ pounds shrimp, peeled,
   deveined, cooked over medium
   heat in boiling water to cover 5
   minutes, and chopped
1 cup cracker meal (see page 7)
   or fine bread crumbs
1 large egg, lightly beaten
Peanut or vegetable oil for frying
Fresh lime juice to taste

1. Place the potatoes in a saucepan, cover with salted water, bring to a boil over medium-high heat, cook until tender, 15 to 20 minutes, and drain.

2. In a mixing bowl combine the potatoes, egg yolk, butter, salt, pepper, onion, and parsley. Mash thoroughly using a potato masher or fork. Add the cooked shrimp and mix well.

3. Sprinkle a light layer of cracker meal on a work surface. Take a large tablespoonful of the mixture in the palms of your hands, form it into a ball or a cylinder, and roll it first in the beaten egg and then in the crumbs; repeat with the remaining mixture, renewing the crumbs when necessary. Refrigerate the balls at least 30 minutes.

4. In a large, heavy-bottomed skillet or deep fryer over medium-high heat, heat 2 to 3 inches of oil to 375° F, or until a drop of batter sizzles when it touches the oil, and fry the puffs until golden brown on all sides, turning with a slotted spoon. Do not fry too many at once, or the oil temperature will fall and they will be soggy rather than crisp. Place the puffs on a paper-towel-lined platter in the oven until all have been cooked, and serve hot, sprinkled with lime juice.

MAKES 25 PUFFS

Empanadas al Horno de Titi

TITI'S BAKED TURNOVERS

These turnovers are baked, not fried, and they are simple and versatile. Fill them with *Picadillo* (Cuban Beef Hash, see pages 122–23), cooked, minced chorizo, crabmeat, chicken, or any of your own favorite fillings. This sturdy dough can be used immediately, without refrigerating, and the recipe can be doubled easily.

FOR THE DOUGH:

1 cup all-purpose flour
1 teaspoon baking powder
¼ teaspoon salt
1 tablespoon sugar

2 tablespoons vegetable
*   shortening, chilled*
1 tablespoon salted butter
1 tablespoon dry sherry
1 large egg

FOR THE FILLING:

¾ to 1 cup Picadillo, crabmeat
*   filling (see pages 91–93) or*
*   chicken filling (see pages*

51–53) or ¼ pound chorizo or
*   other spicy sausage, finely*
*   chopped (see pages 6–7)*

TO BRUSH THE TURNOVERS:

1 large egg, lightly beaten and
*   mixed with 1 tablespoon water*

1. To prepare the pastry, sift the flour together with the baking powder, salt, and sugar in a large bowl. Make a well in the center of the dry ingredients and cut in the shortening and butter with a pastry cutter or two knives. Add the sherry and egg and combine the ingredients with your fingers. Knead until the dough is smooth and stiff, holds together, and comes away from the sides of the bowl, adding a few drops of water if necessary.

2. Preheat the oven to 375° F and flour a work surface. Divide the dough into quarters and with a floured rolling pin roll out one quarter to a thickness of ⅛ inch, and, using a pastry cutter or the top of a glass, cut the dough into 4- to 4½-inch circles. Place 1 tablespoonful of filling in the center of each pastry circle, moisten the edges with a finger dipped in water, fold the pastry into a semicircle, enclosing the filling, and crimp the edges with a fork to seal. Repeat with the remaining three portions of pastry dough. Place the pastries on a lightly oiled baking sheet and brush the tops with the egg-and-water mixture.

3. Bake the turnovers 10 minutes or until golden brown. The baked turnovers can be refrigerated and reheated in a 375° F oven until heated through before serving.

MAKES ABOUT 12 TURNOVERS

Croquetas de Jamón de Titi

TITI'S HAM CROQUETTES

Ham croquettes are Cuba's national appetizer—they are served at parties, picnics, weddings, and christenings and they are eaten any time of day in the cafés, accompanied by Cuban coffee. My favorite aunt, Titi, taught me how to make them, spending many evenings with me until she was sure I had the technique down perfectly.

½ stick salted butter	2 cups milk, scalded
1 cup all-purpose flour	3 cups finely chopped cooked ham

1 teaspoon salt
½ teaspoon freshly ground black
  pepper
½ teaspoon freshly grated
  nutmeg
3 teaspoons fresh lime juice, plus
  extra for sprinkling

1 tablespoon finely chopped fresh
  parsley
2 cups very fine bread crumbs
1 large egg, lightly beaten
Peanut or vegetable oil for frying

1. In a large skillet over low heat, melt the butter. When it begins to foam, blend in the flour, then gradually whisk in the milk until the mixture thickens into a smooth paste. Do not overcook or it will get lumpy. Add the ham, salt, pepper, nutmeg, lime juice, and parsley, and continue cooking over low heat for 2 minutes, stirring constantly with a wooden spoon. Remove from the heat.

2. Spoon the mixture into a pan or platter and let it cool thoroughly. (After it has reached room temperature, it can be refrigerated.)

3. Sprinkle a light layer of bread crumbs on a work surface. Scoop up 1 tablespoon of the cooled ham mixture and shape it into a cylinder about 1½ inches long and ¾ inch in diameter. Dip it in the beaten egg and then in the crumbs, and repeat with the remaining mixture, renewing the crumbs when necessary. (The recipe can be prepared to this point one day ahead of time and refrigerated overnight.)

4. Preheat the oven to 250° F. In a large, heavy-bottomed skillet or deep fryer over medium-high heat, heat 2 to 3 inches of oil to 375° F, or until a drop of the mixture sizzles when it touches the oil, and fry 5 to 6 croquettes at a time until golden on all sides, turning with a slotted spoon. Do not fry too many at once, or the oil temperature will fall and they will be soggy rather than crisp. Transfer them to a paper-towel-lined platter to drain, keep warm in the oven until you have finished frying the rest, and serve sprinkled with fresh lime juice.

MAKES 45 TO 50 CROQUETTES

Croquetas de Pescado

FISH CROQUETTES

Fridays meant fish in most Catholic Cuban households, and Fridays were when we enjoyed these fish croquettes rather than the usual ham croquettes. Served as an appetizer, they were generally followed by a main course of crisp-skinned roasted fish.

1 pound firm white fish fillets, such as sole or cod
2 tablespoons salted butter
1/4 cup minced onion
1 clove garlic, finely chopped
1/4 cup all-purpose flour
1 cup milk, scalded
3 teaspoons fresh lime juice, plus extra for sprinkling
1 teaspoon salt
1/2 teaspoon freshly ground black pepper

1/2 teaspoon freshly grated nutmeg
1 tablespoon finely chopped fresh parsley
Few dashes of Tabasco sauce, optional
1 cup very fine bread crumbs or cracker meal (see page 7)
1 large egg, lightly beaten
Vegetable or peanut oil for frying

1. Place the fish in a saucepan, cover with water, and bring to a slow simmer over low heat. Poach, covered, until tender, 10 to 15 minutes. Drain, let cool, then flake the fish and set it aside.

2. In a skillet over low heat, melt the butter. When the butter begins to foam, add the onion and garlic and cook, stirring, until tender. Add the flour and continue cooking and stirring until the mixture turns a golden color. Gradually whisk in the milk, still cooking over low heat, until the mixture thickens into a smooth paste.

3. Add the fish, lime juice, salt, pepper, nutmeg, and parsley, and cook over low heat 2 minutes, stirring constantly with a wooden

spoon, until the paste comes away from the sides of the pan. Correct the seasonings, add the Tabasco, and remove from the heat. Spread the mixture on a baking sheet or large platter, allow it to cool thoroughly to room temperature, then refrigerate it until cold.

4. Sprinkle a light layer of crumbs on a work surface. Take 1 tablespoon of fish mixture in the palm of your hand and form it into a cylinder about 1½ by ¾ inches, then roll it in the crumbs, in the beaten egg, and once again in the crumbs. Repeat with all the fish mixture, renewing the crumbs when necessary.

5. Preheat the oven to 250° F. In a large, heavy-bottomed skillet or deep fryer over medium-high heat, heat 2 to 3 inches of oil to 375° F, or until a drop of mixture sizzles when it touches the oil, and fry 5 to 6 croquettes at a time until golden brown on all sides, turning with a slotted spoon. Do not fry too many at once, or the oil temperature will fall and they will be soggy rather than crisp. Transfer them to a paper-towel-lined platter in the oven until all have been cooked, and serve hot, sprinkled with lime juice.

MAKES 30 TO 35 CROQUETTES

Cangrejitos

FILLED CRESCENT PASTRIES

These savory pastries are the Cuban forerunners of today's croissant sandwiches. They are immensely popular and are served at every celebration, usually filled with ground ham or chorizo.

FOR THE DOUGH:

1½ cups all-purpose flour
1½ teaspoons salt
1 tablespoon sugar

Three 3-ounce packages cream
 cheese
¼ pound (1 stick) salted butter

FOR THE FILLING:

2 cups finely ground ham or
 chorizo (see page 6)

TO BRUSH THE TURNOVERS:

1 large egg, beaten lightly with
 ¼ teaspoon water

1. Sift the flour, then sift it again with the salt and sugar, and set aside.

2. In a large bowl, using a hand or electric mixer, cream the cheese and butter together until well blended. Add the flour mixture and mix with your fingers or a pastry blender until smooth. Cover and refrigerate at least 30 minutes.

3. Preheat the oven to 400° F and lightly flour your work surface. Divide the dough into 4 balls and, working with one ball at a time, with a floured rolling pin roll out the dough ⅛ inch thick. Cut the dough into 3-inch squares, then cut them in half, into triangles, and place a teaspoonful of filling in the center of each triangle. Gently roll up the dough from the base of the triangle to the tip, curving the ends slightly toward the center, to form a crescent.

4. Place the pastries on an ungreased cookie sheet 2 inches apart, brush with the egg wash, and bake until lightly browned, 15 to 20 minutes. They can be made ahead of time and reheated in a 250° F oven for 4 to 6 minutes.

MAKES 24 PASTRIES

Dip de Frijoles Negros

BLACK BEAN HUMMUS

My dear friend Harold Streitman once led me on a tour of New York's organic food restaurants in search of the perfect hummus, a classic Middle Eastern chick-pea puree. The dish lends itself to black beans as well as to chick-peas, as Harold and I found when I put together this winning variation. Cuban hummus is great as a dip for *Mariquitas de Plátanos* (green plantain chips, see page 24), toasted baguette rounds, or fresh vegetable chunks.

My Cuban friends have adopted this recipe warmly, even though it is innovative, because it is firmly based upon Cuban ingredients and flavors. The optional tahini is the only departure from Cuban tradition.

One 16-ounce can black beans, drained
1 tablespoon tahini (sesame paste, available at Middle Eastern groceries and many supermarkets), optional

3 tablespoons pure Spanish olive oil
Juice of 1 lime
1 to 2 cloves garlic, sliced
Salt and freshly ground black pepper to taste
1 teaspoon ground cumin

In a food processor fitted with a steel blade, combine all the ingredients and process until smooth. Cover and refrigerate until ready to use. Bring to room temperature before serving. It will keep in the refrigerator for one week.

MAKES 1 1/2 CUPS

Pan Cubano

CUBAN BREAD

Cuban bread is a favorite for sandwiches and a special treat for breakfast, when it is cut into long strips, buttered on all sides, and toasted in the oven or on a grill. Cubans dip these crisp, buttery lengths of bread into either steaming coffee with milk or hot chocolate.

This recipe for Cuban bread, one of the best, comes from the late James Beard.

1 package (¼ ounce) yeast
2 cups lukewarm water
1¼ tablespoons salt

1 tablespoon sugar
6 to 7 cups sifted all-purpose
flour

1. Dissolve the yeast in the water and add the salt and sugar, stirring thoroughly.

2. Add the flour, one cup at a time, beating it in with a wooden spoon, or use the dough hook on an electric mixer at low speed. Add enough flour to make a fairly stiff dough.

3. When the dough is thoroughly mixed, shape it into a ball, place in a greased bowl, and grease the top. Cover with a dry, clean towel and let stand in a warm place (80° to 85° F) until doubled in bulk.

4. Turn the dough out onto a lightly floured board and shape into two long, French-style loaves or round, Italian-style loaves. Arrange on a baking sheet heavily sprinkled with cornmeal and allow to rise five minutes.

5. Slash the tops of the loaves in two or three places with a knife or scissors. Brush the loaves with water and place them in a cold oven. Set the oven control at hot (400° F) and place a pan of boiling water on the bottom of the oven. Bake the loaves until they are crusty and done, about 40 to 45 minutes.

MAKES 2 LOAVES

SNACKS

Bocaditos

TEA SANDWICHES

When is a sandwich more than a sandwich? When it is a *bocadito*, a savory little mouthful in traditional Cuban style. Basically, a *bocadito* is constructed like any other tea sandwich, with a filling spread between two slices of white bread. Then the crusts are trimmed and the sandwich is cut into squares, triangles, or rounds.

For a variation, a loaf of white bread can be trimmed of crusts and cut lengthwise into three or four slices, and each slice can be spread with filling, rolled like a jelly roll, wrapped tightly in aluminum foil or plastic wrap, and refrigerated. Just before serving, the rolls are unwrapped and cut into twelve pinwheel *bocaditos*.

You can assemble *bocaditos* a few hours ahead of time, arrange them on a platter, and refrigerate, covered with a damp dish towel or paper towels.

The fillings are what make *bocaditos* special. Here are four delicious traditional spreads.

Pasta de Queso Crema

CREAM CHEESE AND OLIVE
FILLING

One 8-ounce package cream cheese, at room temperature
¼ cup finely chopped drained pimientos
½ cup pimiento-stuffed green olives, drained and finely chopped

Salt and freshly ground black pepper to taste
Milk to thin the filling

Mix all the ingredients together thoroughly by hand or by pulsing in a food processor fitted with a metal blade and correct the seasonings. Cover and refrigerate until ready to spread, then bring to room temperature and thin with a little milk if necessary.

MAKES ENOUGH FILLING FOR ABOUT 20 *BOCADITOS*

Pasta de Jamón
HAM FILLING

¼ pound boiled ham, finely
  ground
Two 4½-ounce cans deviled ham
½ cup pimiento-stuffed green
  olives, drained and finely
  chopped

½ cup mayonnaise to taste
Salt and freshly ground black
  pepper to taste
¼ cup sweet relish, drained,
  optional

Mix all the ingredients together thoroughly by hand or by pulsing in a food processor fitted with a metal blade, and correct the seasonings. Cover and refrigerate until ready to spread.

MAKES ENOUGH FILLING FOR 25 *BOCADITOS*

Pasta de Pollo

CHICKEN FILLING

1 large all-purpose potato, halved
and cooked over medium-high
heat in salted, boiling water to
cover until tender, 20 to 25
minutes, drained, cooled and
cut into 1/4-inch cubes

2 cups finely ground cooked
chicken (pulsed in a food
processor if desired)

1/2 cup canned early sweet peas (I
prefer LeSueur), thoroughly
drained

2 large eggs, hard-boiled and
finely chopped

3/4 cup mayonnaise or to taste

Salt and freshly ground black
pepper to taste

Mix all the ingredients together thoroughly by hand, correct the
seasonings, cover, and refrigerate until ready to spread.

MAKES ENOUGH FILLING FOR 35 TO 40 *BOCADITOS*

Pasta de Pollo y
Esparragos

CHICKEN AND ASPARAGUS FILLING

2 cups finely ground cooked
chicken

One 15-ounce can green
asparagus, drained and finely
chopped

3 tablespoons finely chopped
onion

3/4 cup mayonnaise or to taste

Salt and freshly ground black
pepper to taste

Mix all the ingredients together thoroughly by hand, correct the seasonings, cover, and refrigerate until ready to spread.

MAKES ENOUGH FILLING FOR 30 TO 35 *BOCADITOS*

Cake de Bocadito

RIBBON SANDWICH LOAF

The ubiquitous ribbon sandwich found its way to Cuba in the 1950s where it was dubbed *Cake de Bocadito, Sandwich Gigante,* or *Sandwich Camagüeyano* (in the Camagüey region of the island), and was served at teas, card games, showers, and similar social gatherings. Its style varied: sometimes white and dark bread were alternated or bread slices were rolled to form pinwheels and then sliced. Loaves were usually frosted with cream cheese and filled with chicken, egg, and asparagus salads, or, as in the old-fashioned recipe below, ham, Swiss cheese, salami, and strawberry preserves, a common accompaniment to smoked meats in Cuba. Spread the filling thin, so the sandwiches don't tumble when the layers are stacked.

1 loaf white bread, unsliced
  (available at most bakeries)
1 tablespoon strawberry preserves
4 thin slices boiled ham

1 tablespoon mayonnaise
2 slices muenster or Swiss cheese
1 teaspoon prepared mustard
4 slices salami

FOR THE FROSTING:
1 cup whipped cream cheese
1/2 cup mayonnaise

6 to 8 pimiento-stuffed green
  olives, each sliced crosswise into
  about 3 slices
1 pimiento, cut into narrow strips

1. Using a serrated or electric knife, cut the crusts off the bread and slice the loaf into 4 horizontal slices. Spread one slice with the strawberry preserves and 2 slices of the ham, place another bread slice on top of it and spread with the mayonnaise and cheese, place another bread slice over this and spread it with the mustard and salami, place 2 slices ham on top, and cover with the last slice. Make sure the slices are stacked neatly, press down gently on the loaf, cover with damp paper towels, and refrigerate ½ to 2 hours.

2. To prepare the frosting, mix the cream cheese with the mayonnaise until smooth and well blended. Unwrap the bread, spread the top and sides with the frosting, and decorate with olives and pimiento strips. Cut the loaf into ¾-inch slices but do not separate the slices before serving.

MAKES 8 TO 10 SANDWICHES

Sandwich Miramar

MIRAMAR YACHT CLUB SANDWICH

The snack bar at the Miramar Yacht Club in Havana was in the open air right next to the boat slips where the sailboats were moored. The salt air was delicious—as was this sandwich, an entire breakfast on a roll. For brunch in the country I make platters of Yacht Club Sandwiches, preparing the fried potatoes ahead of time and placing the eggs in a warm oven as I cook them, until all are done.

6 hamburger buns, cut in half
2 medium-size all-purpose
  potatoes, peeled, grated, and
  placed in cold water to cover
Peanut or vegetable oil for frying
  the potatoes
Unsalted butter or vegetable oil
  for frying the eggs

6 large eggs
3 tablespoons ketchup
6 slices boiled or baked ham, at
  room temperature
Salt and freshly ground black
  pepper to taste

1. Preheat the oven to 200° F and place the buns in the oven to
warm. Drain and squeeze dry the potatoes and set aside.

2. In a large, heavy-bottomed skillet or deep fryer over medium-
high heat, heat 1 to 2 inches of oil to 375° F, or until a piece of
potato sizzles when it hits the oil. Carefully pour the grated potatoes
into the skillet and fry until crisp, 1 to 2 minutes. Remove from the
oil with a slotted spoon, drain on a paper-towel-lined platter, and
keep warm in the oven while you complete the recipe.

3. In another large skillet, over medium heat, heat the butter or
oil until fragrant, then fry the eggs to taste. Drain on a paper-towel-
lined platter and keep warm in the oven until all are finished.

4. Remove the potatoes, buns, and eggs from the oven, spread
the bottom halves of the buns with ketchup, and place on each a
slice of ham, an egg, salt and pepper, and a handful of fried potatoes. Cover with the top half of each bun, forming sandwiches.

MAKES 6 SANDWICHES

Media Noche

MIDNIGHT SANDWICH

Midnights are made with soft egg buns, which are available in Spanish markets. Midnights are made commercially in a sandwich grill, but the home cook will have excellent results using an oven.

2 soft egg buns or egg dinner rolls, halved
1 tablespoon mayonnaise
1 teaspoon prepared mustard
2 small dill pickles, thinly sliced lengthwise
2 slices Swiss cheese

4 ounces thinly sliced cooked pork loin or roast pork
4 ounces sliced boiled or baked ham
½ teaspoon salted butter for brushing

1. Preheat the oven to 375° F. Spread one half of each bun with mayonnaise, and the remaining halves or slices with mustard. Distribute the filling ingredients equally between the mayonnaise-spread halves, starting with the pickle, followed by the cheese, pork, and ham, and top with the mustard-spread halves, making 2 sandwiches.

2. Place the sandwiches on a lightly oiled baking sheet and brush the tops lightly with butter. Place a heavy cast-iron skillet over both sandwiches to weigh them down and bake until crisp and hot, 15 to 20 minutes.

MAKES 2 SANDWICHES

Sandwich Cubano

CUBAN SANDWICH

Here is the favorite grilled sandwich in South Florida—with Americans as well as Cubans. It has begun appearing, as well, on the menus of many trendy New York City restaurants, and its popularity is swiftly growing all over the United States.

1 loaf Cuban (see page 44) or
    Italian bread
2 tablespoons mayonnaise
2 small dill pickles, thinly sliced
    lengthwise

2 slices Swiss cheese
4 ounces sliced roast pork
4 ounces sliced boiled or baked
    ham
1 tablespoon butter, melted

1. Preheat the oven to 350° F. Trim the ends off the loaf and slice the bread in half lengthwise. Spread both cut surfaces with mayonnaise, layer one half with pickle slices, cheese, pork, and ham, cover with the second slice of bread, and cut down the middle into two sandwiches.

2. Place the sandwiches on a lightly oiled baking sheet and brush the tops with butter. Place a heavy cast-iron skillet over both sandwiches to weigh them down, and bake until crisp and hot, about 20 minutes.

MAKES 2 SANDWICHES

Variation: For a Miami Sandwich, toast the bread, assemble the sandwich as for a Cuban sandwich, and add 4 slices fried bacon, 2 large leaves lettuce, and 4 tomato slices, before cutting in two. Do not bake the sandwiches.

Elena Ruz

CUBAN TURKEY SANDWICH

There really is an Elena Ruz. She lives in Miami, where the sandwich that bears her name is served in every Cuban sandwich shop. Legend has it that she originated this unusual sandwich of cream cheese, strawberry preserves, and sliced turkey at El Carmelo restaurant in Havana, where she was a regular patron.

*2 slices white bread, toasted and
  crusts removed
1 tablespoon cream cheese*

*1 tablespoon strawberry preserves
4 ounces sliced cooked fresh
  turkey*

Spread 1 slice of toasted bread with the cream cheese and the other slice with the strawberry preserves, place the turkey on one slice, and close with the other to make a sandwich.

MAKES 1 SANDWICH

Platillos Voladores

FLYING SAUCERS

To make flying saucers you will need a sandwich grill or toasting iron, available at grocery stores in Miami or in any department store or cookware shop. The traditional flying saucer grill is round, but square grills will work. A double shell-shaped (croque monsieur) toasting iron is available by mail order through the Williams-Sonoma *A Catalog for Cooks*. An electric sandwich maker is also a good substitute.

*2 slices white bread, crusts
    removed*
1 teaspoon mayonnaise

1 teaspoon strawberry preserves
2 to 3 slices baked or boiled ham
1 slice Swiss or muenster cheese

1. Spread one slice of bread with mayonnaise and one with strawberry preserves. Place the ham and cheese between the bread slices, and close the sandwich. Place the entire sandwich over the bottom cavity of a lightly oiled sandwich grill and bring down the top, closing the grill (this will crimp the sandwich). Secure the grill with the latch at the handle and trim the excess bread with a knife.

2. Place the grill over a stove burner (electric or gas) over medium-high heat for 2 to 3 minutes on each side, turning frequently. Open the grill to make sure the bread is nicely toasted, remove from the heat, and invert the sandwich onto a plate.

MAKES 1 SANDWICH

Pan con Bistec

STEAK SANDWICH

Since Cuban steaks are especially thin, they are ideal sandwich material. With tomatoes, lettuce, and chopped onion, they make a hearty lunch.

1 tablespoon mayonnaise
*One 6-inch section from a loaf of
    Cuban (see page 44) or
    Italian bread, cut in half
    lengthwise and toasted*
1 leaf lettuce

3 thin slices ripe tomato
1 tablespoon finely chopped onion
*Salt and freshly ground black
    pepper to taste*
*1 small Bistec de Palomilla (see
    page 118)*

Spread the mayonnaise on both cut surfaces of the bread, place the lettuce on one half, cover with the tomatoes, and then sprinkle with the onion. Season with salt and pepper, place the steak on top, and cover with the second bread slice to make a sandwich.

MAKES 1 SANDWICH

Pan con Lechón

CREOLE PORK SANDWICH

Much like the *porchetta* sandwiches common in the hill towns of Umbria in Italy, but uniquely Cuban because of the addition of *Mojo Criollo* (Creole Garlic Sauce), this is a hearty peasant sandwich for pork lovers. It is also an excellent way to use leftover *Pierna de Puerco Asada* (Roast Leg of Pork Creole, see pages 136–37).

Two 6-inch sections from a loaf of Cuban (see page 44) or Italian bread, cut in half lengthwise
6 tablespoons Mojo Criollo (see page 26)

16 thin slices Pierna de Puerco Asada
Salt and freshly ground black pepper to taste
1 tablespoon salted butter, melted

1. Preheat the oven to 350° F. Spread the cut sides of the bread with the *mojo*, then cover with the pork slices, season to taste, and cover with the other bread slices, forming two sandwiches.

2. Place the sandwiches on a baking sheet and brush the tops with the butter. Place a heavy cast-iron skillet over both sandwiches to weigh them down and bake until crisp and hot, about 20 minutes.

MAKES 2 SANDWICHES

Choripan

SAUSAGE IN A BAGUETTE

This spicy sausage sandwich should be made with the finest quality chorizos. *Choripan* may be a simple concept, but it is a truly great sandwich.

1 tablespoon vegetable oil,
  optional
½ small onion, sliced into thin
  rings, optional
1 large chorizo, cut on the
  diagonal into ¼-inch-thick
  slices (see pages 6–7)

One 4-inch section from a loaf of
  Cuban (see page 44) or
  Italian bread, sliced lengthwise
  and toasted
1 tablespoon mayonnaise

1. If you are including the onion, heat the oil over medium heat in an iron skillet until it is fragrant, add the onion, and cook, stirring, 2 minutes. Add the chorizo and cook, stirring, 6 to 8 minutes. (You do not need the oil if you are cooking only the chorizo.)

2. Spread both cut sides of the bread with the mayonnaise, place the cooked chorizo over one bread slice, and cover with the other slice to make a sandwich.

MAKES 1 SANDWICH

Fritas

CUBAN FRIED HAMBURGERS

As children, our favorite drive-in restaurant was El Recodo, where we stuffed ourselves with *fritas*, small hamburgers that were fried and then topped with a nest of "angel-hair" fried potato threads. Sad to say, authentic fried potatoes are hard to find in Miami restaurants these days; most chefs make do with canned shoestring potatoes, which can be disappointing to those of us who remember the real thing.

When I serve *fritas* topped with fried potatoes to my friends, I make them by the platterful because they go very fast.

FOR THE FRITAS:

Two 2-inch sections of Cuban (see page 44) or Italian bread

⅓ cup milk

1 pound ground beef chuck

1½ cups finely ground chorizo (4 small sausages—see pages 6–7)

1 large egg, lightly beaten

1 tablespoon ketchup, plus more for the finished hamburgers

Few dashes of Tabasco sauce

2 teaspoons Worcestershire sauce

1 teaspoon hot paprika

½ teaspoon freshly ground black pepper

1 teaspoon salt

14 to 16 dinner rolls, sliced in half lengthwise

FOR THE FRIED POTATOES:

Peanut or vegetable oil for frying

2 large all-purpose potatoes, peeled and finely grated (the food processor does a good job) or 2 cups good-quality commercial shoestring potatoes

1. Preheat the oven to 250° F. In a small bowl, soak the bread in the milk, and set aside. In a large bowl, combine the remaining *fritas* ingredients, except the buns. Squeeze any excess milk from the bread and add the bread to the meat mixture, mix thoroughly, shape the meat into walnut-size balls, and set aside.

2. In a large skillet over medium-high heat, heat 2 to 3 inches of oil to 375° F, or until a piece of potato sizzles when it touches the oil. Fry as much of the grated potatoes as will fit comfortably in the pan until crisp, 1 to 2 minutes, remove with a slotted spoon, and drain on paper towels.

3. Wipe out the skillet with paper towels and return it to the stove over medium heat. Once it's heated, fry as many meat patties as will fit comfortably. Press down on the patties with a spatula to flatten them, cooking 3 to 4 minutes on each side.

4. Meanwhile, place the buns on an ungreased cookie sheet and heat in the warmed oven 6 to 8 minutes. Remove the buns from the oven and spread the bottom halves with a little ketchup, place a cooked beef patty on top, heap with fried potatoes, and close with the top half to make a sandwich.

MAKES 14 TO 15 HAMBURGERS

Note: As most dinner rolls come stuck together and uncut, slice the entire cluster in half, prepare as directed, and then separate into individual rolls.

Papas Rellenas
STUFFED MASHED POTATO BALLS

Comfort food in a ball, these wonderful potatoes are sold at most Cuban snack bars in Miami. Biting into mashed potatoes and finding the tasty meat hash makes for a gastronomic surprise.

2 pounds all-purpose potatoes, peeled and diced (to make 4 cups pureed potatoes)
Salt and freshly ground black pepper to taste

¾ to 1 cup Picadillo (see pages 122–23)
1 large egg, lightly beaten
½ cup cracker meal (see page 7) or fine bread crumbs
Peanut or vegetable oil for frying

1. In a large pot, cook the potatoes in salted water to cover until tender, 20 to 25 minutes, then drain. Place them back in the pot over medium heat and shake the pot until all the remaining moisture has evaporated.

2. In a food processor fitted with a steel blade, puree the potatoes, pulsing on and off until smooth. Do not overprocess. Season with salt and pepper, and allow the mixture to rest 30 minutes at room temperature.

3. Take a handful of pureed potatoes and shape into a 3-inch ball. Push down with a tablespoon to make a well, fill with 2 tablespoons *picadillo,* and then reshape into a ball; repeat with the remaining potato mixture. Roll the balls first in the beaten egg and then in the cracker meal, place on a platter, cover, and refrigerate 1 hour.

4. In a large, heavy-bottomed skillet or deep fryer over medium-high heat, heat 2 to 3 inches of oil to 375° F, or until a drop of mixture sizzles when it touches the oil, and fry the balls 2 or 3 at a time until golden brown on all sides, turning with a slotted spoon. Do not fry too many at once, or the oil temperature will fall and they will be soggy rather than crisp. Drain the balls on a paper-towel-lined platter and serve hot.

MAKES SIX TO EIGHT 3-INCH BALLS

Carne Fría

COLD BEEF ROLLS

Savory miniature meatloaves, or *carne fría,* are served cold at picnics and luncheon buffets. My Aunt Titi's original recipe calls for the loaves to be tied in cheesecloth and poached in beef stock, and many Cuban cooks still use her method, but I prefer this newer, quicker baked version. Strawberry preserves make a surprisingly good accompaniment to the cold meat.

1 pound ground sirloin or chuck
1 pound ground pork
1 pound ground ham
1 teaspoon salt
1 tablespoon prepared mustard
1 small onion, grated
1 tablespoon Worcestershire sauce
1/4 teaspoon freshly ground black
  pepper

1/8 teaspoon freshly grated
  nutmeg
1/8 teaspoon dried oregano
1/8 teaspoon ground cumin
4 large eggs, lightly beaten
1 cup cracker meal (see page 7)
  or very fine bread crumbs

1. Preheat the oven to 350° F. In a large bowl, combine the meats, kneading to mix thoroughly. Add the remaining ingredients except the eggs and cracker meal, and knead until well mixed. Add the eggs and continue kneading, then add the cracker meal a little at a time, using only ¾ cup; the mixture should be firm enough to hold its shape.

2. Divide the mixture into quarters and form each into a small meatloaf. Roll the loaves in the remaining crumbs. Wrap each loaf separately in aluminum foil and place them in a large roasting pan. Pour ½ inch of water around them and bake for 1 hour. Allow to cool to room temperature, then refrigerate until cold.

3. Unwrap the loaves and slice thinly but do not separate the slices, and arrange on a serving platter. Serve each loaf with saltine crackers or toasted baguette rounds, accompanied by mustard, mayonnaise, or strawberry preserves.

MAKES 14 TO 16 APPETIZER SERVINGS

Pudín de Pescado

FISH PUDDING

A beautiful loaf of fish pudding appears at all our family gatherings when our meal consists of Cuban snacks served buffet style. Aunt Titi lightly frosts the unmolded pudding with pimiento mayonnaise and sprinkles the top with a confetti of parsley and pimientos. With the precision of a surgeon, she slices the loaf thin, leaving it intact, and surrounds it with stalks of white and green asparagus. What a sweet reminder of the 1950s!

6 slices white bread, crusts removed and torn into small pieces

2/3 cup milk

1 medium-size onion

4 sprigs fresh parsley, stems removed

Two 6½-ounce cans chunk light tuna in oil, drained, or one 16-ounce can red sockeye salmon, drained and picked over for bones and skin

¼ pound (1 stick) salted butter, at room temperature

2/3 cup prepared tomato sauce

6 large eggs

Salt and freshly ground black pepper to taste

Fine bread crumbs for the mold

1 recipe Mayonesa Rosada (recipe follows)

½ teaspoon minced fresh parsley for garnish

1 tablespoon minced drained pimiento for garnish

6 to 8 stalks canned asparagus for garnish, optional

1. Preheat the oven to 350° F. Place the bread in a bowl, cover with the milk, and let soak until the bread is softened. Squeeze the excess milk from the bread and set aside.

2. In a food processor fitted with a steel blade, process the onion and parsley until finely chopped. Add the bread and the remaining ingredients, except for the bread crumbs, mayonnaise, and garnish, and process until well blended.

3. Butter a 6-cup loaf pan or fish-shaped mold, sprinkle it with the bread crumbs, and pour in the fish mixture. Tap the pan on a table or counter to level the loaf, then put in the oven and bake until a toothpick inserted in the center comes away clean, about 1 hour.

4. Unmold the pudding while hot onto a serving platter. Cool to room temperature, then refrigerate until cold. When the pudding is cold, frost the top and sides with the *mayonesa rosada*, decorate with the minced parsley and pimiento, and surround with the asparagus. Serve cold or at room temperature.

MAKES 12 TO 14 SERVINGS

Mayonesa Rosada

PIMIENTO MAYONNAISE

This is my version of the classic *mayonesa rosada,* a smooth and colorful sauce that makes a rich frosting for *Pudín de Pescado* (Fish Pudding, see page 61) as well as an excellent dip for crunchy, raw vegetables.

¼ cup drained pimientos
1 tablespoon tomato paste
Few dashes of Tabasco sauce,
  optional

1 cup mayonnaise
1 teaspoon fresh lime juice
Salt to taste

In a blender or food processor, puree the pimientos and tomato paste. Add the remaining ingredients and pulse off and on until thoroughly blended. Correct the seasonings, cover, and refrigerate until ready to use.

MAKES 1 CUP

Pastel de Pollo

CHICKEN PIE

This pie is a popular take-out item at grocery stores and bakeries in Miami's Cuban neighborhoods, being almost essential for picnics, baseball games, and boating afternoons. You will find it wonderful for summer luncheons, accompanied by your favorite salad and a bottle of good Rioja.

FOR THE PASTRY:
4 cups all-purpose flour
3 tablespoons sugar
2 teaspoons salt
2 teaspoons baking powder
3/4 cup vegetable shortening, chilled

4 tablespoons (1/2 stick) salted butter, chilled and cut into 1/2-inch pieces
3 large eggs, lightly beaten
3 tablespoons dry sherry

FOR THE FILLING:
One 3-pound chicken, cut into 8 pieces and skin removed
Salt and freshly ground black pepper to taste
2 tablespoons fresh lime juice
3 tablespoons pure Spanish olive oil
1 large green bell pepper, finely chopped
1 large onion, finely chopped
4 cloves garlic, finely chopped
1 bay leaf

1/4 cup chopped drained pimientos
1/2 cup dry sherry
2/3 cup drained and chopped canned whole tomatoes
1/2 cup chopped pimiento-stuffed green olives
1/2 cup dark raisins
2 large eggs, hard-boiled and sliced
1/2 cup drained canned early sweet peas (I prefer LeSueur)
1 large egg, lightly beaten

1. To prepare the pastry, in a large bowl sift together all the dry ingredients, add the chilled shortening and butter, and combine,

using your fingertips, until the mixture resembles coarse meal. Add the eggs and sherry and knead the pastry using the heel of your hand. Shape into 2 balls, making one a little larger, wrap the dough in waxed paper, and refrigerate until ready to use.

2. Wash and dry the chicken and season liberally with salt, pepper, and the lime juice.

3. In a large saucepan, heat the oil over medium heat until fragrant, then cook the chicken pieces, uncovered, until golden brown, about 20 minutes. Transfer the chicken to a platter and set aside.

4. Place the onions, green bell peppers, and garlic in the same saucepan and cook over low heat, stirring, until tender, 6 to 8 minutes, adding more oil if necessary. Add the bay leaf, pimientos, sherry, tomatoes, olives, and raisins. Return the chicken to the pan, cover, and simmer over low heat 35 minutes. Transfer the chicken to a plate and allow it to cool. If the tomato mixture has not thickened, continue cooking over medium heat until thick.

5. When the chicken is cool enough to handle, remove the meat from the bones, shred it into bite-size pieces, and add it to the tomato mixture, stirring well.

6. Preheat the oven to 450° F. Remove the dough from the refrigerator, place it on a floured work surface, and with a floured rolling pin roll out the larger ball to a ¼-inch thickness and fit it into a greased 3-quart ovenproof casserole 9½ × 13½ × 2 inches, allowing the excess dough to drape over the edges. Fill with the chicken-tomato mixture and arrange the peas and sliced eggs on the top.

7. Roll out the second ball of dough and place it over the top, pressing firmly around the edges. Crimp the edges to seal, puncture the dough in several places to allow steam to escape, and brush with beaten egg. Bake at 450° F 10 minutes, then lower the temperature to 350° F, and bake an additional 30 to 40 minutes until golden brown. Serve hot or at room temperature.

MAKES 6 TO 8 SERVINGS

Churros

SPANISH DOUGHNUTS

Spanish settlers brought their national snack to Cuba, where it quickly became popular. *Churros* and *chocolate*—hot chocolate milk—are favorites of Cuban children, while adults prefer to dunk their doughnuts in *café con leche*—espresso with hot milk. I find *churros* a special treat for winter Sunday breakfasts.

2 cups water
1 teaspoon salt
2 tablespoons salted butter
2 cups all-purpose flour, sifted

1 tablespoon anise-flavored
   liqueur (Anis del Mono or any
   fine brand)
Peanut or vegetable oil for frying
Sugar for dusting

1. In a heavy-bottomed saucepan over medium-high heat, bring to a boil the water, salt, and butter. Remove the pan from the heat and quickly mix in the flour and liqueur. Stir the mixture until it comes away from the sides of the saucepan, and set it aside to cool to room temperature.

2. In a large, heavy-bottomed skillet or deep fryer, heat 1½ to 2 inches of oil to 400° F over medium-high heat, or until a drop of batter sizzles when it touches the oil. Fill a metal biscuit press fitted with the star disk with the mixture and press down, forming circles that fall into the hot oil, and fry 2 to 3 *churros* at a time, turning with a slotted spoon, until golden. (Frying any more at a time will lower the oil temperature and the *churros* will be soggy, not crisp.) Drain on paper towels, dust with sugar, and serve warm.

MAKES 14 TO 16 CHURROS

Magdalenas

MADELEINES

How these Proustian scallops got to Cuba is a mystery, yet they were popular at Havana snack shops and kiosks—and they have migrated to Miami as well. Although they are easily purchased, I still make them at home according to my grandmother's recipe, and they are the favorite treat of my stepdaughter Nicole.

2 large eggs, at room
*   temperature*
Pinch of salt
½ cup sugar
½ teaspoon grated lemon peel
½ teaspoon vanilla extract

½ teaspoon rum or cognac
½ cup all-purpose flour, sifted
½ teaspoon baking powder
¼ pound (1 stick) unsalted
*   butter, melted and cooled*

1. Preheat the oven to 400° F. Grease and flour 2 madeleine pans.

2. Using an electric mixer, beat the eggs with the salt and gradually add the sugar until the mixture has thickened and is pale yellow. Add the lemon peel, vanilla, and rum, and stir to combine. Gradually add the flour and baking powder, stirring to blend after each addition. Add the cooled butter and stir lightly to blend.

3. Reduce the oven temperature to 325° F, fill each mold in both pans two thirds full, and bake on the top oven rack for 8 to 10 minutes, until golden brown. Remove the cakes from the pan and allow them to cool on a rack.

MAKES 24 MADELEINES

COFFEE

Cubans love coffee. They consume it dark, strong, and aromatic, in thimble-size cups throughout the day. Around coffee counters in Miami, the rapid conversation, loud, generous laughter, and aroma of coffee are infectious. While the espresso machines hiss and the cups clink, spirited conversations cover politics, current news, food, home life, and the favorite topic, anything having to do with Cuba.

Offering coffee is synonymous with hospitality. Upon arriving at a beauty salon, doctor's office, or place of business, the visitor is immediately offered a thimbleful of rich *café*. At the nearest kiosk, merchants purchase coffee to go in a six-ounce cup, accompanied by a stack of thimble cups so it can be served to customers. This ritual goes on all day, wherever you happen to be in the Cuban community.

When added to hot milk, coffee becomes *café con leche*, the break-fast beverage of choice for children and adults alike, usually accompanied by large slivers of grilled Cuban bread with butter. (The bread is cut lengthwise, spead with butter, and toasted in a sandwich grill or in the oven.) *Café con leche* can be made darker or lighter according to preference, and can be served *cortadito*—cut in half—for a mini-portion. Dark coffee is enjoyed at the end of a meal espresso style, but is never accompanied by lemon peel.

The best coffee is made in large steam pressure machines (usually of Italian make), resulting in a rich and foamy brew. To prepare it at home, use the two-part Moka coffeepot, which is based on the same principle. These screw-top pots are available in 3-, 6-, 9-, and 12-cup capacity.

For Cuban coffee, the beans are more finely ground than for Italian espresso, although a good espresso grind may be substituted. Some brands available at Hispanic markets and supermarkets are: Bustelo, Pico, Goya, Pilon, and Medaglia D'Oro (an Italian blend).

Café Cubano

CALI'S CUBAN COFFEE

My youngest sibling, Cali, is the only one in our family who was born in the United States, yet he makes the best Cuban coffee. His recipe is genuinely sweet and is topped with a rich foam, referred to as *espuma*.

To make this coffee, you don't have to measure—simply fill the coffee and water compartments up to the fill lines on the pot. This recipe is for a six-cup pot, which means six demitasse servings.

To add sugar to coffee prepared in pots of other sizes, the rule of thumb is 1¼ teaspoons sugar per demitasse.

FOR A 6-CUP POT

Cold water, to reach the fill line   *8 teaspoons sugar*
Cuban or espresso grind coffee, to
reach the fill line

1. Fill the bottom half of the pot with water up to the bottom of the screw. Fill the top half loosely with coffee—do not pat it down.

2. Place the pot over medium heat. As the water heats, the pressure will push the water up into the top half. If you are making the coffee without sugar, keep the pot on the heat until it stops gurgling and the top half is filled with brewed coffee.

3. If you are making the coffee with sugar, place the sugar in a 2-cup glass measuring cup. When the coffee begins to rise to the upper half of the pot, take out 2 teaspoonfuls and add it to the sugar. With a spoon, whip the sugar and coffee into a smooth, beige paste.

4. When the coffee is fully brewed, pour it into the measuring cup until almost full, and stir until the sugar is fully absorbed. Pour into demitasse cups.

MAKES 6 DEMITASSE SERVINGS

La Majagua
Tobacco Ranch:
Soups and Stews

José Besu Polier, my father's great-great grandfather, was a Catalan who established a fifteen-hundred-acre tobacco plantation, naming it for an indigenous hardwood tree, *La Majagua*. The plantation prospered beyond his wildest dreams, for it was located in the region of Vuelta Abajo, on the west side of the island, which was uniquely suited to growing superlative tobacco. Although La Majagua was not the largest plantation in the region, it was known for producing the finest quality Cuban leaf. Vuelta Abajo at one time was the purveyor of tobacco to the royal houses of Spain and Italy.

When I was a child, La Majagua was owned by my father's uncle, José Antonio Besu, who was my godfather and whom I lovingly called *Tata*. Under his stewardship, about eight hundred people lived and worked on the property, making it a conglomeration of very busy, colorful, small neighborhoods. The farm itself was divided into sections, each under the supervision of a *partidario*, or manager, who was paid one quarter of his harvest's profit.

A tobacco ranch in Pinar del Río, Vuelta Abajo, the famous tobacco-growing region in the west of Cuba. Reprinted with permission of the Richter Library of the University of Miami.

Partidarios were free to grow crops and raise cows and pigs for their own consumption, which they did in great quantities, but should their crops and products be sold, the same shared percentage applied.

The wives of the *partidarios* made dried beef *(tasajo)* and lard and other pork products, and they grew sweet potatoes, yuca, tomatoes, eggplant, and green peppers. They often had their own small businesses as well, selling butter, eggs, and dry goods to one another. They were remarkably self-sufficient and rarely shopped in town except for staples like salt and sugar. These families lived in their own homes in an area of the plantation called La Sabana, where the younger children had a school whose teacher was hired by the plantation owners and who stayed in a small house they provided. Many of the older children went to school in the neighboring town of Puerta de Golpe.

DAILY LIFE AT MAJAGUA

Besu's son Mario supervised the daily farm operations, but since the plantation had been running well and profitably for years, he and the other men in the family had lots of time for conversation, for politics, and for other pastimes, like organizing matches for their favorite fighting roosters.

The tobacco they raised was highly prized. My cousins remember visits from a man they called *El Suizo,* the representative of the important Davidoff tobacco firm, a major buyer of Majagua's crop. Early each season, brokers also came from other tobacco companies and looked at the seedlings; later they returned to look at the half-grown plants. At that point they could tell whether the leaves were good, so that by the time the tobacco was fully grown, the whole crop would have been sold. At harvest time the *partidarios* hired a force of extra workers, women who picked the leaves and strung them on long wooden sticks that were later transferred to the drying barns.

A view of a drying barn on the farm, where harvested leaves were taken after they had been strung on long strings to dry.

A cigar factory in Vuelta Abajo, near La Majagua.

Besu lived in the main house, a large, white Spanish colonial that had been built at the turn of the century. The shiny tile floors of its generous rooms reflected the clear Cuban sunlight. In front, eight stout porch columns were entwined with pink bougainvillea, whose hardy trunks had been clipped for decades, forcing the flowers to bloom all around the second story of the house. The gardens were lush with tropical flowers and silvery green topiary pines pruned into pyramid shapes, which always reminded me of Hershey's choc-olate kisses on sticks. Behind the house was a trickling cobble-stoned fountain, mossy, green, and cool, and beyond that stretched fragrant mango, pomegranate, and orange orchards.

Besu shared the house with his wife and his unmarried son and daughters, while his married children and their families lived nearby in Puerta de Golpe (where we lived) or in Havana. The house was always filled with relatives and friends, and many, many children.

Each day at lunchtime, the enormous dining room table was spread with a custom-made linen cloth long enough to accommo-date its great length. On the sideboards were arranged ceramic bowls filled with colorful fresh, poached, and candied fruit, crystal

A supervisor in the field at Majagua, 1953.

bowls of marmalades, serving dishes laden with puddings, and long boards covered with fresh cheeses. Lunch was the main meal of the day, starting at 12:30 or 1:00 and lasting for hours. Several conversations went on simultaneously at the table, and in addition to the gossip, there was a lot of political debate, since so many family members were involved in politics. After this leisurely meal, the family liked to move outdoors to the spacious porch. The men in their white linen suits and Panama straw hats and the women in their fine, simple white linen dresses settled into comfortable rattan chairs and chatted over coffee, beneath a gentle, aromatic haze of cigar smoke. As the bright afternoon faded to dusk, they quietly enjoyed the magnificent sunset. The sun went down slowly at La Majagua, a huge ball of fire descending into the blazing pink and purple gardens.

We children were free to roam all day as we wished, often riding horseback with the farmhands and exploring the far reaches of the plantation. With bathing suits, towels, and fat inner tubes bouncing along, tied to our saddles, we rode to Río Hondo, about ten minutes from the main house, where we fished and swam and rafted. Or we took the longer ride to El Colorado, the most scenic area of the plantation, to swim near the majestic waterfall that cascaded down the tall cliffs of reddish earth.

In the evenings, the house emptied and the scene shifted, as everyone trooped into town to visit Besu's sister, who was my godmother. She was a surprisingly lively old woman who loved cards and who drank a nightcap of cognac, even in her nineties. The mother of ten, she lived in an imposing white stone Regency house with balustrades, high on a hill overlooking the railroad station far below. This may not sound like a prime location, but it was. The railroad was the business heart of the area and she was the first to know when the trains were coming, who was arriving and departing, and who was buying and selling livestock and crops. Many local landowners lived in this picturesque town in grand homes not far from the railroad.

The family spent their evenings on her comfortable veranda where, joined by neighbors and relatives, they sat for hours chatting and watching the parade of townspeople out for a stroll. They played fierce games of dominoes, checkers, and pachisi and sipped coffee, hot chocolate, and cognac until two in the morning. The only variations in this easygoing routine were provided by the frequent turnover of visitors.

MAJAGUA'S KITCHEN

Food—produce, fish, and livestock—from its raising to its preparation and enjoyment, was a big part of life at La Majagua. The main farmhouse employed thirty workers who were fed three meals daily by Pepe, Mariano, and Anastasio, the cooks. A variety of vegetables was grown especially for these workers and for the household, including corn, peppers, sweet potatoes, squash, and taro.

Cooking for thirty hard-working, hungry people every day, the cooks had to rely on hearty soups such as *puré de frijoles negros* (black bean soup), *potaje de garbanzos* (chick-pea soup), *sopa de ajos* (garlic soup), *sopa de plátanos criolla* (Creole plantain soup), *potaje de judias* (navy bean soup), and *caldo gallego* (Galician bean soup).

Robust stews were perfect for the workers' lunches, especially *ajïaco criollo* (Cuban creole stew), a traditional dish of slowly simmered short ribs, flank steak, corn, sweet potatoes, yuca, and taro. Equally hearty was *rabo encendido* (oxtail stew), with its fiery bite of ground pepper. When corn was in season, the cooks made *guiso de maíz* (a rich corn stew), thick with fresh vegetables and spicy sausage. What set Majagua's stews apart from the usual beef or vegetable stew was that they were complete meals in themselves, needing no accompaniments.

At the family table, deer and other game were abundant during hunting season. And the fish in Río Hondo, especially *viajaca*, with a soft, flaky texture similar to St. Peter fish, or John Dory, were simply grilled and served fresh and glistening with just a squeeze of lime juice. Lunch for the family usually lasted until 3:00 in the afternoon and by the time everyone finished talking, dessert had run into teatime, *merienda*.

The kitchen was enormous and constantly busy; the kitchen staff seemed to be cooking every minute of the day, filling the air with a mixture of aromas, from sweet to savory to incendiary. When the cooks woke up early in the morning, the first thing they did was fill a huge pot with small, white-fleshed sweet potatoes and a little water, cover the pot with brown paper, and steam it for hours. The potatoes stuck together and caramelized, as if they had been steamed over coals, and by 11:00 their sweet, heavy fragrance hung over the kitchen and dining room. These delicious *boniatos asados*, served hot with melted butter, were a daily staple.

Cattle were raised for beef and a herd of dairy cows supplied the needs of the family and staff. One resident cow, a sweet, spotted creature named Vaca Cuca, was used solely to provide fresh milk for the children—my sisters, my brothers, and me, and our many second cousins—who lived in Puerta de Golpe. The milk was poured into large metal containers, each labeled for the house to which it was going. Then it was delivered on horseback by a gentle man whose nickname, Comején, or Termite, always inspired giggles in us children. The slow, rocking journey on horseback caused a heavy layer of rich cream to rise to the top, and we had to cut through it before the milk would pour freely.

Besu's daughters made their own cheeses, which were exceptionally soft and velvety. *Queso blanco,* one of my favorites, resembled a fine pot cheese and was served with sweet guavas, mangoes, oranges, and *dulce de toronja* (sweetened grapefruit shells). It was made by draining fresh milk mixed with rennet in large colanders. When the resulting cheese was inverted onto platters, the top was speckled with little marks left from the drain holes.

Comején, the man who delivered fresh milk to all the children in the family, and our spotted cow—almost a family pet— Vaca Cuca.

Besu's daughter Ana Rosa planned all the meals with her mother and was an especially talented dessert chef. She had her own private area of the kitchen where I spent many fascinating afternoons watching her prepare sumptuous flans of coconut, sweet potato, and pineapple, bread puddings, and sweet potato puddings. Everyone still talks about her *coco quemado* (crispy coconut), a confection that was truly heavenly.

Majagua was a place of abundance, generosity, and the riches of nature. It is no wonder that I remember it as a Garden of Eden. Its kitchen produced a variety of Creole dishes that any restaurant kitchen today could be proud of, yet they are all simple, robust preparations that are easy to reproduce. I include my favorite classic soups and stews in the recipes that follow, as well as a few that are more modern, such as the yuca and ham soup that my mother and I created, and light, cold mango and avocado soups.

Caldo de Res

CUBAN BEEF STOCK

The flavors of cumin and saffron give this beef stock a Cuban twist.

1 pound flank steak, cut into
    chunks
2 pounds beef bones
3 quarts water
1½ teaspoons salt
6 black peppercorns
4 cloves garlic, crushed
1 bay leaf

1 large onion, quartered
1 large green bell pepper, seeded
    and quartered
Few sprigs fresh parsley
3 large ripe tomatoes, quartered
½ teaspoon ground cumin
¼ teaspoon powdered saffron, or
    3 to 4 saffron threads, crushed

1. Place all ingredients in a large stockpot and bring to a boil over medium-high heat, skimming the scum from the surface until no more appears. Reduce the heat to low and simmer, partially covered, until the meat falls apart, 1½ to 2 hours.

2. Remove from the heat and cool to room temperature, skimming any fat that rises to the surface. Remove the meat and bones, then strain the stock through a colander, pushing down on the solids to extract the stock, and refrigerate or freeze for later use. The meat can be used for Ropa Vieja (Old Clothes, see pages 121–22) or Vaca Frita (Stir-fried Beef, see pages 120–21), if you halve the recipes.

MAKES 10 CUPS

Caldo de Pollo

CHICKEN STOCK

The smell of gently cooking chicken stock is another reminder of Rosalie, our beloved cook, and our lively kitchen in Puerta de Golpe, where stockpots simmered perpetually.

One 5- to 6-pound fowl,
*   quartered, including the giblets*
*   but without the liver*
3 quarts water
1½ teaspoons salt
½ teaspoon ground cumin
6 black peppercorns
4 to 5 cloves garlic, crushed

¼ teaspoon powdered saffron or 3
*   to 4 saffron threads, crushed*
2 bay leaves
1 large onion, quartered
Few sprigs fresh parsley
4 to 5 ripe plum tomatoes or 2
*   large, ripe tomatoes, quartered*

1. Place all the ingredients in a large stockpot and bring to a boil over medium-high heat, skimming the scum from the surface until

no more appears. Reduce the heat to low and simmer, partially covered, 2 hours.

2. Remove from the heat and cool to room temperature, skimming any fat that rises to the surface. Remove the meat and bones, then strain the stock through a colander, pushing down on the solids to extract the stock. The stock will keep in the refrigerator 2 to 3 days and can be frozen. Reserve the chicken for another use.

MAKES 8 CUPS

Caldo de Pescado

FISH STOCK

My paternal grandmother, Abuela Ina, lived in the fishing town of Mariel and was famous in our family for her fish cookery. Grandmother always had gallons of fish stock on hand because fish carcasses and trimmings were easy to come by in Mariel. This is her stock recipe.

2 to 3 pounds fish trimmings (no skins)	6 black peppercorns
	1 bay leaf
2 quarts water	1 large onion, quartered
1½ teaspoons salt	1 large green bell pepper, seeded
2 large, ripe tomatoes	and cut into strips
4 to 5 cloves garlic, crushed	Few sprigs fresh parsley

1. Place all the ingredients in a large stockpot and bring to a boil over medium-high heat, skimming any scum that accumulates. Reduce the heat to low and simmer, partially covered, 30 minutes.

2. Remove from the heat and allow to cool. Strain the stock through a fine strainer. The stock will keep in the refrigerator 1 to 2 days and can be frozen.

MAKES 8 CUPS

Potaje de Pescado

GRANDMA'S FISH SOUP

This is the easiest and most wonderful fish soup you can make, a recipe I learned from my grandmother, Abuela Ina. She had to put all the ingredients for this soup through a food mill but, today, a food processor does an equally fine job of pureeing. You can use her stock recipe (see the preceding recipe) or substitute clam juice, if you prefer.

I often serve this soup as a spring or summer lunch, accompanied by a red snapper salad and crusty baguettes.

⅓ cup pure Spanish olive oil
1 large Spanish onion, quartered
4 cloves garlic, crushed
4 large, ripe tomatoes, chopped
10 sprigs fresh parsley
½ teaspoon ground cumin
3 large all-purpose potatoes, peeled and chopped

1 teaspoon salt
Few dashes of Tabasco sauce, optional
2 pounds firm fish (cod or sole) fillets, tied in cheesecloth
Juice of 1 lemon
6 cups fish stock or clam juice
1 lime, cut into wedges

1. In a large casserole, heat the oil over low heat, then cook the onion, stirring, until tender, about 5 minutes. Add the garlic and tomatoes and cook, stirring, 10 minutes. Add the remaining ingredients, except the lime, bring to a boil, cover, and simmer over low heat for 20 to 25 minutes, until potatoes are tender.

2. Remove the fish with a slotted spoon and flake. Set it aside.

3. In a food processor, puree the soup in several batches. Correct the seasonings, add the flaked fish, and serve hot or cold with a wedge of lime.

MAKES 8 SERVINGS

Sopa Isleña

MOM'S ISLAND SOUP

Every year, when our family gathers on Sanibel Island, Florida, Mom's first priority is visiting the fish store in search of fish trimmings for her favorite soup. While there are several versions of *Sopa Isleña*, I find Mom's recipe light and full of the essence of fish.

You may garnish the soup with crisp croutons or, if you choose, mix the untoasted bread cubes into the simmering soup for extra texture.

3 pounds fish trimmings (no skins)
One 3-pound snapper, cleaned, boned, and cut into chunks (sole, halibut, or grouper may be substituted)
2 large onions, quartered
6 large, ripe tomatoes, quartered
1 large green bell pepper, seeded and coarsely chopped
½ teaspoon ground cumin
Several sprigs fresh parsley
¼ teaspoon dried oregano
1 bay leaf
4 cloves garlic, crushed
Salt to taste

5 black peppercorns
Pinch of powdered saffron or one saffron thread, crushed
2 quarts water
1 cup dry white wine
4 medium-size all-purpose potatoes, peeled and diced
½ loaf day-old Cuban, Italian, or French bread, cut into ½-inch cubes
4 tablespoons (½ stick) salted butter or pure Spanish olive oil
1 tablespoon finely chopped fresh parsley
8 lime wedges for garnish

1. Place the fish trimmings and the fish in a large stockpot and add the onions, tomatoes, bell pepper, cumin, parsley sprigs, oregano, bay leaf, garlic, salt, peppercorns, saffron, water, and wine. Bring to a boil over medium-high heat, then reduce the heat to low and simmer, covered, 30 to 45 minutes. Remove the stock from the heat and allow it to cool.

2. Remove the fish with a slotted spoon and flake. Set it aside.

3. Strain the stock through a fine strainer into a large pot and discard the other solids. Add the potatoes to the stock and simmer over low heat, covered, 15 to 20 minutes, until they are tender. Add the flaked fish. If you prefer not to brown the bread cubes (see step 4), you can add them to the soup halfway through the cooking of the potatoes.

4. To prepare the croutons, melt the butter over medium heat in a medium-size saucepan, then add the bread cubes and cook, stirring, until golden brown. Serve hot, garnished with the chopped parsley, lime wedges, and croutons.

MAKES 8 SERVINGS

Puré de Frijoles Negros

BLACK BEAN SOUP

For black bean soup, prepare *Frijoles Negros* (Mom's Black Beans, pages 222–23). Pulse the beans in batches in a food processor fitted with a steel blade until smooth, then simmer in a large saucepan over medium heat 5 to 10 minutes, until heated through. For a thinner soup, add Cuban Beef Stock (pages 77–78) or canned beef broth to taste.

MAKES 8 SERVINGS

Variation: For a quicker version, prepare *Frijoles de Lata* (Quick and Easy Black Beans, pages 224–25) and follow the directions above.

Potaje de Frijoles Colorados

THICK AND RICH RED BEAN SOUP

Hearty and filled with red beans, potatoes, and squash, this is the classic recipe for red bean soup.

1 pound dried red kidney or pink beans, rinsed in cold water, picked over, and soaked in water to cover overnight

2 quarts water

1 bay leaf

1 large green bell pepper, seeded and quartered

One 2-ounce piece salt pork, rind removed

FOR THE SOFRITO:

¼ cup pure Spanish olive oil

¼ pound slab bacon, diced

3 to 4 cloves garlic, finely chopped

1 large onion, finely chopped

1 large green bell pepper, seeded and finely chopped

1 cup drained and coarsely chopped canned whole tomatoes

1 tablespoon red wine vinegar

½ cup dry sherry

½ teaspoon dried oregano

½ teaspoon ground cumin

Salt and freshly ground black pepper to taste

TO COMPLETE THE DISH:

2 medium-size all-purpose potatoes, peeled and diced

1 cup peeled, seeded, and diced calabaza (see page 6) or butternut squash

Pure Spanish olive oil to taste

1. Pour the beans and their soaking water into a large pot, then add the additional water, the bay leaf, green bell pepper, and salt pork. Bring to a boil over medium-high heat, reduce the heat to low, and simmer over low heat, covered, 1½ to 2 hours, until the beans are tender. Add more water if needed.

2. To prepare the *sofrito,* heat the oil in a medium-size skillet over medium heat until fragrant. Add the bacon, garlic, onion, and bell pepper, and cook, stirring, until the vegetables are tender. Add the tomatoes, vinegar, sherry, oregano, cumin, salt, and pepper and cook 10 minutes, until thickened.

3. When the beans are tender, add the *sofrito,* potatoes, and calabaza, stir to blend, and cook over low heat, covered, 30 to 35 minutes, until the potatoes and calabaza are tender. Correct the seasonings and serve hot, or remove the salt pork and puree the soup in a food processor fitted with a steel blade, and serve hot. Drizzle some olive oil over each serving.

MAKES 6 TO 8 SERVINGS

Caldo Gallego
GALICIAN BEAN SOUP

Since my maternal grandmother's cook, María, was born in the part of Spain known as Galicia, she was referred to as *la Gallega* María, which separated her, I suppose, from the other Marías we knew. The Galician María often made this classic soup, a staple in most Cuban kitchens.

1 cup dried white kidney beans, rinsed in cold water, picked over, and left in water to cover overnight

3 quarts water
1 pound flank steak, cut into chunks

One ½-pound ham hock

One 2-ounce piece salt pork, rind
  removed

1 medium-size onion, coarsely
  chopped

1 teaspoon salt

1 large green bell pepper, seeded
  and coarsely chopped

3 medium-size chorizos or other
  spicy garlic sausage (see
  page 6–7)

2 large all-purpose potatoes,
  peeled and diced

½ pound turnip greens, stems
  removed, washed and shredded
  (or substitute collard or
  mustard greens)

Freshly ground black pepper to
  taste

1. Drain the beans and place them in a stockpot with the water, flank steak, ham hock, salt pork, onion, salt, and bell pepper. Bring to a boil over medium-high heat, then reduce the heat to low and simmer, covered, about 1½ hours.

2. Add the chorizo, potatoes, and turnip greens and continue to simmer over low heat until the beans are tender, about 30 minutes. Remove the ham hock, cut the meat from the bone, and return the meat to the pot. Remove the chorizo, slice it about ¼ inch thick, and return to the pot. Remove the flank steak, shred it finely with a fork, and return to the pot. Discard the salt pork, correct the seasonings, and serve the soup in warmed soup bowls.

MAKES 6 TO 8 SERVINGS

Potaje de Judias

NAVY BEAN SOUP

Each Cuban cook has a personal recipe for navy bean soup. In my mother's kitchen the soup resembles the Spanish *fabada Asturiana*—Asturian stew—while other chefs add cabbage and pumpkin to produce a dish more Creole than Spanish. Regardless of the variations, this thick, rich *potaje* is a meal in itself.

1 cup dried navy beans, rinsed in cold water, picked over, and left in water to cover overnight

2½ quarts water

1 bay leaf

One 2-ounce piece salt pork, rind removed

¼ cup pure Spanish olive oil

2 cloves garlic, finely chopped

1 medium-size onion, finely chopped

½ pound boneless smoked ham, diced

2 cups drained and chopped canned whole tomatoes

1 medium-size all-purpose potato, peeled and sliced ½ inch thick

¼ teaspoon powdered saffron or 3 to 4 saffron threads, crushed

Salt and freshly ground black pepper to taste

½ teaspoon ground cumin

1 cup shredded cabbage, optional

1 cup peeled, seeded, and diced pumpkin (calabaza, page 6), or Hubbard or butternut squash, optional

2 tablespoons finely chopped fresh parsley for garnish

1. Drain the beans, place them in a large saucepan with the water, bay leaf, and salt pork, and bring to a boil over medium-high heat. Reduce the heat to low and simmer, covered, until tender, 1 to 1½ hours, adding additional water if necessary.

2. Meanwhile, in a medium-size skillet, heat the olive oil over low heat until fragrant and cook the garlic, onions, and ham, stirring, 6 to 8 minutes, until the vegetables are soft. Add the tomatoes and cook until thickened, about 10 minutes.

3. When the beans are tender, add the tomato mixture, potato, saffron, salt, pepper, cumin, cabbage, and pumpkin, and continue cooking another 30 minutes, adding more hot water if necessary. Remove the salt pork and discard. Mix well and serve garnished with the parsley.

MAKES 8 SERVINGS

Puré de Calabaza

CREAMY PUMPKIN SOUP

Anastasio, one of the cooks at La Majagua tobacco ranch, always prepared this soup for his young lunch guests. He would garnish each bowl with two hard-boiled egg slices for eyes and a curved strip of pimiento for a smile and tell us it was "Sunshine Soup." Since the pumpkins had just been picked and the cream had come from cows grazing a few feet from the kitchen, the soup was marvelously fresh and fragrant.

3 tablespoons pure Spanish olive oil
1 large onion, chopped
2 cloves garlic, chopped
2 pounds calabaza (see page 6) or butternut squash, peeled, seeded, and cut into chunks

4 cups chicken stock (see pages 78–79)
1 cup half-and-half or light cream
Freshly ground black pepper to taste or dash of Tabasco sauce
Salt to taste
Hard-boiled egg slices and pimiento strips for garnish

1. In a large, heavy saucepan, heat the olive oil over low heat, then add the onion and garlic and cook, stirring, until tender.

2. Add the pumpkin chunks and chicken stock, cover, and simmer over low heat until the pumpkin is very soft, 40 to 50 minutes.

3. In a food processor fitted with a steel blade, process the soup in several batches until smooth, then return it to the saucepan. Add the half-and-half and season with the pepper and salt.

4. Pour into a warmed soup tureen or 6 individual bowls and garnish with hard-boiled eggs and pimiento strips.

MAKES 6 SERVINGS

Puré de Lentejas

CREAM OF LENTIL SOUP

Abuela Ina, my paternal grandmother, often served this creamy Spanish soup accompanied by thin slices of toasted Cuban bread brushed with garlic and olive oil. In those days before food processors, she pureed the vegetables in a food mill.

1 pound dried quick-cooking lentils, rinsed in cold water and picked over

2 quarts water

1 ham bone

1 medium-size onion stuck with 3 cloves

1 rib celery, without leaves, chopped

2 medium-size ripe tomatoes, quartered

1 clove garlic

1 large leek, the white bulb and tender part of the green stem, cleaned well and sliced

1 medium-size carrot, scrubbed and diced

1 medium-size all-purpose potato, peeled and diced

1 bay leaf

1 teaspoon ground cumin

1 tablespoon red wine vinegar

Salt and freshly ground black pepper to taste

2 cups milk

1. In a large saucepan, over low heat, combine all the ingredients except the salt, pepper, and milk, and simmer, covered, 45 minutes to 1 hour, adding more water if necessary.

2. Remove the ham bone, onion, and bay leaf, and discard. Pour the soup, in batches, into a food processor fitted with a steel blade, and process until smooth. Return the soup to the saucepan and add the salt and pepper.

3. Over low heat, gradually add the milk, stirring to blend. Cook 10 to 15 minutes, correct the seasonings, and serve. The soup thickens upon standing, so to reheat, thin it out with a little stock or milk.

MAKES 6 TO 8 SERVINGS

Potaje de Garbanzos

CHICK-PEA SOUP

This hearty soup easily can be served as a main course, thick with chick-peas and accented by spicy sausages. Some Cubans add cabbage to the soup as well.

½ pound dried chick-peas, rinsed in cold water, picked over, and left in water to cover overnight
2½ quarts water
1 bay leaf
One ½-pound smoked ham hock
2 medium-size chorizos or any spicy garlic sausage (see pages 6–7)
2 large all-purpose potatoes, peeled and cubed
¼ cup pure Spanish olive oil

1 large onion, finely chopped
1 large green bell pepper, seeded and chopped
3 cloves garlic, finely chopped
2 cups drained and chopped canned whole tomatoes
1 tablespoon tomato paste
Salt and freshly ground black pepper to taste
1 cup shredded cabbage, optional
Minced fresh parsley for garnish

1. Drain the chick-peas and place them in a large stockpot with the water, bay leaf, and ham hock. Bring to a boil over medium-high heat, then reduce the heat to low and simmer, partly covered, 2½ to 3 hours. Add the chorizos and potatoes and cook another ½ hour, until the chick-peas are tender, adding more water if necessary. (The time and amount of water needed will depend upon the freshness of the chick-peas.)

2. Meanwhile, in a large skillet, heat the oil over low heat until it is fragrant, then add the onion, pepper, and garlic, and cook, stirring, 6 to 8 minutes, until tender. Add the tomatoes and tomato paste and cook until thickened, 10 to 15 minutes.

3. When the chick-peas are tender, add the tomato mixture and combine well, then add the salt, pepper, and cabbage, and cook 15 minutes, covered, over low heat.

4. Remove the bay leaf and discard. Remove the ham hock, cut the meat from the bone, and return the meat to the pot. Remove the chorizos, cut them into ½-inch slices, and return to the pot. Serve the soup hot, garnished with minced parsley.

MAKES 6 SERVINGS

Potaje de Yuca y Jamón

YUCA AND HAM SOUP

One late December day in Miami, when the temperature fell to a nontropical low, Mom and I decided that a kettle of rich, steaming soup would be welcome. The refrigerator yielded some yuca left over from Christmas Eve dinner and part of a roasted ham that remained from Christmas day luncheon. Our palates led us to this hearty creation, easy to duplicate any time of the year.

2 large or 3 small fresh yuca, peeled (about 1 pound) or one 16-ounce package frozen yuca (see page 11)

Salt to taste

3 tablespoons pure Spanish olive oil

2 large leeks, white part only, cleaned well and finely chopped

2 cloves garlic, finely chopped

1 medium-size onion, coarsely chopped

½ pound boneless ham, skin removed and diced

6 to 8 cups chicken stock (see pages 78–79) or canned chicken broth

2 cups whole or skim milk

Freshly ground black pepper to taste

Finely minced fresh coriander (cilantro) for garnish

1. If you are using frozen yuca, do not defrost it. Place the yuca in a large saucepan over medium heat with salted water to cover and simmer, covered, until tender, 30 to 35 minutes.

2. Meanwhile, in a small skillet, heat the oil over low heat until fragrant, then add the leeks and cook, stirring, for 8 to 10 minutes. Add the garlic, onion, and ham, and cook, stirring, an additional 5 minutes.

3. Remove the center core of the yuca and discard. Cut the remaining yuca into chunks and puree in a food mill or food processor fitted with a steel blade. Return it to the saucepan and add the leek mixture.

4. Place the saucepan over low heat and gradually add the stock and milk, whisking until smooth and well-blended. Correct the seasonings, heat through, and serve sprinkled with coriander. (If the soup is too thick, add more stock or milk and correct the seasonings.)

MAKES 6 SERVINGS

Sopa de Plátanos Verdes

PLANTAIN SOUP

An unusual preparation based on fried plantain chips pulverized into a coarse meal and combined with a rich beef stock, this soup has a delicious, uniquely Cuban flavor.

To increase or decrease the amount of soup you prepare, remember that one pound of plantain yields two cups of fried chips and that you need ½ cup of fried chips for each cup of stock.

1½ to 2 large green plantains (1 pound), peeled (see pages 9–10) and cut into paper-thin slices, or 3 to 4 cups commercial plantain chips (or more to taste)
Peanut or vegetable oil for deep frying

6 cups Cuban Beef Stock (see pages 77–78) or canned beef broth
Salt and freshly ground black pepper to taste
Fresh lime juice to taste

1. Place the plantain slices in a large bowl, cover them with cold water, and soak for 30 minutes.

2. Drain the slices and pat dry with paper towels. In a frying pan or deep fryer, heat 2 to 3 inches of oil to 375° F, or until a piece of plantain sizzles when it is thrown in. Fry the plantain chips a handful at a time, turning them with a slotted spoon until they are golden brown. Drain on paper towels. Do not fry too many chips at once, or the temperature of the oil will fall and the chips will be soggy rather than crisp.

3. Using a mortar or a food processor fitted with a steel blade, crush the plantain chips into a thick paste. In a large saucepan, heat the stock over medium heat, gradually stir in the crushed plantain chips, blending thoroughly, and season.

4. Simmer over low heat, stirring frequently to prevent sticking, until the soup has thickened, 20 to 25 minutes. Serve hot, sprinkled with lime juice. The soup can be cooled, refrigerated, and reheated, but it will thicken considerably. If you reheat, add an additional 1½ to 2 cups stock.

MAKES 6 SERVINGS

Sopa de Plátanos Rapido

QUICK AND EASY PLANTAIN SOUP

This hearty, thick soup can be made in minutes with frozen *tostones*—plantain rounds. It's a bit of a cheat on the original, but it is delicious and very quick.

One 16-ounce package frozen tostones (green plantain rounds, available in Hispanic markets)
6 cups Cuban Beef Stock (see pages 77–78) or canned beef broth

Salt to taste
1 clove garlic, crushed, optional
Few sprigs fresh coriander (cilantro), optional
Lime wedges for garnish

1. Place all the ingredients, except the garnish, in a large saucepan and bring to a boil over medium-high heat. Reduce the heat to low, cover, and simmer 15 minutes.

2. Remove the solids with a slotted spoon, place in a food processor fitted with a steel blade, and pulse on and off 2 or 3 times to chop coarsely. Or coarsely mash the solids in a bowl, using a fork. Return to the stock, stir to blend, correct the seasonings, and simmer over low heat an additional 5 minutes. Serve each portion with lime wedges on the side for squeezing into the soup. The soup can be cooled, refrigerated, and reheated, but it will thicken considerably. If you reheat, add an additional 1½ to 2 cups stock.

MAKES 6 SERVINGS

Sopa de Plátanos Criolla

CREOLE PLANTAIN SOUP

This classic Creole recipe, still widely enjoyed today, uses a paste of almonds and bread to thicken and give texture to a soup of boiled green plantains, and adds coriander to impart a unique flavor. It appeared in the 1856 *Manual del Cocinero Cubano* (Manual of Cuban Cuisine), from which I have translated and adapted it.

2 large green plantains, peeled (see pages 9–10) and sliced into 1-inch rounds.

10 cups Cuban Beef Stock (see pages 77–78) or canned beef broth

12 leaves fresh coriander (cilantro), finely minced

2 to 3 tablespoons fresh lime juice

Salt and freshly ground black pepper to taste

One 2-inch slice toasted Cuban (see page 44), Italian, or French bread

6 almonds, shelled and blanched

Lime wedges for garnish

1. In a large, heavy saucepan, simmer the plantains and stock over medium heat until the plantains are tender. (The time needed will depend upon the ripeness of the plantains.)

2. Remove the plantains to a bowl and mash into a thick paste. Gradually add the plantain paste to the stock, stirring to blend well, and then add the coriander, lime juice, salt, and pepper. Bring the soup to a boil over medium-high heat, then reduce the heat to low and simmer, covered, 15 to 20 minutes.

3. In a mortar or a food processor fitted with a steel blade, mash or grind the bread and almonds into a thick paste. Add to the soup just before serving and serve hot, with the lime wedges on the side for squeezing into the soup.

MAKES 4 TO 6 SERVINGS

Sopa de Ajos

GARLIC SOUP

This Mediterranean peasant soup is also a staple in the Cuban kitchen. This version comes from my godmother, Rosita Arocha-Ferrán, who thickens the soup by whisking one egg into the simmering broth. She poaches the other eggs in the broth and then breaks them up, as she stirs it.

¼ cup pure Spanish olive oil
8 large cloves garlic, mashed into a paste with ½ teaspoon salt
4 to 6 thick slices day-old Cuban (see page 44), French, or Italian bread with crusts, coarsely crumbled

5 cups water
Salt and freshly ground black pepper to taste
4 large eggs, 1 of them lightly beaten
1 teaspoon finely chopped fresh parsley for garnish

1. In a large saucepan, heat the oil over very low heat until it is fragrant. Add the garlic and cook, stirring, 3 to 4 minutes, taking care that it does not brown. Add the bread crumbs, raise the heat to medium, and cook, stirring, 3 minutes. Add the water, salt, and pepper and bring to a boil, stirring to break up the bread.

2. Reduce the heat to low, whisk in the beaten egg, and then add the remaining eggs, one at a time. When each egg is floating on the broth, pinch it to break the yolk, so that it poaches with the white and yolk blended. Simmer over low heat, uncovered, 20 to 25 minutes, stirring several times, and breaking up the eggs. Remove from the heat and serve immediately in warmed bowls sprinkled with the parsley.

MAKES 6 SERVINGS

Sopa Fría de Mango

COLD MANGO SOUP

My brother Ralph, who lives in Miami, is the proud owner of a large and bountiful mango tree. In mango season he makes chutneys, jams, preserves, salads, and innovative fish and chicken dishes with his large crop. Some of his creations, like this cold soup, may not be traditional, but they are certainly delicious. Using frozen or fresh fruit, this recipe couldn't be simpler.

4 cups peeled, pitted, and chopped ripe mango, or an equal amount of frozen mango (see page 8)
2 tablespoons sugar
2 cups Goya mango nectar (a thick fruit juice, available in supermarkets)

1 cup plain yogurt
¾ cup heavy cream or half-and-half
Dash of Cointreau or other orange-flavored liqueur
6 mango slices for garnish
6 fresh mint sprigs for garnish

1. Puree the mango in a food processor fitted with a steel blade or in a blender. Add the remaining ingredients, except the garnishes, and process until smooth. Process in batches, if necessary.

2. Remove to a bowl, cover, and refrigerate 1 hour.

3. Serve in chilled bowls garnished with a mango slice and a sprig of mint.

MAKES 4 TO 6 SERVINGS

Sopa Fría de Aguacate

COLD AVOCADO SOUP

Our garden in Miami had an avocado tree that produced abundantly, and this soup was always plentiful during avocado season. The original recipe, clipped by Mom from the *Miami Herald,* calls for heavy cream and sour cream, but I have substituted skim milk and yogurt, both healthier for the heart. Avocados are so rich and creamy that you don't miss the heavier ingredients. I find this version even more refreshing and delicious than the original.

*3 large, ripe Florida avocados, or
   6 smaller Haas avocados,
   peeled, pitted, and cut into
   chunks
Juice of 1 lime
Salt to taste
Pinch of cayenne (red) pepper
1 teaspoon dry sherry or dry
   white wine*

*2 cups skim milk
2 cups plain yogurt
1 teaspoon finely chopped fresh
   mint or coriander (cilantro)
Chopped fresh coriander
   (cilantro), chives, or tomatoes
   for garnish, optional*

Place the avocado chunks in a food processor fitted with a steel blade or in a blender, sprinkle with the lime juice, add the remaining ingredients (except the garnish), and process until smooth (you may have to do this in batches). Refrigerate at least 1 hour and serve in chilled bowls garnished with chopped coriander.

MAKES 6 SERVINGS

Gazpacho

COLD VEGETABLE SOUP

There are no hard and fast rules for making a good *gazpacho*—basically all you need are crisp, fresh vegetables. Let your palate be your guide for seasonings and texture. Any of the vegetables in the soup makes a good garnish, but my mother always topped each serving with avocado slices or chunks.

4 large, ripe tomatoes, peeled, seeded, and coarsely chopped

½ small red onion, finely chopped

½ medium-size yellow or green bell pepper, seeded and finely chopped

1 large cucumber, peeled, seeded, and finely chopped

¼ cup pure Spanish olive oil

1 clove garlic, crushed

2 tablespoons red wine vinegar

2 cups tomato juice

½ teaspoon ground cumin

Few dashes of Tabasco sauce, optional

1½ cups cubed Cuban (see page 44), Italian, or French bread, toasted or sautéed until golden brown in pure Spanish olive oil with 1 clove garlic, quartered, for garnish

1 large Florida avocado, or 2 smaller Haas avocadoes, peeled, pitted, and cut into slivers or chunks, for garnish

2 tablespoons chopped fresh parsley or mint for garnish

1. Combine all the ingredients, except the garnishes, in a large bowl, cover, and refrigerate until thoroughly chilled, 2 to 3 hours.

2. When ready to serve, remove the garlic, correct the seasonings, and ladle into chilled soup bowls. Garnish with the croutons, avocado, and parsley and serve.

MAKES 4 TO 6 SERVINGS

Vichyssoise de Yuca

YUCA VICHYSSOISE

This soup is not traditional—in fact, the only thing about it that is Cuban is the yuca. But cold potato soup was popular in Cuba, and this recipe substitutes our famous tuber for the potato. Skim milk thins the soup (a necessity, since the pureed yuca tends to make it very thick), and yogurt adds the perfect light texture.

2 large or 3 small fresh yucas, peeled and left whole, or 1 pound frozen yuca (see page 11)
3 tablespoons salted butter
2 cloves garlic, finely chopped
2 leeks, white part only, cleaned well and finely chopped

4 cups chicken stock (see pages 78–79) or canned chicken broth
2 cups skim milk
Salt to taste
Freshly ground black pepper to taste or few dashes of Tabasco sauce, optional
2 cups plain yogurt
Chopped fresh chives or coriander (cilantro) for garnish

1. Place the yuca in a medium-size saucepan with salted water to cover and simmer over medium heat until tender, 30 to 35 minutes. Drain and set aside.

2. In a small skillet, melt the butter over low heat, then add the garlic and leeks and cook, stirring, over low heat until tender, 10 to 15 minutes.

3. Cut the yuca into small pieces, removing the stringy core, and puree it in a food mill, in a food processor fitted with a steel blade, or in a blender. Return it to the saucepan and add the garlic and leeks.

4. Over low heat, gradually add the stock and skim milk, whisking vigorously until the soup is smooth and well blended. Remove from the heat and correct the seasonings.

5. Cover the soup and refrigerate it several hours, until it is thoroughly chilled. Whisk in the yogurt and correct the seasonings. (If you prefer a thinner soup, add more skim milk and, once again, correct the seasonings.) Serve in chilled bowls sprinkled with chives.

MAKES 6 SERVINGS

Guiso de Maíz

CORN STEW

Part stew and part soup, this rich combination is wonderful in late summer when corn is in season. If you want to make it during colder months, you can substitute frozen corn, but never canned.

2 tablespoons pure Spanish olive oil

¼ pound bacon, rind removed and finely diced

2 medium-size chorizos or other spicy sausage, sliced ½ inch thick (see pages 6–7)

1 medium-size onion, finely chopped

1 medium-size green or red bell pepper, seeded and finely chopped

2 cloves garlic, finely chopped

1 cup drained and chopped canned whole tomatoes, or prepared tomato sauce

3 tablespoons cooking sherry

8 cups chicken stock (see pages 78–79) or canned chicken broth

1 medium-size all-purpose potato, peeled and cut into ½-inch dice

1 cup peeled and diced calabaza (see page 6) or Hubbard or butternut squash

4 cups fresh corn kernels (from 8 large ears)

Salt and freshly ground black pepper to taste

1 tablespoon chopped fresh parsley

1. In a large saucepan, heat the oil over medium-high heat until fragrant, then fry the bacon until crisp. Reduce the heat to low, add the chorizos, onion, pepper, and garlic, and cook, stirring, until the vegetables are tender, 6 to 8 minutes. Add the tomatoes, sherry, stock, potato, and pumpkin and cook, covered, an additional 20 minutes.

2. Add the corn, salt, and pepper, and cook, partially covered, until all the vegetables are tender, about 20 minutes. Correct the seasonings and garnish with the parsley. Serve in warmed bowls.

MAKES 8 SERVINGS

Guiso de Quimbombó

OKRA STEW WITH PLANTAIN DUMPLINGS

This thick stew, one of our cook Rosalie's specialties, is typical of Creole cooking, with its combination of Cuban and African ingredients and its plantain dumplings. You may substitute skinless, boneless chicken breast for the pork.

1 pound lean, boneless pork (shoulder or chops), cut into bite-size pieces

Salt and freshly ground black pepper to taste

Juice of 1 lime

¼ pound slab bacon, rind removed and cut into ¼-inch dice

3 tablespoons pure Spanish olive oil

1 large onion, diced

1 large green bell pepper, seeded and diced

3 cloves garlic, finely chopped

1 cup drained and chopped canned whole tomatoes

4 cups water, Cuban Beef Stock (see pages 77–78), or canned beef broth

½ cup dry sherry

1½ teaspoons salt

Freshly ground black pepper to taste
2 cups sliced small okra, fresh or frozen

2 medium-size very ripe plantains, peeled (see pages 9–10) and cut into 4 pieces (about 2 pounds)
Lime wedges for garnish

1. Season the pork liberally with the salt, pepper, and lime juice. Place it in a large saucepan with the bacon, and cook, stirring, over medium heat about 10 minutes. Reduce the heat to low, add the oil, onion, bell pepper, and garlic, and cook, stirring, about 5 minutes. Add the tomatoes, water, sherry, salt, and pepper and bring to a boil. Reduce the heat to low, and cook, uncovered, 10 minutes, until the meat is tender. Add the okra and cook until tender, 10 to 12 minutes.

2. Meanwhile, place the plantains in a medium-size saucepan with water to cover and bring to a boil over high heat. Reduce the heat to low and simmer, covered, until the plantains are tender, about 20 minutes. Drain.

3. Using a potato masher or a fork, mash the plantains until smooth. Roll the pulp into walnut-sized balls and add to the simmering broth. Correct the seasonings, cook 5 to 10 minutes to heat through, and serve with lime wedges.

MAKES 6 SERVINGS

Rabo Encendido

OXTAIL STEW (TAIL ON FIRE)

The Besu family, owners of La Majagua tobacco ranch, were famous for this delicious family recipe, which came from their kitchen in huge quantities, ready to serve to hungry farm workers at lunch. It was served hot and it had a sharp, peppery taste, hence the fiery name.

3 to 3½ pounds oxtails, trimmed of fat, disjointed, and cut into 2-inch pieces

Salt and freshly ground black pepper to taste

Juice of 2 limes

½ cup pure Spanish olive oil

1 large onion, finely chopped

1 large green bell pepper, seeded and finely chopped

4 cloves garlic, finely chopped

1 cup drained and chopped canned tomatoes or prepared tomato sauce

½ cup dry sherry

1 cup dry red wine

2 cups Cuban Beef Stock (see pages 77–78) or canned beef broth

¼ teaspoon dried oregano

¼ teaspoon ground cumin

½ teaspoon freshly ground black pepper, or more to taste

1 bay leaf

2 medium-size chorizos, or other spicy sausage, sliced 1 inch thick, optional (see pages 6–7)

4 medium-size all-purpose potatoes, peeled and quartered

1. Sprinkle the oxtails with the salt, pepper, and lime juice. In a large soup kettle or casserole over medium heat, heat ¼ cup of the oil until fragrant, then brown the oxtails on all sides. Transfer them to a platter and discard the oil. In the same kettle, heat the remaining oil over low heat until fragrant, then cook the onion, bell pepper, and garlic, stirring, until tender, 6 to 8 minutes.

2. Return the oxtails to the kettle and add everything but the potatoes. Stir well and bring to a boil over medium heat. Reduce the heat to low, cover, and simmer 2 hours. Add additional stock if needed. Add the potatoes and cook an additional 30 minutes, until the oxtails and potatoes are done, and serve hot.

MAKES 6 TO 8 SERVINGS

Ajiaco Criollo
CUBAN CREOLE STEW

In the 1500s a Spanish settler in colonial Cuba described the food of the "Creoles" in a letter home. This letter was quoted in 1857 by Dr. José María de la Torre in his book *Lo Que Fuimos y lo Que Somos* (*Who We Were and Who We Are*):

"They have this dish which is a union of fresh meats cut up in small pieces that stew with diverse root vegetables that are stimulated by means of a caustic pepper called 'aji-aji,' that they give color with a seed called 'vija' that grows plentiful. This is their main dish, by way of not saying their only dish, that these primitive inhabitants serve themselves."

The settler is describing *Ajiaco*, a peasant stew that can be found in most countries in Central and South America and whose ingredients vary according to what is available in each place. In our home, variety was the secret; we added one of every kind of root vegetable we could get. To make a really good *ajiaco*, take advantage of the entire spectrum available at your nearest Hispanic market. The meats are varied too—a little bit of dried beef, flank steak, and short ribs.

1/4 pound tasajo (salt-dried beef), desalted (see pages 10–11)

3 1/2 quarts water

1/2 pound flank steak, cut into 2-inch chunks

1 pound beef short ribs, sawed into 1-inch slices (ask your butcher to do this)

1 bay leaf

1 medium-size malanga amarilla (yellow taro), peeled and quartered (see page 8)

1 medium-size yuca, peeled and cut into 2-inch rounds (see page 11)

1 large green plantain, peeled (see pages 9–10) and cut into 2-inch rounds

1 large white sweet potato

(boniato), peeled and cut into 2-inch chunks (do not substitute American sweet potato or yam—see pages 5–6)

1 large white malanga (taro), peeled and quartered (see page 8)

1 tropical yam (ñame), about the size of a medium white potato, peeled and quartered (do not substitute American sweet potato or yam—see page 9)

1 large very ripe plantain, peeled (see pages 9–10) and cut into 6 rounds

1 cup peeled and seeded 2-inch chunks calabaza (see page 6) or butternut or Hubbard squash, optional

2 large ears of corn, husked and cut into 2-inch rounds

FOR THE SOFRITO:

1/4 cup pure Spanish olive oil
1 large onion, finely chopped
1 to 2 cloves garlic
1/2 medium-size green bell pepper, seeded and finely chopped

1/4 cup drained and chopped canned whole tomatoes or prepared tomato sauce
1/2 teaspoon ground cumin

1. In a large stockpot over medium-high heat, combine the dried beef and water, bring to a boil, and simmer, covered, 1 hour. Add the flank steak, short ribs, and bay leaf, reduce the heat to low, and cook for another hour, skimming off any scum that comes to the surface.

2. Meanwhile, prepare the *sofrito*. In a large skillet over medium heat, heat the oil until fragrant, then reduce the heat to low, and cook the onion, garlic, and bell pepper, stirring, until tender, 6 to 8 minutes. Add the tomatoes and cumin and cook for an additional 5 minutes.

3. Over low heat, add the *sofrito* to the meats, stir, and add the vegetables in 5-minute intervals in the order listed. Simmer, covered, 45 minutes, then add the corn, and cook an additional 10 to 15 minutes. Serve hot.

MAKES 8 TO 10 SERVINGS

The sitting room in the house at Puerta da Golpe at the turn of the century.

El Chamizo Cattle Ranch:
Meat and Poultry

My maternal great-grandmother, María Cecilia Diaz Tabares, was a beautiful and impressive woman. With a grandfather who had been the mayor of Havana and a father who owned large sugar mills and sugar warehouses, she grew up in Havana surrounded by wealth and privilege. When she married in 1900, she moved with her new husband, Rafael Díaz, from Havana to the western province of Pinar del Río so they could manage his cattle ranch, El Chamizo. A land grant of 14,000 acres from the King of Spain had given his family extensive property, which had been divided into four farms: San Rafael, San Lorenzo, Los Pinares, and Chamizo. The young couple built a spacious new home in Puerta de Golpe, a small town near the railroads where all the other landowners lived, about one hour by horseback from the ranch. (This house became my grandmother's home in her early years, and later, when my parents were married, it became their home, as well.)

María Cecilia had been a city girl, enchanted with everything the sophisticated capital offered, and she didn't care much for living in the country. She determined not to change her life-style to fit her new surroundings, continuing to dress in the height of fashion and filling her home with treasured antiques. Her splendid leather saddles and boots were custom made, and she bought her hats and dresses at Havana's elegant *El Encanto* department store, having them sent by train to Puerta de Golpe for her selection, along with delicacies from Havana: nougats (*turrones*) and imported strawberries and grapes. At least once every year, she made the crossing to Europe by ocean liner.

Her aristocratic ways notwithstanding, *Mamaita* (as we called her) was more than equal to her responsibilities as mistress of El Chamizo. Every day at noon, when the train from Havana pulled into the station at Puerta de Golpe, she could be reasonably sure

My grandmother and her brother at Puerta da Golpe.

that friends and business associates would step off that train and make their way to her home. There were no telephones, so she could never know just how many would be arriving for lunch, but her kitchen was always prepared to lavishly feed anyone arriving dusty and hungry at her doorstep. Not only did she run her household to perfection, she was also a witty conversationalist with a strong interest in local politics.

Many years later, when her husband died and the management of El Chamizo fell to her, her competence was astounding. At about the same time, my grandmother was separated from her husband, Dr. Ildefonso Mas, and she joined her mother in running the ranch. These two women, inexperienced in business, managed to turn a profit running their properties and selling cattle every single year.

When *Mamaita* left Cuba and settled in Miami, her circumstances were reduced, but her style did not change. She had to make do with just a few dresses and one or two pairs of shoes, but these she had custom made by Cuban-American seamstresses and shoemak-

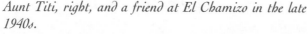

Aunt Titi, right, and a friend at El Chamizo in the late 1940s.

ers. She zealously avoided exposure to the sun, and she dabbed a face powder containing crushed pearls on her delicate white skin. She died in 1971 at the age of ninety-two, an elegant lady to the end.

Mamaita's daughter, my grandmother, entered her nineties still possessed of a sharp mind and excellent memory. In our most recent conversation in Miami, she spoke at length about the cattle ranch, explaining to me the different types of cattle and how the farm was run years ago, when she and her mother were in charge.

When she was two years old, my grandmother rode in the first automobile in Cuba, bought by her father; as an elderly woman, she sat with us in front of the television set to watch the first man landing on the moon. With great joy and pride, she became a U.S. citizen during the centennial celebration of the Statue of Liberty. She has lived a full life, and has nine grandchildren and fourteen great-grandchildren.

THE CATTLE ROUNDUP

My mother has colorful memories of her many visits to *El Chamizo* during school vacations, where she was given unusual freedom for a young Cuban girl, riding horseback from an early age and participating in the rough and tumble of ranch life.

El Chamizo was a beautiful place, vast and flat, except for the deep ravines that led to its many rivers. During the rainy season the rivers were high and turbulent and almost impossible to cross. When Mom was a little girl, there were twice-yearly cattle round-ups during dry weather, when the herds could be moved en masse to one special area, *la lechería* (the dairy). The roundup was Mom's favorite event at the ranch. She loved the noise and excitement, the magnificent food, and the challenge of an early morning horseback ride across the sprawling terrain.

The day of the roundup, my great-grandfather and my mother would leave Puerta de Golpe long before sunrise in a bustle of excitement. An early start was essential, because they had a ride of several hours ahead of them, and they wanted to arrive in plenty of time for the roundup and auction.

Their large entourage set out with much clatter along the winding trails. In addition to the family, there were ranch hands (*monteros*) with their families, supervisors, cooks, and a caravan of horses carrying food and other supplies. Freshly killed wild pigs were part of that cargo, destined to be spit-roasted later for a lavish picnic lunch. As the riders passed through chestnut groves so dense they overhung the road, they reached up and picked quantities of nuts, adding them to the sacks of food.

Everyone arrived at *la lechería* to find the cattle in corrals surrounded by specially built wooden bleachers. Into the bleachers my mother would climb, sitting with her grandfather and the cattle brokers who had come to purchase the best of the herd.

They all watched as the penned cattle were counted, branded, checked for illness, and selected for sale. Cattle were presented to

Riding on the ranch about 1906. The women in hats are my grandmother and great-grandmother.

the viewers, who raised their hands to bid, auction style. If the famiy wanted to keep any of the best animals, then negotiations became fast and furious. Once the choices were made, herds of cattle were led off to trains that would take them to slaughterhouses or other farms. It was a noisy, hot, and dusty scene, with an inter-mission at noon.

By then, Mom was thinking of nothing but lunch—an extraor-dinary event at every roundup. The air was heavy with the aroma of food that had been cooking outdoors all morning. As soon as the party arrived, the cooks had dug a large barbecue pit, in which they had built a fire of fresh wood. They placed the wild pigs on a spit over the fire, brushed them with a mixture of garlic, olive oil, and lime juice, covered them with green banana leaves pulled from the nearby trees, and slowly roasted them to a golden brown. They threw fresh chestnuts on the fire as well, and everyone snacked on them throughout the morning. The aroma of the roasting pigs was so intoxicating that my mother and the other children ran to snatch bits of crisp, brown skin. As the pigs turned on the spit, the cooks and *monteros* arranged long tables and benches under the trees and set them with blue-and-white enameled tin plates and cups.

At noon, everyone sat down to lunch—the family, the ranch hands with their wives and children, the cattle brokers and their ranch hands. There could easily have been two hundred for lunch under the trees. They feasted on the garlic-flavored roasted pig accompanied by rice, and for dessert ate crispy coconut, *coco que-mado*, made by the wives of the ranch hands. While the ranch hands drank *aguardiente*, a kind of moonshine made from sugar cane, the women and children drank frosty lemonade made from fresh fruit and thick, sticky brown sugar.

After lunch the roundup and auction resumed, not ending until early evening. Mom and her grandfather rode slowly to the small farmhouse that belonged to the estate supervisor, Matildo Lugo. Here everyone magically sprang back to life. All day long the su-pervisor's wife and daughters had been in the kitchen cooking on their massive brick stove, and the savory results waited on tables lit by kerosene lamps and spread with their best tableclothes and crockery.

Dinner was a traditional Cuban peasant dish, *ajiaco criollo,* a stew bursting with the flavors of short ribs, flank steak, corn, sweet potatoes, yuca, and taro, that had simmered on the wood-burning stove. Everyone lingered over this bountiful meal, talking, laughing, and recounting the high points of the day. It was late at night before they finally finished and the family cars (two Lincolns, open at the sides in front) came from Puerta de Golpe to take them home. The little girl who was my mother struggled to stay awake as this very long day wound down, but it seemed hours and hours before she finally got to sleep again.

CUBAN MEAT AND POULTRY COOKERY

On the farms and in the small, inland towns, the poorer people raised livestock for their own tables and the women butchered pigs and rendered lard, which was used to fry meat and poultry and to preserve sausages. (Fish was obtained from local rivers.) Before refrigeration, people cooked their meat as soon as it was butchered, and often the best method was to simmer or roast it outdoors. But while many classic Cuban meat recipes, such as *boliche* (stuffed pot roast), *carne con papas* (beef stew), *lechón asado* (roast suckling pig), and *puerco asado* (roast pork loin) call for stewing or roasting, still more call for quick frying in lard. For the sake of more healthful eating, I've changed the lard to olive or vegetable oil in all the recipes—for example, in *filete de palomilla* (Cuban fried steak), *masitas de puerco fritas* (fried pork chunks), and *masitas de pollo fritas* (fried chicken morsels).

Of course, in the cities, where life was more sophisticated, people ate European-style dishes, and all sorts of meat and fish were available in the markets. But on the cattle ranch, and on other farms, fresh meat either had to be cooked or somehow preserved. A popular method was to marinate it in lime juice (*limón*), a tradition that survives today, because the lime imparts a delicious flavor to meat and poultry—one that I consider uniquely Cuban. Another method was salt drying: cuts of meat that were hung and salted could be stored for long periods of time, then soaked, and cooked exactly like fresh meat. *Tasajo a la Cubano,* stir-fried dried beef, is prepared very much like *ropa vieja,* "old clothes," except the first is dried and the second is fresh. Flavorful *tasajo* is still popular among Cubans, and it is worth a try to expand your culinary horizons.

Most of our poultry dishes are fricaseed and cooked in a *sofrito* base, like *Tambor de Maíz* (Corn and Chicken Pie), or stewed Creole style, like *Pollo Criollo en Cazuela* (Mom's Farm-style Chicken), *Guinea Africana* (Guinea Hen African Style), and *Chilindrón de Pollo* (Basque Chicken), and they are more peasant than haute cuisine. It would be hard to ruin any of these recipes—if you cook them a little too long, or add more or less garlic or pepper, they will still be delicious.

Boliche

CUBAN STUFFED POT ROAST

Boliche is the name of the Spanish cut of beef used for this roast, but eye of round or rump roast makes a perfect substitute. The meat is stuffed with chunks of smokey ham, making a dramatic presentation when it is sliced and served.

One 4-pound eye of round or rump roast, with a 1½-inch pocket (the width of 2 fingers) cut through the center

¾ pound ham steak, cut into 1-inch squares
5 to 6 cloves garlic
½ teaspoon dried oregano

Salt and freshly ground black
   pepper to taste
1 cup sour (Seville) orange juice
   (see page 9), or ½ cup sweet
   orange juice mixed with ¼ cup
   lime juice and ¼ cup lemon
   juice
½ cup pure Spanish olive oil

2 large onions, thickly sliced
2 bay leaves
1 cup dry sherry
3 cups water or Cuban Beef Stock
   (see pages 77–78)
4 medium-size all-purpose
   potatoes, peeled and halved

1. Starting at either end and working toward the center, stuff the roast tightly with the ham, pushing it in with the handle of a wooden spoon. Pierce the roast all over with the point of a knife.

2. In a mortar, mash into a paste the garlic and oregano, and rub over the surface of the meat. Sprinkle the roast liberally with salt and pepper, pour the orange juice over it, cover, and refrigerate 3 to 4 hours or, preferably, overnight.

3. About 3 hours before serving, remove the meat from the marinade and pat it dry. In a large, heavy-bottomed casserole that will hold the meat comfortably, heat the oil over medium heat until fragrant, and brown the roast on all sides. Remove the meat from the casserole and set it aside.

4. Add the onions to the casserole and cook, stirring, over low heat 4 to 6 minutes, taking care that they do not brown. Return the meat to the casserole and add the bay leaves, sherry, water, and reserved marinade. Bring to a boil over medium-high heat, then reduce the heat to low and simmer, covered, 2 hours. Add the potatoes and simmer, covered, an additional 30 minutes, adding more stock if necessary.

5. Remove the roast from the casserole, allow it to stand 10 minutes, and slice it just under ½ inch thick. Arrange the meat on a serving platter surrounded by the potatoes, strain the sauce over it, and serve.

MAKES 8 SERVINGS

Carne con Papas

CUBAN BEEF STEW

Boneless chuck is the best cut for this classic, since it cooks fork tender. Subtly flavored with Spanish capers, paprika (called pimentón in Cuba), and oregano, Cuban Beef Stew is a fragrant company dish and a very easy one to prepare

½ cup pure Spanish olive oil
2 pounds boneless chuck, cut into 1-inch cubes
1 large onion, finely chopped
1 large green bell pepper, seeded and finely chopped
4 cloves garlic, finely chopped
2 teaspoons salt
1 tablespoon hot paprika
2 bay leaves
¼ teaspoon dried oregano
1 cup drained and chopped canned whole tomatoes

1 cup dry sherry
1 cup water or Cuban Beef Stock (see pages 77–78)
4 large all-purpose potatoes, peeled and cut into 1-inch dice
¼ cup brine-packed Spanish capers, drained
¼ cup loosely packed finely minced fresh parsley for garnish
½ cup drained canned early sweet peas (I prefer LeSueur), for garnish

1. In a large, heavy-bottomed saucepan, heat the oil over medium heat until fragrant, then brown the meat on all sides. Add the onions, bell pepper, and garlic, and cook, stirring, over low heat, until the onion is tender, 6 to 8 minutes. Add the remaining ingredients, except for the potatoes, capers, and garnishes, and cook, covered, 1 hour.

2. Add the potatoes and capers and cook another hour, until the meat and potatoes are tender. If extra liquid is needed, add equal parts water and dry sherry. Transfer to a deep serving bowl, sprinkle with the parsley and peas, and serve immediately.

MAKES 6 TO 8 SERVINGS

Carne Guisada con Plátanos

BEEF AND PLANTAIN STEW

This is a hearty country dish, but the contrast of sweet plantain and savory beef is quite subtle and delicious.

½ cup pure Spanish olive oil
2½ pounds boneless chuck, cut
    into 2-inch chunks
1 large onion, thickly sliced
1 large green bell pepper, seeded
    and diced
4 cloves garlic, finely chopped
2 cups drained and chopped
    canned whole tomatoes or 4 to
    6 medium-size, ripe tomatoes,
    coarsely chopped
1 cup dry sherry
1 cup Cuban Beef Stock (see
    pages 77–78)
1 tablespoon salt

1 tablespoon Spanish paprika
    (available at gourmet
    shops)
½ teaspoon freshly ground black
    pepper
¼ teaspoon cumin seeds, crushed
    in a mortar
Pinch of dried oregano
1 bay leaf
3 medium-sized plantains of
    medium ripeness (yellow with
    black spots — see pages 9–10)
2 tablespoons finely chopped fresh
    parsley

1. In a large, heavy-bottomed casserole, heat the oil over medium heat until fragrant, then brown the beef on all sides. Reduce the heat to low, add the onions, bell pepper, and garlic, and cook, stirring, until the onions are lightly browned, 4 to 5 minutes. Add the remaining ingredients, except for the plantains and parsley, cover, and simmer 1½ hours, stirring frequently. Add more stock if necessary.

2. Cut the tips off the plantains, peel, and slice 1 inch thick. Add them to the casserole and cook over low heat, until the plantains are tender, another 20 to 30 minutes. Transfer the stew to a serving bowl, sprinkle with parsley, and serve hot.

MAKES 6 TO 8 SERVINGS

Bistec de Palomilla
CUBAN FRIED STEAK

In Cuban kitchens, this is the most popular way to prepare steaks. The meat is pounded thin, marinated, and fried. The onion and parsley used to top the steak should be chopped by hand to achieve the proper crunchiness.

6 top round steaks, 4 to 6 ounces each
2 cloves garlic, finely chopped
Juice of 2 limes
Salt and freshly ground black pepper to taste

3 to 4 tablespoons pure Spanish olive oil or salted butter
1 medium-size onion, finely chopped by hand
3 tablespoons fresh parsley, finely chopped by hand

1. Pound the steaks on both sides, using a mallet, until ¼-inch thin. Season with garlic, lime juice, salt, and pepper, and allow to marinate at least 1 hour, refrigerated.

2. Remove the steaks from the marinade and pat dry. In a large frying pan, heat the oil over medium heat until very hot, and brown each steak for 2 to 3 minutes on each side.

3. Transfer the steaks to a serving platter and keep warm. Add the marinade and onion to the pan and cook until the onion is slightly wilted, 3 to 4 minutes. Garnish the steaks with the onion and parsley and serve immediately.

MAKES 6 SERVINGS

Bistec en Cazuela

CASSEROLED STEAK

In this simple, delicious dish, the meat simmers until it is fork tender, absorbing the tangy marinade. The potato is my mother's addition.

Six 6- to-8-ounce beef steaks, palomilla (a thin cut of round, available at Hispanic markets), round, or rump, pounded with a mallet to 1/2-inch thickness

Salt and freshly ground black pepper to taste

1/2 cup sour (Seville) orange juice (see page 9) or 1/4 cup sweet orange juice mixed with 1/8 cup each fresh lime and lemon juice

1/4 cup vegetable or peanut oil

1 large onion, thinly sliced

1 large green bell pepper, seeded and cut into thin strips

1 bay leaf

1/2 cup drained and chopped canned whole tomatoes or prepared tomato sauce

1/2 cup dry sherry

1 cup Cuban Beef Stock (see pages 77–78) or canned beef broth

6 medium-size all-purpose potatoes, peeled and halved

2 tablespoons finely chopped fresh parsley

1. Season the steaks liberally with salt and pepper, place in a nonreactive bowl, pour the orange juice over them, cover, and refrigerate at least 1 hour.

2. Remove the steaks from the marinade and pat dry, reserving the marinade. In a large, heavy-bottomed casserole, heat the oil over medium heat until fragrant, and brown the steaks for 4 to 6 minutes on each side. Remove the steaks from the casserole and set aside.

3. In the same casserole, over low heat, adding more oil if necessary, cook the onion, bell pepper, and garlic, stirring, until tender, 8 to 10 minutes. Add the reserved marinade, bay leaf, tomatoes, sherry, stock, steaks, and potatoes, and simmer, covered, over low heat for 30 minutes or until the steaks and potatoes are fork tender. Transfer the steak, vegetables, and sauce to individual shallow bowls, and sprinkle with the parsley.

MAKES 6 SERVINGS

Vaca Frita

STIR-FRIED BEEF (''FRIED COW'')

My husband votes this his favorite Cuban recipe. Although he has tried it in many of Miami's Cuban restaurants, he likes our homemade version the best.

One 2½-pound flank steak, cut in half
1 bay leaf
¼ cup fresh lime juice
¼ cup fresh lemon juice
3 cloves garlic, finely chopped

Salt and freshly ground black pepper to taste
½ cup pure Spanish olive oil
1 large onion, cut in half and each half thinly sliced
2 tablespoons finely chopped fresh parsley

1. Place the beef and bay leaf in a large saucepan, cover with salted water, and cook over low heat, covered, until the meat is tender, 1 to 1½ hours. Remove the meat from the stock and allow to cool at room temperature (*save the stock for another use*).

2. When the meat is cool, cut it into 2-inch chunks, shred it using your fingers, and place in a large nonreactive bowl. Add the citrus juices, garlic, salt, and pepper, cover, and refrigerate at least 1 hour, or overnight.

3. Remove the meat from the marinade and squeeze out the excess liquid. In a large skillet, heat the oil over medium-high heat until fragrant and cook the beef shreds, stirring, 6 to 8 minutes. Add the onions and cook, stirring, 5 minutes. Stir well, and cook until the beef is crisp, another 5 minutes. Sprinkle with the parsley and serve with *Arroz Blanco* (Perfect White Rice, pages 200–202).

MAKES 4 TO 6 SERVINGS

Ropa Vieja
OLD CLOTHES

If you tell your guests that the dinner entree is Old Clothes, you may get some strange glances, but this classic Cuban beef dish is a winner. Odd as its name may be, on the plate it translates into steak hash in tomato sauce.

One 2½-pound flank steak, cut in half
2 bay leaves
¼ cup pure Spanish olive oil
1 large onion, cut in half and each half thinly sliced
1 large green bell pepper, seeded and cut into thin strips
2 to 3 cloves garlic, finely chopped

2 cups drained and chopped canned whole tomatoes or prepared tomato sauce
½ cup cooking sherry
Salt and freshly ground black pepper to taste
½ cup finely chopped drained pimientos for garnish
½ cup drained canned early sweet peas (I prefer LeSueur), for garnish, optional

1. Place the beef and 1 bay leaf in a large saucepan, cover with salted water, and cook over low heat, covered, until the meat is tender, 1 to 1½ hours. Remove the meat from the stock (save the stock for another use), allow to cool at room temperature, then cut the meat into 2-inch chunks.

2. Meanwhile, in a large skillet, heat the oil over low heat until fragrant, then cook the onions, bell pepper, and garlic, stirring, or until the onions are tender, 6 to 8 minutes. Add the tomatoes, sherry, and the remaining bay leaf, and cook, uncovered, an additional 15 minutes.

3. When the meat is cool, shred it with your fingers, season with salt and pepper, add it to the tomato mixture, cover, and simmer over low heat for 30 minutes. Remove the bay leaves, garnish with the pimientos and peas, and serve with *Arroz Blanco* (Perfect White Rice, pages 200–202). The dish can be prepared a day or two in advance, cooled, and refrigerated, and then simmered, covered, over low heat until heated through, 30 to 35 minutes.

MAKES 6 TO 8 SERVINGS

Picadillo

CUBAN BEEF HASH

The spicy aroma and sweet accents of this delicious dish magically evoke childhood adventures at my grandmother's cattle ranch. This is a perfect dish for feeding a large group because it can be made days ahead and its flavor will improve and mellow as it waits. (My brother Tony and I add a little Worcestershire sauce and Tabasco sauce to the classic recipe, for an even tastier dish.)

Versatile *picadillo* is the filling for *Empanadas al Horno de Titi,* (Titi's Baked Turnovers, pages 32–33). Layered with mashed potatoes it becomes *Tambor de Picadillo* (Beef Hash and Mashed Potatoes, pages 124–25) and topped with a sweet plantain crust, *Tambor de Picadillo y Plátano* (Beef Hash and Plantain Pie, pages 125–26).

¼ cup pure Spanish olive oil

1 medium-size onion, chopped

1 medium-size green bell pepper, seeded and chopped

2 to 3 cloves garlic, finely chopped

1 pound ground beef, chuck or rump

¼ cup dry sherry

½ cup canned crushed tomatoes or prepared tomato sauce

1 tablespoon salt

1 tablespoon Worcestershire sauce, optional

½ teaspoon Tabasco sauce, optional

1 small all-purpose potato, peeled and cut into ¼-inch cubes

¼ cup dark raisins

½ cup pimiento-stuffed green olives (may be cut in halves), drained

¼ cup vegetable or peanut oil

FOR THE GARNISH:

1 large egg, hard-boiled and finely chopped

½ cup drained canned early sweet peas (I prefer LeSueur)

1 pimiento, chopped

1. In a casserole, heat the oil over low heat until fragrant, then add the onion, bell pepper, and garlic, and cook, stirring, 10 minutes. Add the beef and cook, stirring, until brown, 10 to 15 minutes, breaking up any large chunks with a wooden spoon. Drain off any excess fat.

2. Add the sherry, tomatoes, salt, Worcestershire and Tabasco, stir, and cook, uncovered, over medium heat for 15 to 20 minutes.

3. Heat the vegetable oil in a small skillet over medium-high heat until fragrant, then fry the chopped potato until golden, 10 minutes. (If you prefer not to fry the potato, boil it over medium-high heat, unpeeled and halved, in salted water to cover until tender, 20 minutes, and omit the vegetable oil.) Add the potato, raisins, and olives to the meat, correct the seasonings, and continue cooking until most of the liquid is absorbed, 10 to 15 minutes.

4. Transfer the *picadillo* to a large bowl or platter, place the chopped egg in the center, outline the border with peas, and sprinkle the entire dish with the pimiento.

MAKES 4 TO 6 SERVINGS

Tambor de Picadillo

BEEF HASH AND MASHED POTATOES

This layered casserole is undoubtedly my favorite Cuban comfort food. It is also a fine dish for company because it benefits from being made ahead of time, and I usually prepare it in stages, as the directions below reflect. You can embellish it as our cook did, by piping the potato topping in swirls around the meat hash and decorating it with pimientos and olives.

1 recipe Picadillo (see pages 122–23)

3 pounds all-purpose potatoes, peeled and quartered

2 to 3 tablespoons salted butter, at room temperature

1 cup milk or half-and-half, scalded

Salt and freshly ground black pepper to taste

¼ cup freshly grated Parmesan cheese

1. Prepare the *picadillo* one day in advance. The day of serving, bring it to room temperature.

2. Place the potatoes in a large saucepan, cover with cold, salted water, bring to a boil over medium-high heat, and boil until tender, 15 to 18 minutes. Drain the potatoes well and transfer them to a large bowl.

3. Add the milk, butter, salt, and pepper and mix with an electric mixer until the potatoes are smooth. Allow to cool 5 to 10 minutes.

4. Lightly butter a round ovenproof 3-quart casserole, spread the bottom with half the mashed potatoes, cover with all the *picadillo*, then spread with the rest of the mashed potatoes. Cover and refrigerate until ready to cook.

5. Bring the casserole to room temperature and preheat the oven to 350° F. Cover with aluminum foil or the casserole cover, place on

the middle oven rack, and bake 30 to 35 minutes. Uncover, sprinkle the top with the Parmesan cheese, and bake an additional 10 minutes. Serve hot from the casserole.

MAKES 6 SERVINGS

Tambor de Picadillo y Plátano

BEEF HASH AND PLANTAIN PIE

Picadillo—Cuban beef hash—is traditionally served with *plátanos maduros fritos*—fried sweet plantains. Here it is sandwiched between plantain layers and baked in a delicious combination of two Cuban classics.

1 recipe Picadillo (see pages 123–23), at room temperature
10 medium-size, ripe (almost black) plantains (see pages 9–10)
½ cup vegetable or peanut oil
1 large egg, lightly beaten

1. Cut the tips off the plantains, peel, and slice on the diagonal, ¼ inch thick. In a large skillet, heat the oil over medium heat until fragrant, then fry the plantain slices until brown, 3 to 4 minutes on each side, turning with a slotted spoon. Drain on a paper-towel-lined platter.

2. Preheat the oven to 350° F. In a large bowl, using a fork or potato masher, mash the plantains until smooth and thick. Divide the mixture in half.

3. Lightly oil a 2½-quart baking dish, and place half the plantain mixture in the dish, spreading it evenly and patting it down with your fingers. Spread all the *picadillo* on top and cover with the remaining plantain mixture, spreading it evenly and patting it down with your fingers. Cover loosely with aluminum foil, bake on the middle oven rack 20 minutes, then remove the foil, brush the top with the beaten egg, and bake another 20 minutes. Serve hot, accompanied by *Ensalada de Aguacate* (Avocado Salad, page 244).

MAKES 8 SERVINGS

Pulpeta

STUFFED MEATLOAF

These savory, braised loaves can be served hot, but they are usually served cold for luncheons or picnics. When they are sliced, they reveal a surprise center of hard-boiled eggs.

1½ pounds ground round
½ pound ground lean pork
½ pound ground ham
1 tablespoon salt
½ teaspoon freshly ground black pepper
1 teaspoon dried oregano
2 cloves garlic, finely chopped
2 teaspoons Worcestershire sauce
4 large eggs, lightly beaten

2 cups cracker meal (see page 7) or fine plain bread crumbs
4 large eggs, hard-boiled
½ cup vegetable or peanut oil
1 large onion, thinly sliced
2 bay leaves
½ cup dry sherry
1 cup water or Cuban Beef Stock (see pages 77–78)

1. In a large bowl, combine the beef, pork, ham, salt, pepper, oregano, garlic, and Worcestershire sauce, and mix well. Add half the beaten eggs and 1 to 1½ cups of the cracker meal and continue mixing (the best way is to use your bare hands) until the mixture is well blended, adding a bit more cracker meal if it is sticky.

2. Shape the meat into two flat rectangles about 10 inches by 4 inches. Place 2 of the hard-boiled eggs in the center of each rectangle, bring the edges of the meat up to enclose the eggs, and shape into 2 cylindrical loaves. Roll each loaf in the remaining cracker meal, brush it with the remaining beaten eggs, and roll again in the cracker meal.

3. In a heavy-bottomed casserole that will fit the loaves comfortably, heat the oil over medium heat until fragrant, then brown the loaves one at a time on all sides, turning very gently. Set the loaves aside.

4. In the same casserole, over low heat, cook the onion, stirring until golden, 4 to 5 minutes. Add the loaves, bay leaves, sherry, and water, raise the heat to high, and bring to a boil. Cover, and simmer over low heat 40 to 45 minutes, turning the loaves once.

5. Remove the bay leaves from the sauce. Transfer the loaves to a platter, and allow to rest 5 minutes before slicing ¼ inch thick. Serve hot, accompanied by the hot sauce. Or allow the loaves to cool to room temperature, then refrigerate and serve cold in sandwiches or accompanied by saltine crackers.

MAKES 8 TO 10 SERVINGS

Note: For a nicer presentation, the hot sauce can be strained.

Tasajo a la Cubana
STIR-FRIED DRIED BEEF

In classic recipes, this dried beef is stir-fried in hot lard, but you can use olive oil (my preference) or your favorite cooking oil without compromising on taste.

2½ pounds tasajo (salt-dried
  beef), desalted and cooked
  until tender (see pages 10–11)
½ to ¾ cup pure Spanish
  olive oil
2 large onions, cut in half and
  each half thickly sliced

1 bay leaf
5 to 6 cloves garlic, crushed
Salt and freshly ground black
  pepper to taste
Pinch of dried oregano

Cut the cooked beef into 2-inch chunks and shred it. In a large
skillet, heat the oil over medium heat until fragrant, and cook the
onions, stirring, 2 to 3 minutes. Add the bay leaf, garlic, and shredded meat, and cook, stirring, until the beef is crisp, 15 to 20 minutes. Season with salt, pepper, and oregano and serve hot with
Arroz Blanco (Perfect White Rice, pages 200–202).

MAKES 6 TO 8 SERVINGS

Note: Remove whole garlic cloves if desired.

Aporreado de Tasajo

SALT-DRIED BEEF STEW

In the days before refrigeration, a colonial Cuban home often was
equipped with a *carnicería*—a cool room where beef was salted and
hung from hooks to dry. Dried salted beef could be stored indefi-
nitely without spoiling, and after soaking it could be prepared like
fresh meat.

Even after refrigeration came to Cuba, salt-dried beef remained
popular and it is still prepared today. Sometimes cookbooks refer to
it as "corned beef" or "beef jerky," both erroneous names. Ask for
salt-dried beef or hung beef, and you will get the proper meat.

½ cup pure Spanish olive oil

2 medium-size onions, halved and thickly sliced

2 medium-size green bell peppers, seeded and cut into thin strips

4 cloves garlic, finely chopped

1 cup drained and chopped canned whole tomatoes or prepared tomato sauce

½ cup dry sherry

Pinch of dried oregano

2½ pounds tasajo (salt-dried beef), desalted, cooked until tender (see pages 10–11), and 1 cup of its cooking liquid reserved

Salt and freshly ground black pepper to taste

1. In a large saucepan, heat the olive oil over low heat until fragrant, then cook the onions, bell peppers, and garlic, stirring, until the onions are tender, about 5 minutes. Add the tomatoes, sherry, and oregano and cook, uncovered, another 10 minutes. Set aside.

2. Cut the cooked beef into 2-inch chunks and shred it. Return the tomato mixture to the stove over low heat, add the beef and reserved cooking liquid, and simmer, uncovered, 25 to 30 minutes. Correct the seasonings and serve hot with *Arroz Blanco* (Perfect White Rice, pages 200–202).

The dish improves in flavor if prepared several days ahead of time, cooled, and refrigerated. To reheat, simmer it, covered, over low heat for 30 to 35 minutes.

MAKES 6 TO 8 SERVINGS

Harina Rellena

STUFFED CORNMEAL PIE

This tasty pie is like a large *tamale* of cornmeal layered with *picadillo*. It is a very inexpensive way to feed a large crowd.

3 tablespoons pure Spanish
  olive oil
2 cloves garlic, finely chopped
1 cup stone-ground yellow
  cornmeal
6 cups water, Cuban Beef Stock
  (see pages 77–78), or canned
  beef broth, cold or at room
  temperature

Salt and freshly ground black
  pepper to taste
1 recipe Picadillo (see pages
  122–23) and note below

1. In a large, nonstick saucepan, heat the oil over low heat until fragrant, then cook the garlic, stirring, 1 minute. Add the cornmeal, water, salt, and pepper, and cook over medium heat, whisking occasionally, after the cornmeal starts to thicken, 20 to 25 minutes. Reduce the heat to low, cover, and simmer until thick, 20 to 30 minutes. (Cooking time for cornmeal can vary considerably.)

2. Preheat the oven to 350° F. Lightly oil a 3-quart baking dish, spread half the cooled cornmeal mixture on the bottom, top with all the *picadillo*, and then spread the remaining cornmeal over it. Bake, covered, until heated through, 40 to 45 minutes. Serve immediately, or keep warm in a 200° F oven until ready to serve.

MAKES 6 TO 8 SERVINGS

Variations: In place of the *picadillo*, use 1 recipe of the chicken filling from *Tambor de Maíz* (Corn and Chicken Pie, pages 151–53), or 1 recipe *Cangrejos Enchilados* (Crab in Creole Sauce, pages 190–91), or its lobster or shrimp variations.

Lechón Asado

ROAST SUCKLING PIG

Christmas Eve, *Noche Buena*, always meant a wonderful feast at our home in Puerta de Golpe. December weather was mild, and we dined in the courtyard overlooking the garden, where extra tables and chairs had been brought in to accommodate the many friends from Havana who traditionally came to celebrate with us. Mom had the tables set with festive linen, china, and silver and the trees decorated with colorful holiday lights. All day long, pigs had been roasting in outdoor barbecue pits on another part of the property, tempting us with their garlicky fragrance, and when they were brought to the tables, their crisp skins were burnished a deep red-brown and their tender meat was practically falling from the bone. Our Christmas Eve party, with festive music and dancing, lasted for hours and, I am told, filled the whole neighborhood with holiday spirit.

In Cuba, the traditional Christmas pigs were roasted over open fires or prepared by local restaurants for families to take home. In Miami, families can buy their roasts ready-cooked, or they can take oven-ready pigs, seasoned at home, to bakeries that prepare the roasts in their large ovens. You can roast this little pig at home, since it weighs only ten to fifteen pounds, but you must order it specially from the butcher and take some care in its preparation. The roast requires a pan with generous sides, so the fat will not splatter. Make sure beforehand that the pan fits comfortably in your oven and reserve enough refrigerator space for the overnight marination—the key to a successful roast pig.

Pigs over fifteen pounds are too large for standard ovens, but you can prepare a larger pig if you have the butcher cut it in half for roasting, and then join the halves together on a platter before serv-ing. In judging doneness, be guided by skin color—Cubans like their suckling pig roasted to a deep cordovan brown—and internal temperature, which should be 185° F to 190° F.

One 10- to 15-pound suckling pig (1 pound per person), prepared by the butcher for roasting
8 to 10 cloves garlic, or to taste
2 teaspoons dried oregano
3 to 4 teaspoons salt
Freshly ground black pepper to taste

2 cups sour (Seville) orange juice (see page 9) or 1 cup sweet orange juice mixed with ½ cup each fresh lime juice and lemon juice
2 bay leaves, crumbled
Pure Spanish olive oil for basting
1 apple, orange, lemon, or lime for garnish

1. One day before cooking, wash the pig inside and out and pat dry with paper towels. In a mortar, combine the garlic, oregano, and salt, and mash to a paste. Place the pig in a large pan, rub it inside and out with the garlic paste, season it liberally with salt and pepper, and pour the sour orange juice over it. Sprinkle with the crumbled bay leaves. Cover the pig with aluminum foil and refrigerate 24 hours.

2. Three to 5 hours before serving, preheat the oven to 375° F, remove the pig from the marinade, and reserve the marinade. Place the pig in a shallow, aluminum foil-lined roasting pan, insert a wad of foil in the mouth to keep it open, cover the ears with foil, and brush the skin with oil. Insert a meat thermometer in the hind leg, making sure it does not touch bone.

3. Roast the pig 1 hour, lower the oven temperature to 350° F, and bake 2 to 5 hours more (depending upon the size of the pig), basting frequently with oil, juices, and reserved marinade. Remove the foil from the ears halfway through the baking time.

4. When the pig is done to an internal temperature of 185° F to 190° F, the skin is a cordovan brown, and the juices run clear when the thigh is pierced with a fork, transfer it to a large platter and allow it to rest 15 to 20 minutes before carving. (The meat will be

very well done and practically falling from the bones.) Remove the foil from the mouth and replace it with your choice of fruit. Serve the carved pig with *Moros y Cristianos* (Black Beans and Rice, pages 204–205), *Yuca con Mojo* (Yuca with Garlic Sauce, page 272), *Ensalada Vasca* (Basque Tossed Salad, pages 242–43), and loads of extra *Mojo Criollo* (Creole Garlic Sauce, page 26).

MAKES 10 TO 12 SERVINGS

Puerco Asado

ROAST PORK LOIN

This is my mother's version of the classic Cuban roast, which is always served accompanied by *Mojo Criollo* (page 26), the forceful garlic sauce. It is delicious simply moistened with its own pan juices and served with *Arroz Blanco* (Perfect White Rice, pages 200–202) and a salad of fresh, ripe avocados.

One 5-pound boneless pork loin, trimmed and tied
2 to 4 cloves garlic
½ teaspoon dried oregano
Salt and freshly ground black pepper to taste
¼ cup fresh lime juice
¼ cup orange juice
1 cup dry red wine

1. Several hours before cooking, score the roast all over its surface with the tip of a knife. In a mortar, combine the garlic and oregano and mash into a paste. Place the roast in a nonreactive dish, rub it with the garlic paste, salt, and pepper, and pour the juices and wine over it. Cover with plastic wrap and refrigerate at least 2 hours, turning the roast several times.

2. Preheat the oven to 350° F, remove the roast from its marinade, pat it dry, discard the bay leaves, and reserve the marinade. Place the meat in a roasting pan and insert a meat thermometer. Roast, uncovered, 2½ hours, to an internal temperature of 165° F. Halfway through the cooking time, pour the reserved marinade over it, and continue cooking, basting frequently with the pan juices.

3. When the roast is done, transfer it to a serving platter, cover it with aluminum foil, and allow it to stand 10 to 15 minutes before carving it into thin slices.

MAKES 8 SERVINGS

Pierna de Puerco Asada

ROAST LEG OF PORK CREOLE

This hearty pork dish is as indigenous to Cuba as black beans. Serve it hot with *Mojo Criollo* (page 26)—the powerful garlic sauce—add it cold to a platter of *entremes variados*—cold meats—or use it to construct the *Media Noche*—a robust midnight sandwich. It is a true Cuban classic.

One 5- to 6-pound leg or shoulder of pork
6 cloves garlic
1 teaspoon dried oregano
1 tablespoon salt
½ teaspoon ground cumin
Freshly ground black pepper to taste

½ cup Seville (sour) orange juice (see page 9) or ¼ cup sweet orange juice combined with ⅛ cup each fresh lime and lemon juice
½ cup dry sherry
2 large onions, thickly sliced

1. The night before serving, remove any excess fat from the leg of pork and pierce the meat all over with the tip of a knife. In a mortar, combine the garlic, oregano, salt, and cumin, and mash into a paste. Place the pork in a nonreactive pan and rub it well with the paste, sprinkle liberally with pepper, add the orange juice, sherry, and onions, cover with plastic wrap, and refrigerate overnight, turning the meat several times.

2. About 4½ hours before serving, preheat the oven to 350° F. Remove the meat from the marinade, pat it dry, and reserve the marinade. Place the pork in an aluminum-foil-lined roasting pan. Roast 1 hour, turning the roast to brown on all sides. Insert a meat thermometer, making sure it doesn't touch bone. Lower the oven temperature to 325° F, pour the reserved marinade over it, cover loosely with aluminum foil, and cook another 3 hours or so, turning the meat once and basting frequently with pan juices, until the meat reaches an internal temperature of 180° F. Remove the foil during the last 30 minutes of roasting, adding sherry if the meat becomes dry.

3. When it is done, remove the leg of pork to a serving platter and allow it to stand, covered with the foil, 15 minutes before carving. Serve with *Mojo Criollo* (Creole Garlic Sauce).

MAKES 8 SERVINGS

Pierna Rellena

STUFFED ROAST LOIN OF PORK

This simple roast is my mother's recipe. The contrasting flavors of the sweet prunes and salty ham highlight the delicate flavor of the pork. The roast can also be served cold as part of a platter of cold cuts for a buffet luncheon or dinner.

One 4- to 5-pound boneless pork
    loin, cut with a lengthwise
    pocket for stuffing
Salt and freshly ground black
    pepper to taste
1/2 pound ham steak, cut in
    1/2-inch chunks
1 cup pitted prunes

1 1/2 cups firmly packed dark
    brown sugar
Two 7-ounce bottles Malta
    Hatuey, a nonalcoholic malt
    drink available in Hispanic
    markets
Fresh sprigs parsley for garnish

1. Preheat the oven to 350° F. Season the roast liberally inside and out with salt and pepper and stuff the pocket with alternating layers of ham and prunes, using the handle of a wooden spoon to push the stuffing into the meat. Tie the roast with kitchen twine and place in a shallow baking pan. Insert a meat thermometer.

2. In a small bowl, combine the sugar and Malta and pour the mixture over the roast. Set the baking pan on the middle oven rack and roast uncovered, 2 to 2½ hours (or 25 to 30 minutes per pound), to an internal temperature of 160° F, turning to brown all sides of the meat and basting frequently.

3. When the roast is done, remove it from the oven and allow it to stand, covered with aluminum foil, 15 to 20 minutes before carving it into thin slices. Arrange the meat on a serving platter, spoon the pan juices over, and sprinkle with parsley.

MAKES 8 SERVINGS

Chuletas de Puerco Criollas

CUBAN PORK CHOPS

The marriage of pork, sherry, and sour orange juice, plus generous additions of garlic, sautéed onions, and herbs, makes this a truly delicious Creole dish.

8 thin, center-cut pork chops,
   about 4 ounces each
Salt and freshly ground black
   pepper to taste
4 cloves garlic
¼ teaspoon dried oregano
¼ teaspoon ground cumin

½ cup sour (Seville) orange juice
   (see page 9) or ¼ cup sweet
   orange juice mixed with ⅛ cup
   each fresh lime and lemon juice
2 large onions, thinly sliced
¼ cup pure Spanish olive oil
½ cup dry sherry

1. Season the chops with salt and pepper. In a mortar, crush the garlic, oregano, and cumin together into a paste. Rub the chops with the garlic paste, place in a nonreactive bowl, pour the orange juice over, and cover with the sliced onions. Cover and refrigerate 2 to 3 hours.

2. Remove the chops from the marinade, pat dry with paper towels, and reserve the marinade. In a large skillet, heat the oil over medium heat until fragrant, then brown the chops on both sides. Add the sherry and reserved marinade, including the onions, cover, and cook until the chops are tender, about 20 minutes. Serve hot, accompanied by *Moros y Cristianos* (Black Beans and Rice, pages 204–205) or *Boniatos Fritos* (Fried Sweet Potato Rounds), pages 267–68).

MAKES 4 SERVINGS

Masitas de Puerco Frita

FRIED PORK CHUNKS

We always served these crisp and succulent pork chunks with *Moros y Cristianos* (pages 204–205), the Cuban combination of black beans and white rice, and *Mojo Criollo* (Creole Garlic Sauce, page 26).

When frying the pork chunks, remember to start them on high heat, lower the temperature when the oil is very hot, and turn up the heat again when they are almost finished, to ensure crispness.

2 pounds lean boneless pork (shoulder or leg), cut into 2-inch cubes
Salt and freshly ground black pepper to taste
4 cloves garlic

½ cup sour (Seville) orange juice (see page 9) or ¼ cup sweet orange juice mixed with ⅛ cup each fresh lime and lemon juice
Vegetable or peanut oil for frying

1. Sprinkle the meat liberally with salt and pepper. In a mortar, crush the garlic into a paste and rub the pork with the garlic paste. Place the pork in a nonreactive bowl and pour over the orange juice. Cover and refrigerate 2 to 3 hours.

2. Drain the pork cubes. In a large saucepan, over medium heat, heat 2 inches of oil until very hot but not smoking, then add the pork cubes, without crowding them, raise the heat to high, and brown the cubes, turning with a slotted spoon. (The pork will release some moisture, lowering the oil temperature considerably.) When oil temperature rises again, lower the heat a little and cook the cubes, turning frequently, until they are a rich, golden brown, another 10 minutes. Occasionally turn up the heat when necessary to crisp the cubes. As the cubes are finished, transfer them to a paper-towel-lined platter to drain; keep warm in a 200°F oven until all the cubes are fried. Serve immediately, with *Moros y Cristianos* (Black Beans and Rice) and *Mojo Criollo* (Creole Garlic Sauce).

MAKES 4 SERVINGS

Tamal en Cazuela

CORNMEAL STEW

For this modernized version of a traditional Cuban dish, I usually make the meat and tomato sauce ahead of time and blend it with the cornmeal at the last minute. *Tamal en Cazuela* is very flexible, so feel free to substitute chicken or beef for the pork and ham for the chorizo. Any way you prepare it, you will have a great main dish for a winter's evening.

1 pound lean boneless pork shoulder cut into bite-size cubes
Salt and freshly ground black pepper to taste
Juice of 1 lime
2 to 3 tablespoons pure Spanish olive oil
1 large onion, finely chopped
1 large green bell pepper, seeded and finely chopped
3 cloves garlic, finely chopped

1 chorizo or other spicy sausage, diced, optional (see pages 6–7)
2 cups drained and chopped canned whole tomatoes or prepared tomato sauce
1/2 cup dry sherry
1/2 teaspoon ground cumin
Dash of Tabasco sauce

*1 cup stone-ground yellow
  cornmeal*
6 cups cold water
*2 tablespoons pure Spanish
  olive oil*

3 teaspoons salt
*Freshly ground black pepper to
  taste*

1. In a nonreactive bowl, sprinkle the pork with the salt, pepper, and lime juice, cover, and let marinate 2 hours, refrigerated.

2. In a large skillet over high heat, heat the oil until fragrant. Drain the pork cubes (reserving the marinade) and pat them dry, add them to the skillet, and cook, turning often with a slotted spoon, until golden brown, 15 to 20 minutes. Reduce the heat to low, add the onion, bell pepper, and garlic, and cook, stirring, until the onion is tender, 6 to 8 minutes. Add the chorizo, tomatoes, sherry, cumin, Tabasco, and reserved marinade and simmer 30 minutes, stirring frequently. (Can be prepared ahead up to this point and refrigerated.)

3. In a large, nonstick saucepan over medium heat, combine the cornmeal, 5 cups of the water, the oil, salt, and pepper, and cook, whisking frequently, until the mixture starts to thicken. Add the remaining water, whisk to blend, and cover. Reduce the heat to low and simmer until thickened, 20 to 30 minutes. (Cooking time for cornmeal can vary considerably.)

4. Add the tomato mixture to the cornmeal, blend well, correct the seasonings, and serve.

MAKES 4 TO 6 SERVINGS

Higado a la Italiana

ITALIAN-STYLE LIVER

Despite its name, this standard of the Cuban kitchen bears no resemblance to any of the classic Italian liver preparations. This recipe originally comes from my sister-in-law Yolanda's mother, Yolanda Balais, whose husband, Dr. Miguel Balais, is a Cuban history buff.

1½ pounds calf or beef liver, skin removed, thinly sliced, and cut into pieces approximately 1½-inch square
Salt and freshly ground black pepper to taste
2 cloves garlic
¼ cup red wine vinegar
¼ cup dry sherry
1 tablespoon flour
1 bay leaf
¼ cup pure Spanish olive oil
1 large onion, thinly sliced
1 medium-size green bell pepper, seeded and cut into thin strips

1. Sprinkle the liver with salt and pepper. In a mortar, crush the garlic into a thick paste and rub the paste into the liver. In a small bowl, combine the vinegar, sherry, and flour, and pour over the liver in a nonreactive bowl. Add the bay leaf, cover, and refrigerate 2 hours.

2. In a large skillet, heat the oil over low heat until fragrant, then cook the onions and bell peppers, stirring, 3 to 4 minutes. Raise the heat to high, add the liver and marinade (discarding bay leaf), and cook, stirring, to desired doneness, about 10 minutes. Serve at once.

MAKES 4 SERVINGS

Chilindrón de Carnero

LAMB STEW

Although my paternal grandmother, Abuela Ina, is most famous for her fish and shellfish recipes, she also produced a marvelous Cuban lamb stew, which she always made with ripe tomatoes.

2½ pounds boneless shoulder of
  lamb, cut into 2-inch cubes
Salt and freshly ground black
  pepper to taste
Juice of 2 limes
Flour for dredging
¼ cup pure Spanish olive oil
½ pound tocino (slab bacon),
  rind removed and cut into
  ¼-inch dice
1 large onion, thinly sliced
1 large green bell pepper, seeded
  and thinly sliced

3 to 4 cloves garlic, finely
  chopped
6 medium-size ripe tomatoes, or
  2 cups drained and chopped
  canned whole or crushed
  tomatoes
1 cup dry sherry
¼ teaspoon dried oregano
½ teaspoon cumin seeds
1 teaspoon hot paprika
1 bay leaf
3 tablespoons finely chopped fresh
  parsley

1. In a large nonreactive bowl, sprinkle the lamb chunks liberally with salt, pepper, and lime juice, cover, and refrigerate 2 hours.

2. Drain the lamb (reserving the marinade) and pat it dry, then roll the lamb chunks in the flour. In a large, heavy-bottomed casserole, heat the oil over medium heat until fragrant, then brown the lamb on all sides, turning it with a slotted spoon, and transfer it to a plate when done.

3. In the same casserole, brown the bacon over medium heat 3 to 4 minutes, then add the onion, bell pepper, and garlic, reduce the heat to low, and cook, stirring, until tender, 5 to 6 minutes. Return

the lamb to the casserole, add the reserved marinade, the tomatoes, sherry, oregano, cumin seeds, paprika, and bay leaf, cover, and simmer until the lamb is tender, 1 to 1½ hours. Transfer to a serving bowl, discard the bay leaf, stir in the parsley, and serve with *Arroz Blanco* (Perfect White Rice, pages 200–202).

MAKES 6 SERVINGS

Sesos Fritos

FRIED BRAINS

No Cuban cookbook would be complete without at least one recipe for brains, for there are many in Cuban cuisine. This is my mother's recipe.

1½ pounds lamb or calf brains, soaked 1 hour in cold water, changing the water twice, skin and membranes then removed (you need not refrigerate when soaking)

3 tablespoons mild vinegar or juice of 1 lemon

Salt and freshly ground black pepper to taste

2 large eggs, lightly beaten

1 cup cracker meal (see page 7) or fine bread crumbs

Vegetable or peanut oil for frying

1 tablespoon finely chopped fresh parsley

2 limes, cut into wedges, for garnish

1. Place the prepared brains in a medium-size saucepan with salted water to cover and the vinegar, and simmer over low heat, uncovered, 15 minutes. Drain, rinse in cold water, pat dry with paper towels, and allow to cool at room temperature.

2. Place the cooled brains in a nonreactive bowl, sprinkle with salt and pepper, and allow to stand, covered, at room temperature 1 hour. Cut into bite-size pieces. Drain, pat dry with paper towels, dip in the beaten eggs, and roll in the cracker meal.

3. In a large skillet, heat 2 inches of oil to 375° F, or until the oil sizzles when a piece of meat touches it. Fry the brains until lightly golden, and drain on paper towels. Transfer to a serving platter, garnish with the parsley and lime wedges, and serve hot.

MAKES 6 SERVINGS

Pollo Criollo en Cazuela

MOM'S FARM-STYLE CHICKEN

A favorite in our family, this dish features chicken that simmers on the stove until the meat practically falls off the bones. Organic or free-range chickens are perfect for this recipe, since they are similar to the farm chickens in Cuba.

One 3-pound roasting chicken, cut into quarters or serving pieces, or 3 pounds chicken breasts and thighs
Salt and freshly ground black pepper to taste
3 to 4 cloves garlic
½ teaspoon ground cumin
½ cup sour (Seville) orange juice (see page 9) or ¼ cup sweet orange juice mixed with ⅛ cup each fresh lime and lemon juice

¼ cup pure Spanish olive oil or vegetable oil
½ cup dry sherry
1 large onion, thinly sliced
½ cup chicken stock (pages 78–79) or canned chicken broth
1 tablespoon flour, optional
2 tablespoons finely chopped fresh parsley

1. Wash the chicken, pat it dry with paper towels, and season liberally with salt and pepper. In a mortar, crush the garlic into a paste with the cumin and rub the garlic paste into the chicken. Place the chicken in a nonreactive bowl, pour the orange juice over it, cover, and refrigerate at least 1 hour, or overnight.

2. Remove the chicken from the marinade (reserving the marinade) and pat dry. In a heavy-bottomed casserole, heat the oil over medium heat until fragrant, then brown the chicken on all sides. Add the reserved marinade, the sherry, onion, and stock, reduce the heat to low, cover, and simmer until the chicken is fork tender, 35 to 45 minutes. Transfer the chicken to a serving platter. Strain the sauce through a colander and return it with the flour to the casserole. Cook the sauce over low heat, stirring, until it has thickened, 5 to 6 minutes, correct the seasonings, pour over the chicken, and garnish with the parsley.

MAKES 4 SERVINGS

Chilindrón de Pollo

BASQUE CHICKEN

My paternal grandfather was Basque and he adored this earthy native dish, which was often prepared at his home. If it is too hot for your palate, you can alter the intensity by using less hot chili; or if you are Basque yourself, you can add more.

One tip: When doubling or tripling this recipe for a large group, brown the chicken in several batches. Then divide the chicken and the *sofrito* among two or three casseroles.

2 chickens, 3½ to 4 pounds each, each cut into 6 to 8 pieces, skin removed

Salt and freshly ground black pepper to taste

¼ cup pure Spanish olive oil

FOR THE SOFRITO:

4 to 6 cloves garlic, finely chopped

2 medium-size onions, cut in half lengthwise and thinly sliced

1 medium-size green bell pepper, seeded and cut into thin strips

¼ pound smoked ham, cubed

2 chorizos or other spicy sausage, cut into ½-inch slices (see pages 6–7)

2 cups canned crushed tomatoes

½ cup dry sherry

½ teaspoon red pepper flakes or 1 teaspoon Tabasco sauce or more to taste

½ cup green Spanish olives, pitted

1. Wash the chicken pieces, dry them with paper towels, and season them with salt and pepper.

2. In a large skillet, heat the oil over medium heat until fragrant, then brown the chicken on all sides, a few pieces at a time. Transfer the browned pieces to a platter.

3. To prepare the *sofrito*, add the garlic, onions, and bell pepper to the oil remaining in the skillet and cook over low heat, stirring frequently, until the onions are soft but not browned. Add the ham and sausage and cook until browned, about 5 minutes. Add the tomatoes, sherry, and pepper flakes and cook over medium heat about 10 minutes.

4. Return the chicken to the skillet, cover, and cook over low heat 45 minutes to 1 hour, stirring frequently to prevent sticking. Add the olives, correct the seasoning, and cook another 10 minutes.

5. Transfer to a large platter and serve with *Arroz Blanco* (Perfect White Rice, pages 200–202).

MAKES 8 SERVINGS

Guinea Africana

GUINEA HEN AFRICAN STYLE

This recipe was given to my mother by her sister-in-law, our Tia (Aunt) Yeya, from a yellowed Havana newspaper clipping that had been in her recipe file for forty years. The original recipe calls for yam chunks to be cooked along with the hen, but Mom considers the result too mushy. Therefore she advises boiling or baking the yams separately and serving them alongside the hen. If you cannot find guinea hen, you may substitute chicken.

One 2½- to 3-pound guinea hen, cut into 6 to 8 serving pieces
Salt and freshly ground black pepper to taste
3 tablespoons pure Spanish olive oil
3 tablespoons salted butter
1 large onion, finely chopped
2 cloves garlic, finely chopped
½ cup dry sherry

1 cup chicken stock (pages 78–79) or canned chicken broth
1 tablespoon flour
3 medium-size, ripe tomatoes, peeled, seeded, and chopped or 1 cup drained and chopped canned whole tomatoes
1 bay leaf
4 medium-size yams, cooked (see note below)

1. Wash and dry the hen and season liberally with salt and pepper. In a heavy casserole over medium heat, heat the oil and butter until fragrant. Brown the hen pieces on all sides, remove them from the casserole, and set aside.

2. Add the onion and garlic to the oil remaining in the casserole and cook, stirring, until softened but not brown, about 5 minutes. Add the sherry, chicken stock, and flour, raise the heat to high, mix well, and add the tomatoes and bay leaf.

3. Return the hen to the casserole, reduce the heat to low, cover, and cook until very tender, 40 to 50 minutes, stirring frequently.

Transfer the hen to a serving platter, top with the sauce (discarding the bay leaf), and serve with the boiled or baked yams.

MAKES 4 SERVINGS

Note: Boil the scrubbed unpeeled yams over medium heat, uncovered, in salted water to cover until tender, 30 to 40 minutes. Drain, return to the pan, reduce the heat to low, and shake the pan over the heat until any remaining moisture has evaporated. Or bake the yams at 400° F until tender, 40 to 45 minutes. Cut the unpeeled yams in half after cooking.

Pollo de Rancho Luna

CHICKEN RANCHO LUNA

Rancho Luna was a *campestre* — an outdoor country-style restaurant — on the outskirts of Havana, famous for chicken and pork that were cooked to perfection over a wood fire. Rancho Luna provided my first al fresco dining experience, as I sat on a wooden picnic bench with my family and friends, and the speakers hung among the trees filled the air with "Unforgettable," sung by Nat King Cole. That day is still unforgettable.

Two 2½-pound roasting chickens, each cut into quarters, backbone removed

Salt and freshly ground black pepper to taste

FOR THE MARINADE:
6 to 8 cloves garlic
¼ teaspoon dried oregano
½ teaspoon ground cumin
⅓ cup fresh lime juice

3 teaspoons Worcestershire sauce
¼ cup dry sherry
¼ cup pure Spanish olive oil

1 small onion, finely sliced, for garnish

2 tablespoons finely chopped fresh parsley, for garnish

1. Wash the chicken, pat dry, and sprinkle liberally with salt and pepper. In a mortar, mash to a paste the garlic, oregano, and cumin. Combine the remaining marinade ingredients with the garlic paste and rub the chicken well with the mixture. Place in a large non-reactive bowl, cover, and refrigerate for several hours or preferably overnight.

2. Remove the chicken from the marinade (reserving the marinade) and pat dry. Place the chicken on a lightly oiled aluminum-foil-lined broiler pan, bone side up, 5 to 6 inches from the heat source. Broil 13 to 15 minutes on each side, basting frequently with the marinade. If the skin cooks too rapidly, lower the broiler rack. Transfer the chicken to a serving platter, brush with any remaining marinade, and garnish with the onion and parsley.

MAKES 4 TO 6 SERVINGS

Pollo Borracho

DRUNKEN CHICKEN

Many countries have a version of this dish, using the most popular local wines or liqueurs. This particular recipe comes from a Cuban friend, Billie Taylor, who is a television stylist. I have found it excellent for parties and easy to double or triple for a large group or a buffet. I usually make it a day in advance or the morning of the party and reheat it in the oven, covered, just before serving, or in the original pan, on top of the stove. Serve with *Arroz Blanco* (Perfect White Rice, pages 200–202) or *Arroz Amarillo* (Yellow Rice, pages 202–203).

One 4- to 5-pound frying chicken, cut into serving pieces and skin removed

Salt and freshly ground black pepper to taste

1/2 teaspoon dried oregano

1/4 cup pure Spanish olive oil

2 to 3 cloves garlic, minced

1 large onion, thickly sliced

1 bay leaf

1/2 cup dry white wine

1/2 cup light rum

3/4 cup unpitted large green Spanish olives, drained

1. Wash the chicken pieces, pat dry with paper towels, and season with salt, pepper, and oregano.

2. In an ovenproof skillet large enough to hold the chicken pieces without crowding, heat the olive oil over medium heat until fragrant, and brown the chicken pieces well on all sides. Remove the chicken from the pan and set it aside. Reduce the heat to low, add the garlic and onions, and cook, stirring, until tender, 6 to 8 minutes, adding more oil if necessary. Add the bay leaf, wine, rum, and olives and stir to incorporate. Return the chicken to the pan, cover, and cook over low heat until tender, about 45 to 60 minutes or, if you prefer, place the covered skillet in a 350° F oven for 45 minutes. Remove the bay leaf and serve.

MAKES 4 SERVINGS

Masitas de Pollo Frito

FRIED CHICKEN MORSELS

Long before there were Chicken McNuggets, we were enjoying our own Creole deep-fried chicken morsels.

2 1/2 to 3 pounds boneless breast of chicken, cut into 1 1/2-inch chunks

Salt and freshly ground black pepper to taste

3 cloves garlic

½ teaspoon dried oregano
½ teaspoon ground cumin
Juice of 2 limes
⅔ cup all-purpose flour
1 teaspoon paprika

Vegetable or peanut oil for frying
2 tablespoons finely chopped fresh
   parsley for garnish
1 recipe Mojo Criollo (page 26)

1. Wash the chicken, pat dry with paper towels, and season liberally with salt and pepper. In a mortar, crush the garlic to a paste with the oregano and cumin and rub the chicken pieces with the mixture. Place the chicken in a nonreactive bowl and sprinkle with the lime juice. Cover and refrigerate 2 to 3 hours.

2. Preheat the oven to 200° F. Drain the chicken, pat it dry with paper towels, and discard the marinade. On a plate, combine the flour and paprika, roll the chicken pieces in the mixture to coat, and set aside.

3. Meanwhile, in a large skillet over medium-high heat, heat 1 inch of oil until hot but not smoking, or until a small piece of chicken sizzles when it touches the oil, and fry as many pieces of chicken as can fit comfortably in the skillet, turning with a slotted spoon, until until golden and crisp, about 5 minutes on each side. Transfer the finished pieces to a paper-towel-lined plate and keep warm in a low oven until all the chicken has been fried.

4. Transfer to a serving platter, garnish with the parsley, and serve accompanied by the garlic sauce and your favorite rice dish.

MAKES 6 SERVINGS

Tambor de Maíz

CORN AND CHICKEN PIE

This layered pie, one of our cook Rosalie's specialties, goes especially well with a refreshing *Ensalada de Aguacate* (Avocado Salad, page 244). It is a rich, traditional preparation, calling for grated fresh corn thickened with egg yolks. When I serve it to company, I prepare the chicken-tomato mixture the night ahead and put the entire pie together the next day—always a good strategy for entertaining.

One 2- to 3-pound chicken, cut into serving pieces and skin removed

Salt and freshly ground black pepper to taste

2 tablespoons fresh lime juice

½ cup pure Spanish olive oil

2 medium-size onions, finely chopped

2 medium-size green bell peppers, seeded and finely chopped

3 large cloves garlic, finely chopped

2 cups drained and chopped canned whole tomatoes

¼ teaspoon ground cumin

¼ cup chopped drained pimientos

½ cup dry sherry

½ cup pimiento-stuffed green olives, drained and chopped

2 tablespoons drained brine-packed Spanish capers

3 cups fresh (from 6 ears of corn) or frozen corn kernels

1 cup milk

1 teaspoon salt

1 tablespoon sugar

6 large egg yolks

1 cup grated muenster cheese

1. Wash and pat dry the chicken, and season it liberally with the salt, pepper, and lime juice. In a large, heavy-bottomed casserole, heat the oil over medium-high heat until it is fragrant. Cook the chicken pieces, turning them occasionally, until golden brown, and transfer to a platter to cool at room temperature.

2. Using the same casserole, adding a little oil if necessary, cook, stirring, the onion, bell pepper, and garlic over low heat until tender, 6 to 8 minutes. Add the tomatoes and cook, stirring occasionally, another 15 to 20 minutes. Measure out 1 cup of the tomato mixture and set aside. To the remaining mixture, add the cumin, pimientos, sherry, olives, and capers, cover, and simmer over low heat 35 minutes. If the sauce is watery, reduce until thickened over medium-high heat.

3. Remove the sauce from the heat. When the chicken is cool enough to handle, cut it into bite-size pieces and discard the bones. Add the chicken to the tomato sauce and blend thoroughly. (Can be made ahead up to this point and refrigerated.)

4. Preheat the oven to 350° F and lighly oil a 3-quart ovenproof baking dish. In a food processor fitted with a steel blade or a blender, process the corn kernels until pureed. In a medium-size saucepan over medium-low heat, combine the corn with the milk, salt, pepper, sugar, and the reserved cup of tomato sauce, and cook, uncovered, until the mixture is thick, 20 to 25 minutes. Remove from the heat, mix in the egg yolks, and set aside. Allow to cool slightly.

5. Spread half the corn mixture on the bottom of the prepared baking dish and pat down with your fingers. Cover it with all the chicken mixture and top with the remaining corn. Bake, uncovered, 40 to 45 minutes, then sprinkle with the cheese and bake an additional 5 minutes. Serve hot from the casserole.

MAKES 6 SERVINGS

Variations: In place of the chicken filling, use 1 recipe *Picadillo* (Cuban Beef Hash, pages 122–23).

Pavo Relleno

STUFFED TURKEY, CUBAN STYLE

In Cuba we did not celebrate American Thanksgiving, and although we often ate turkey, ours was traditionally stuffed with *picadillo*—Cuban beef hash, or *Moros y Cristianos*—black beans and rice. This was the way Mom prepared turkey for our family's first Thanksgiving in Miami, and I was mortified. I recall visiting my American neighbors, whose homes were filled with the aromas of turkey with cornbread stuffing, sweet potato casseroles dotted with mini marshmallows, pumpkin pies, and other dishes that seemed to come straight from "Kraft Television Theater" recipes, and begging Mom to change her menu. She would not hear of it, but once we all grew up and started cooking, she lost her vote. For years, our family has celebrated Thanksgiving with course after course of American food, from pumpkin soup to mince pie.

We often ask Mom to prepare Cuban turkey for us during the year, but never on Thanksgiving. We fought too hard to give up that victory.

One 12- to 14-pound turkey, washed inside and out and dried with paper towels
Salt and freshly ground black pepper to taste
4 to 5 cloves garlic, crushed

1 cup sour (Seville) orange juice (see page 9) or 1/2 cup sweet orange juice mixed with 1/4 cup each fresh lime and lemon juice
1/4 pound (1 stick) salted butter, at room temperature

FOR THE STUFFING:
1/2 cup pure Spanish olive oil
1 large onion, finely chopped
1 large green bell pepper, seeded and finely chopped
5 cloves garlic, finely chopped
1 pound ground pork
1 pound ground ham
1 pound ground beef round
1/2 cup drained and chopped canned whole tomatoes, or prepared tomato sauce

1/2 pound slivered blanched almonds
1/2 cup dark raisins
1/2 cup finely chopped drained pimiento-stuffed green olives
4 large eggs, hard-boiled and finely chopped
Salt and freshly ground black pepper to taste
2 teaspoons Spanish paprika or mild paprika

1. In a nonreactive pan, season the turkey liberally with salt and pepper inside and out. In a mortar, crush the garlic into a thick paste and rub it over the turkey, inside and out. Pour the orange juice over the turkey, and set it aside.

2. To prepare the stuffing, heat the oil over low heat in a large skillet until fragrant. Cook the onion, bell pepper, and garlic, stirring, until tender, 6 to 8 minutes. Add the pork, ham, and beef, raise the heat to medium, and cook, uncovered, 15 to 20 minutes, until the meat is cooked through, breaking up any chunks with a wooden spoon. Add the remaining ingredients, reduce the heat to low, and cook, covered, 20 minutes.

3. Preheat the oven to 325° F. Fill the turkey cavity with the stuffing, packing it loosely, rub the butter into the turkey's skin, and close the cavity with trussing skewers or sew with a trussing needle and thread. If there is any stuffing left over, place it in a baking pan and bake it, covered, for 20 to 30 minutes. Place the turkey breast-side up in an aluminum-foil-lined roasting pan, cover loosely with foil, and roast about 2½ hours, basting every 30 minutes with the butter and pan juices. Remove the aluminum foil and continue cooking for another 30 minutes. The turkey is ready when a roasting thermometer inserted in the thigh registers 170° F to 175° F and the thigh juices run clear yellow when pierced with a skewer.

4. When the turkey is done, transfer it to a serving platter and allow it to stand, covered loosely with foil, 30 minutes at room temperature before carving. Remove the stuffing and serve it alongside the carved turkey, on the serving platter.

MAKES 10 TO 12 SERVINGS

Varadero at the turn of the century, the Ferran family and friends.

Varadero and Mariel: Fish and Shellfish

Less than an hour from Havana by superhighway, in the province of Matanzas, lay Varadero Beach, one of the most beautiful seaside resorts in the world. A wide road divided by lush plantings of pink oleander —*flor de Varadero*— and bordered on either side by the crystal blue Caribbean led directly into this sunny town. Built in 1880 as a small vacation hideaway, the hamlet grew steadily and within fifty years its streets were lined with grand hotels and luxurious homes, including the Dupont estate. Its incomparable beaches, their sand white and fine as flour, lured vacationers from Cuba as well as many foreign countries.

Having arrived in Varadero, they were prepared to have fun. Days were spent on the white beaches or boating and fishing in the clear, sunlit sea. Large crowds cheered the Club Nautico de Varadero as it competed against other yachting clubs in the Regatta de Varadero, after which the participants were feted with parties lasting all day and far into the night at the Nautico. Children loved riding around the peninsula on their bikes, visiting friends from

The Varadero beach in the 1800s, with some grand wooden homes in the background.

home, most of whom vacationed here too. Despite its glamour, Varadero was a family resort town.

Havana natives flocked to the Hotel Kawama and its surrounding complex of beachfront bungalows and cabanas. Built by the architects Moenck and Quintana, it was originally owned by a Colonel Silva and later by a Havana lawyer who was a good friend of my husband's family. His son, Gustavo Lopez-Muñoz, Jr., who now lives in Madrid, always reminisces with us about the hotel in its heyday.

The beautiful resort, which was constructed from *piedras de Varadero*, the indigenous stone, was everyone's fantasy of a fun-filled beachfront paradise. Hotel guests, Varadero locals, and summer homeowners filled the hotel for lunch, swimming, and cocktails, and evenings reverberated with the lively sound of Cuban music and dance. The large bar and veranda, extending over the

*The Sampedro family (before Pepe was born) at Varadero,
around 1935.*

My godmother Rosie and my aunts Tit and Tia Main in Varadero.

My father and mother sailing off Varadero, early 1950s.

beach and providing panoramic views of the wide ocean and majestic pines, were the most popular places to socialize.

The hotel was not the only attraction; young people frequented a rustic outdoor ballroom, *La Bolera,* that was built on the beach and covered by a thatched roof, where they danced to the music of the popular orchestra, *Los Chavales de España,* especially at the parties given during Easter and summer school breaks. They also visited *La Patana,* a floating dock and restaurant.

The food at the Kawama was of extraordinary quality, prepared by talented chefs and bakers and delivered by a large army of waiters. Every morning fragrant breads and cakes were baked, orange juice was freshly squeezed, and the finest coffee beans were roasted, ground, and brewed into strong, steaming Cuban coffee. Just-picked vegetables and fruits and freshly butchered meats arrived daily from local farms. The pride of the kitchen was the variety of newly caught fish and shellfish from local waters.

The waiters in their starched white jackets marched between the kitchen and the dining terrace bearing large clay pots engulfed by clouds of fragrant steam. From these caldrons they dipped ladles of *zarzuela de mariscos,* a shellfish stew, for the guests lunching informally in their bathing suits.

The luncheon parade continued with tray after impressive tray. Snapper and grouper caught just that morning were grilled and served crisp and fragrant, garnished with garlicky roasted potatoes. Red spiny lobsters were offered surrounded by creamy lobster salad. Large platters were piled with *cangrejos de Cardenas* (hard-shelled crabs) to be cracked and eaten with fresh mayonnaise. *Camarones al ajillo* (garlic shrimp) were served sizzling in their casseroles. Shiny green avocados were split and heaped with chunks of glistening crab and lobster meat, and garnished with juicy, red plum tomatoes. Lunch al fresco started at three o'clock and continued right through to cocktail hour.

MARIEL

Mariel was not a resort like Varadero, but for our family, seafood is identified first with that old port city on the northern coast of Cuba. Mariel has had some notoriety: Ernest Hemingway spent much time there on fishing expeditions, and his granddaughter is named after it and, more recently, the last influx of Cuban refugees departed from its harbor.

My paternal grandfather, a Basque, was commander of the Cuban Naval Fleet. He and my grandmother, Abuela Ina, lived for a while in Mariel, a pristine, beautifully manicured town, where the white houses stood out in sharp contrast to the blue of the ocean and the sky. Abuela Ina's sister Ana Luz lived there as well, and when we visited, we shifted between the two homes. Ana Luz's son, Luis Fernandez, rode his bike with us all over town.

Grandmother was a slight, soft, kind, and demure lady, with a peaches-and-cream complexion. Like my mother, she cooked only

My brother Tony and I take a moment out from playing in the sun, late 1940s.

a little when she lived in Cuba, relying on servants, but she blossomed as a cook in the United States, and her fish dishes have become part of our family history. She patiently taught me to prepare *escabeche,* an oil-and-vinegar marinated pickled swordfish, with a flawless balance of ingredients. She also made excellent fish soups, based on stock made from fish trimmings and vegetables.

As Cuba is surrounded by water, fish was plentiful. Baked snapper was the most typical Cuban fish dish, but often, fresh fish of any variety was simply fried in olive oil and eaten hot, with a squeeze of lime juice.

Many Cuban fish recipes, like *escabeche,* codfish, and fish with green sauce, are of Spanish origin, while those made with crab and anything in a spicy *enchilada* sauce are Creole. The béchamel-sauced recipes came later in our history and reflect what I think of as city cooking, more European-style than either Spanish or Creole, but Cuban nonetheless.

Pescado al Horno

MOM'S BAKED FISH

A mixture of onions, olives, and pimientos spices up a simple baked fish and turns it into a party dish. You also may bake the fish on a layer of potato slices, following the method of *Pargo al Horno a la Viszcaina* (Baked Whole Snapper Basque Style, pages 164–66).

¼ cup pure Spanish olive oil
1 large onion, thinly sliced
⅔ cup coarsely chopped drained
   pimiento-stuffed green olives
½ cup coarsely chopped drained
   pimientos
¾ cup sour (Seville) orange juice
   (see page 9) or ½ cup sweet
   orange juice and ¼ cup each
   lime and lemon juice

One 4- to 6-pound snapper or
   striped bass or four to six
   1-pound snappers, cleaned and
   prepared for baking, with the
   heads and tails left on
Salt and freshly ground black
   pepper to taste
Lime wedges for garnish

1. Preheat the oven to 350° F. In a large skillet over low heat, heat the oil, then cook the onion, stirring, until tender, 6 to 8 minutes. Add the olives, pimientos, and juice, and cook another 5 minutes, stirring.

2. Wash the fish, pat it dry, and place it in a large roasting pan lined with oiled aluminum foil. Sprinkle it with salt and pepper, pour the onion mixture over it, and bake, uncovered, on the middle oven rack until it flakes easily, about 1 hour. Garnish with lime wedges and serve.

MAKES 4 TO 6 SERVINGS

Pargo al Horno a la Viszcaina

BAKED WHOLE SNAPPER BASQUE STYLE

My mother always planned big lunches on Saturdays—with six children and hordes of relatives and friends to feed, she liked to prepare the largest fish she could find. I recall some snappers so gigantic they could not fit into our oven, their heads and tails having to be sacrificed at the last moment. This Basque recipe, like many of the fish and shellfish recipes in this book, comes from my Abuela Ina, who was married to my Basque grandfather, Calixto Urrutia.

This dish makes a spectacular presentation! Best of all, it can be put together ahead of time and left to wait, ready for roasting, until the guests arrive. Then all you have to do is slide it into the oven.

One 3- to 4-pound snapper, cleaned and prepared for baking, with head and tail left on (or substitute sea bass, striped bass, or pike)

Salt and freshly ground black pepper to taste
Juice of 2 limes
3 thick slices lemon
¼ cup pure Spanish olive oil
3 cloves garlic, minced

FOR THE SOFRITO:
¼ cup pure Spanish olive oil
1 small onion, finely chopped
½ small green bell pepper, seeded and finely chopped
2 cups peeled, seeded, and chopped fresh, ripe tomatoes, or drained and chopped canned whole tomatoes

½ cup chopped, drained pimiento-stuffed green olives
½ teaspoon salt
¼ teaspoon dried oregano
½ cup dry white wine or dry sherry
Freshly ground black pepper to taste or a few dashes of Tabasco sauce

TO COMPLETE THE DISH:
2 tablespoons pure Spanish olive oil
4 medium-size all-purpose potatoes, peeled and sliced into very thin rounds

Salt and freshly ground black pepper
¼ cup chopped fresh parsley for garnish

1. Rinse the fish in cold water, dry it well inside and out with paper towels, and place it in a large, shallow, nonreactive platter that fits it comfortably. Sprinkle it inside and out with salt, pepper, and lime juice. With a sharp knife, make 3 incisions, going right down to the bone, and insert a slice of lemon into each incision. Whisk together the oil and garlic and pour over the fish, rubbing it into the skin. Cover and allow to marinate in the refrigerator several hours or overnight.

2. For the *sofrito*, heat the oil until fragrant in a skillet over low heat, then cook the onion and bell pepper, stirring, until transparent, 6 to 8 minutes. Add the tomatoes, olives, salt, oregano, and wine, and cook, stirring occasionally, 10 to 15 minutes. Season with pepper and set the tomato sauce aside. Just before serving, place the sauce over low heat for 8 to 10 minutes, until heated through.

3. Meanwhile, preheat the oven to 400° F and set the rack in the upper middle position. Rub the bottom of a large baking sheet with 1 tablespoon of the oil, arrange the potato slices evenly on the baking sheet, forming a square, and season with salt and pepper. Place the fish on top of the potatoes and drizzle the remaining tablespoon of oil over it. Wrap the tail in aluminum foil and bake until the fish flakes easily, 45 minutes.

4. When the fish is done, carefully slide it onto a large, heated platter, remove the foil from the tail, and arrange the potatoes around the head and tail. Spoon the tomato sauce along the sides, sprinkle with the parsley, and serve.

MAKES 4 SERVINGS

Pargo Relleno

STUFFED RED SNAPPER

This very old recipe comes from my maternal great-grandmother. The fish is delicious simply served with oven-roasted potatoes.

One 5-pound red snapper, cleaned
   and prepared for baking, with
   backbone removed and head
   and tail left on (or substitute
   sea bass, striped bass, or pike)

Juice of 4 limes
2 cloves garlic, minced
Salt and freshly ground black
   pepper to taste

FOR THE STUFFING:

3 to 4 slices white bread, torn
   into small pieces
1/2 cup milk
2 tablespoons pure Spanish
   olive oil
2 tablespoons salted butter
1 small onion, finely chopped
1/2 small green bell pepper, seeded
   and finely chopped
1 small tomato, seeded and finely
   chopped
1 clove garlic, minced
1/2 cup minced baked ham

3 tablespoons dry sherry
1 teaspoon Worcestershire sauce
1 tablespoon finely chopped fresh
   parsley
Salt and freshly ground black
   pepper to taste
1/2 pound small raw shrimp,
   shelled and deveined
1 lobster tail, simmered in salted
   water to cover over medium
   heat until cooked, about 5
   minutes, and sliced into 3 to 4
   pieces

1. Rinse the fish, pat it dry with paper towels, and place it on a nonreactive platter. Squeeze the lime juice over the skin, and rub the fish inside and out with garlic, salt, and pepper. Cover and refrigerate at least 1 hour.

2. To prepare the stuffing, soak the bread in the milk in a small bowl. In a medium-size skillet over low heat, heat the oil and butter until fragrant, then cook the onion, bell pepper, tomato, garlic, and ham, stirring, until the onion is tender but not brown, 6 to 8 minutes. Add the sherry, Worcestershire, and parsley, mix thoroughly, remove from the heat, and allow to cool slightly. Squeeze the bread to remove the excess milk, stir into the mixture, and add salt and pepper.

3. Preheat the oven to 375° F. Drain the fish and reserve the marinade (there will be a small amount). Stuff the fish with the stuffing mixture, arrange the shrimp and lobster slices on top of the stuffing, and sew up the pocket with needle and thread or secure with toothpicks or skewers. Transfer the fish to a shallow baking pan lined with well-oiled aluminum foil, allowing for enough overlap to pick up the fish. If the tail does not fit in the pan, wrap it in foil. Pour the reserved marinade over the fish, drizzle with a bit of oil, place in the oven, and bake, uncovered, until the fish flakes easily when pierced with a fork, about 1 hour. For an even crisper skin, place in a preheated broiler for the last 3 to 4 minutes of cooking time. Transfer the fish carefully to a serving platter, remove the thread, toothpicks, or skewers, and serve hot.

MAKES 4 TO 6 SERVINGS

Pescado con Salsa Verde

FISH WITH GREEN SAUCE

Whole, baked fish are easy to prepare, and they come out of the oven tender and moist. Although many people cook the green parsley sauce with the fish, my mother always serves it on the side for a more definite herbal flavor.

One 4- to 6-pound snapper, striped bass, or sea bass, cleaned and prepared for baking, with head and tail left on

Salt and freshly ground black pepper to taste
Juice of 3 limes
¼ cup pure Spanish olive oil

FOR THE SAUCE:

2 cloves garlic, finely chopped
1 bunch fresh parsley, stems
   removed and finely chopped
¾ cup pure Spanish olive oil

¼ cup white wine vinegar
Salt and freshly ground black
   pepper to taste

TO COMPLETE THE DISH:

2 tablespoons brine-packed
   Spanish capers, drained, for
   garnish
2 large eggs, hard-boiled and
   coarsely chopped, for garnish

½ cup halved, drained
   pimiento-stuffed green olives
   for garnish

1. Wash the fish thoroughly, pat dry with paper towels, and place on a nonreactive platter. Season with salt and pepper, pour over the lime juice, and refrigerate, covered, 1 hour.

2. Preheat the oven to 400° F. Place the fish in a large roasting pan lined with aluminum foil, cover its tail with foil, drizzle it with olive oil, and bake, uncovered, until it flakes easily, 45 minutes to 1 hour.

3. To prepare the green sauce, in a food processor fitted with a steel blade or in a blender, process the garlic, parsley, oil, vinegar, salt, and pepper until smooth, and set aside.

4. When the fish is done, remove it from the oven, transfer it to a large platter, and carefully remove the top skin.

5. In a small saucepan over low heat, heat the green sauce until heated through, 3 to 5 minutes, and pour it over the fish. Garnish with the capers, eggs, and olives, and serve immediately.

MAKES 4 TO 6 SERVINGS

Variation: Line the baking pan with 2 peeled and thinly sliced large potatoes and place the fish on top. Bake as directed above.

Pescado con Salsa de Aguacate

FISH WITH AVOCADO SAUCE

Whole snapper, poached and topped with avocado sauce, is a summer classic. You can serve the fish hot with the sauce on the side or allow it to cool and then spread it with the sauce.

FOR THE AVOCADO SAUCE:

2 large, ripe avocados, skinned and stone removed (reserve 1 stone)

Juice of 1 lime

½ cup finely chopped, drained pimiento-stuffed green olives

1 tablespoon brine-packed Spanish capers, drained

Salt and freshly ground black pepper to taste

6 tablespoons pure Spanish olive oil

FOR THE FISH:

8 cups water

2 cups dry white wine

2 cloves garlic, crushed

1 bay leaf

Juice of 1 lime

6 black peppercorns

1½ teaspoons salt

One 4- to 6-pound snapper, striped bass, or sea bass, cleaned and prepared for cooking, with the head and tail left on

TO COMPLETE THE DISH:

2 large eggs, hard-boiled, for garnish

2 tablespoons finely chopped fresh parsley for garnish

   1. To prepare the avocado sauce, mash the avocados to a paste with a fork in a nonreactive bowl, then add the lime juice, olives, capers, salt, and pepper, blend well, and mix in the olive oil. Place an avocado pit in the sauce to keep it from darkening, and refrigerate until ready to serve.

2. In a fish poacher or pot large enough to hold the fish, bring to a boil over high heat the water, wine, garlic, bay leaf, lime juice, peppercorns, and salt. Reduce the heat to low.

3. Wrap the fish in cheesecloth and simmer in the broth, covered, 45 to 50 minutes. Take out the fish, unwrap it, and transfer it to a large platter. If you are serving it hot, serve immediately with the avocado sauce and garnishes. If you are serving it at room temperature, set it aside and allow to cool. Remove the top skin and spread the cooled fish with the avocado sauce and garnish with the eggs and parsley.

MAKES 4 TO 6 SERVINGS

Escabeche de Abuela Ina

PICKLED FISH

Watching my grandmother Abuela Ina prepare *escabeche* in her Florida kitchen was a wondrous experience for me as a child. She would sauté the swordfish in a fragrant olive oil, turning each piece until it "got a little color," as she described it, gently patting my cheek to emphasize "color." Removing the fish from the pan, she would take handfuls of evenly sliced onions and peppers and sauté them, intoning "These must be soft and see-through, but they must still have a *crunch*, because they must sit in the oil for a long time and not get mushy." She tapped a garlic clove gently with a knife before she added it to her sauté and told me, "I want only the essence of the garlic." Abuela Ina kept close watch on the flame, fearing that even a slightly burned ingredient would mar her masterpiece. The action turned suddenly dramatic, as she prepared to add vinegar to this sauté. "You must move away from the stove fast, because the splatter will be terrible and you could burn yourself!" she warned me. She rushed to the skillet, threw in a cup of vinegar, and as a loud sizzle cracked the air, she turned and ran as if the house were on fire. Then she giggled with relief: with this behind her, she could get on with the marinating of the swordfish in the heavenly oil-and-vinegar sauce she had just prepared. Arranging the ingredients in a glazed terra-cotta crock, she cautioned that the fish had to "breathe," and could not be locked up in the refrigerator. She covered it with a clean, dry kitchen towel or cheesecloth and whispered, "It's going to sleep," as she left it to marinate.

Abuela Ina never refrigerated *escabeche* and would never dream of covering it with aluminum foil. She left it out, loosely covered with cloth, and served it at room temperature. In fact, she kept adding to the crock, serving the fish from the bottom and adding new fish to the top. I have found as well that refrigerating this dish kills it—*escabeche* from the refrigerator is all but inedible. Since the fish is cooked and then pickled, I have never had any problems with spoilage. And I have learned to avoid the danger of "terrible splatter" by adding the vinegar to warm, not hot, oil.

Escabeche is excellent served as an appetizer.

8 swordfish or kingfish steaks, ¾
   inch to 1 inch thick
Salt and freshly ground black
   pepper to taste
Juice of 1 lime
4 cups pure Spanish olive oil
3 large onions, sliced ¼ inch
   thick
2 large green bell peppers, seeded
   and cut into ¼-inch strips

8 to 10 cloves garlic, crushed
1 cup unpitted green olives,
   drained and cracked with a
   mallet
10 black peppercorns
1 bay leaf
1 cup white vinegar
Flour for dredging

1. On a nonreactive platter, season the fish steaks with salt, pepper, and the lime juice, and allow to marinate an hour or more, refrigerated.

2. Pat dry the fish steaks with paper towels and dredge lightly in the flour. In a large skillet over medium heat, heat 1 cup of the olive oil until it is fragrant, then cook the steaks in several batches until lightly brown, 4 to 5 minutes on each side. Place the steaks in a glass or pottery casserole or large bowl that will fit them comfortably, and allow them to cool completely.

3. In a medium-size saucepan, heat the remaining oil over medium heat until fragrant, then cook the onions, bell peppers, and garlic, stirring, until partly tender, 2 minutes. Reduce the heat to low, add the olives, peppercorns, and bay leaf, and cook another 5 minutes, stirring occasionally. Add the vinegar and cook until the mixture reaches a gentle boil. Remove it from the heat and allow it to cool completely.

4. Pour the cooled mixture over the fish steaks, cover with cheesecloth, and allow the fish to marinate 1 week in a cool place. Do not refrigerate.

5. Turn the fish steaks daily so that they will absorb the marinade. After one week, correct the seasonings, and serve the fish with some of the marinade drizzled over it, accompanied by crusty bread.

MAKES 8 SERVINGS

Pescado a la Parilla con Salsa Vinagreta

GRILLED FISH STEAKS WITH VINAIGRETTE

I have a vivid memory of these aromatic, tangy steaks cooking over a wood fire in a small fishing village outside Pinar del Río, where our grandfather took my brother and me to lunch. Although this dish seems tailored for outdoor grilling, it can be made in the kitchen broiler just as easily.

4 firm-fleshed fish steaks, such as swordfish, kingfish, or snapper, each about 6 to 8 ounces and ½ inch thick
Salt and freshly ground black pepper to taste

Juice of 1 lime
2 tablespoons pure Spanish olive oil
2 cloves garlic, finely chopped

FOR THE VINAIGRETTE:

1 teaspoon salt
¼ teaspoon ground cumin
¼ teaspoon dried oregano
¼ cup pure Spanish olive oil
2 tablespoons cider vinegar

1 tablespoon brine-packed Spanish capers, drained, for garnish
1 tablespoon finely chopped fresh parsley

1. On a nonreactive platter, season the fish steaks with salt, pepper, and the lime juice, rub them with olive oil and garlic, and allow them to marinate at room temperature for at least 1 hour. If grilling, prepare a charcoal or wood fire. If broiling, preheat the broiler. Combine the vinaigrette ingredients in a small bowl and set aside.

2. If grilling, cook on an oiled rack over a charcoal or wood fire 5 to 7 minutes on each side, brushing each side with the marinade before grilling. If broiling, place the fish in a pan lined with lightly oiled aluminum foil and broil 3 to 4 inches from the heat source for 5 to 7 minutes on each side, brushing each side with the marinade before broiling it.

3. Transfer the fish steaks to a heated platter and pour the vinaigrette over them. Sprinkle with capers and serve immediately.

MAKES 4 SERVINGS

Filetes de Pescado al Horno

BAKED FISH FILLETS

A simple, quickly prepared casserole of potatoes and fish, this dish wins raves from my guests. With a green salad (try *Ensalada Vasca*—Basque Tossed Salad—pages 242–43), it is perfect for a casual dinner party.

I partially cook the potatoes before assembling the casserole, but you can slice raw potatoes very thin and cook them with the fish, if you prefer.

6 fish fillets, such as snapper, halibut, perch, or pompano, about 6 ounces each
Salt and freshly ground black pepper to taste
Juice of 1 lime
3 large all-purpose potatoes, unpeeled and cut in half

1 large onion, cut in half and very thinly sliced
2 large, ripe or 6 plum tomatoes, seeded and finely chopped
1/4 cup pure Spanish olive oil
1/4 cup dry sherry or dry white wine
1 tablespoon minced fresh parsley for garnish

1. On a nonreactive platter, season the fillets with salt, pepper, and the lime juice and refrigerate at least 1 hour.

2. In a medium-size saucepan over medium-high heat, boil the potatoes in salted water to cover until partially cooked but still firm, about 20 minutes. Remove the potatoes from the water, allow them to cool, then peel and slice ¼ inch thick.

3. Preheat the oven to 450° F and preheat the broiler, if it is separate. In a large, shallow oiled baking dish, place one layer each of potatoes, onion slices, and chopped tomatoes, seasoning the top with salt and pepper. Drain the fish, discarding the marinade, arrange it on top of the vegetables, and pour the oil and sherry over all. Bake, uncovered, 10 minutes, then transfer the fish to the broiler and broil 5 minutes.

4. Serve from the baking dish or transfer to a heated serving platter and serve, garnished with the parsley.

MAKES 6 SERVINGS

Filetes de Pescado con Camarones

FISH FILLETS WITH SHRIMP

Some cooks prefer these fish fillets breaded and fried, but my mother prepares a more delicate dish by poaching the fish in sherry or white wine and fish stock. After poaching, the fillets are stuffed and sauced for a beautiful and easy main course.

6 fish fillets, such as snapper, halibut, or flounder, about 6 ounces each
Salt and freshly ground black pepper to taste

Juice of 1 lime
¼ cup dry sherry or dry white wine

2 cups fish stock (see pages 79–80) or clam juice, or 1 cup dry white wine mixed with 1 cup water

½ pound small raw shrimp, shelled and deveined

FOR THE SAUCE:

4 tablespoons (½ stick) salted butter

¼ cup all-purpose flour

Pinch of ground nutmeg

1 tablespoon finely chopped fresh parsley

Salt and freshly ground black pepper to taste

1. Season the fillets with salt and pepper, roll them up, and secure each roll with a toothpick. Combine the lime juice, sherry, and fish stock, place the fillets in a large skillet, seam-side down, and pour the liquid over them. Bring to a boil over medium-high heat, then reduce the heat to low, add the shrimp, and simmer, covered, until the shrimp are cooked and the fish is soft, but not flaky, 4 to 6 minutes.

2. Remove the fillets and shrimp from the stock and transfer to a heated platter, reserving the stock.

3. In a saucepan over low heat, melt the butter, gradually add the flour, and cook, stirring, until the flour is absorbed. Do not let the flour brown. Remove from the heat, and whisk to blend. Add the reserved stock and cook, stirring, over medium heat, 1 to 2 minutes. Add the nutmeg and parsley, and correct the seasonings. The sauce should be thin enough to pour easily; if it is too thick, add a bit more stock.

4. Place 2 shrimp in the center of each fillet, pour the sauce over the fish, and serve immediately.

MAKES 6 SERVINGS

Variation: Instead of rolling the fillets, arrange them flat in a single layer in the pan and proceed with the recipe. Place the shrimp over the fish, rather than stuffed in the rolls.

Bacalao a la Viszcaina

BASQUE-STYLE CODFISH

This classic Spanish-Cuban recipe comes from my aunt, Tia Mani, Carmen Sampedro Mas.

2 pounds thick salt cod, desalted and cooked (see page 4), and cut into 2- by 3-inch pieces (reserve 4 cups of the soaking liquid)

Flour for dredging
½ cup pure Spanish olive oil

FOR THE SOFRITO:

¼ cup pure Spanish olive oil
1 large green bell pepper, seeded and finely chopped
6 cloves garlic, finely chopped
2 large onions, finely chopped
1 cup finely chopped drained pimientos

2½ cups canned crushed tomatoes
1 tablespoon Spanish paprika or mild paprika
¼ cup dry white wine
Salt and freshly ground black pepper to taste

TO COMPLETE THE DISH:

4 medium-size all-purpose potatoes, peeled and cut into ½-inch slices

3 pimientos, cut into strips, for garnish
Fried Bread Rounds (recipe follows), as an accompaniment

1. Dredge the cod in the flour. In a large skillet over medium heat, heat the oil until fragrant, then cook the fish until lightly browned, 3 to 4 minutes on each side. Remove the fish from the heat and set aside.

2. For the *sofrito*, in a large saucepan over medium heat, heat the oil until fragrant, then cook the bell peppers, stirring, until slightly softened, 3 to 4 minutes. Reduce the heat to low, add the garlic and onions, and cook, stirring, until tender, 6 to 8 minutes, adding more oil if necessary. Add the pimientos, tomatoes, paprika, and wine and cook, stirring occasionally, until thickened, another 10 to 12 minutes.

3. Place the reserved salt cod soaking water in a medium-size saucepan over medium-high heat and cook the potato slices until partially tender, 10 to 15 minutes.

4. Add the codfish chunks to the *sofrito* and cook over low heat 10 minutes. Arrange the cooked potato slices on top of the fish, do not stir, cover the pan, and shake it several times. Cook over low heat an additional 10 minutes so that the potatoes absorb the fish flavor. Transfer to a large serving platter and garnish with the pimientos. Serve with *Pan Frito* (Fried Bread Rounds) and *Arroz Blanco* (Perfect White Rice, pages 200–202).

MAKES 8 SERVINGS

Pan Frito

FRIED BREAD ROUNDS

¼ cup pure Spanish olive oil
1 clove garlic, crushed, optional

Eight 1-inch slices day-old Cuban (see page 44), French, or Italian bread

In a skillet over medium heat, heat the oil until fragrant with the garlic, then cook the bread slices until lightly browned, 1 to 2 minutes on each side. Add more oil if necessary. The bread can be cooled and stored in a covered container for several days.

MAKES 8 SERVINGS AS AN ACCOMPANIMENT

Variation: Preheat the oven to 325° F. Brush the bread on both sides with oil (flavored with the garlic, if desired), place on a cookie sheet, and bake until light brown, 10 to 15 minutes on each side.

Pudín de Bacalao

CODFISH PUDDING

This delicious casserole, easy to prepare ahead of time and reheat for lunch or dinner, is one of my husband's favorites. The recipe comes from my mother.

4 medium-size all-purpose
  potatoes, cut in half
1 pound salted codfish, desalted,
  cooked, and flaked (page 4)
2 tablespoons salted butter, at
  room temperature
⅓ cup heavy cream
4 large eggs, well beaten

1 cup drained canned early sweet
  peas (I prefer LeSueur)
¼ teaspoon ground nutmeg
¼ cup cracker meal (see page 7)
  or fine bread crumbs
Salt and freshly ground black
  pepper to taste
1 teaspoon finely chopped fresh
  parsley for garnish

1. Preheat the oven to 350° F. Place the potatoes in a medium-size saucepan with salted water to cover over medium heat and cook until tender, 20 to 25 minutes. Drain the potatoes and shake the pan over medium heat to evaporate any remaining moisture.

2. Using a potato masher or a fork, mash the potatoes into a puree. Add the flaked codfish, butter, cream, and eggs, mixing well

after each addition. Add the remaining ingredients except for the garnish, mix well, and set aside. (Recipe can be prepared ahead up to this point and refrigerated for several hours.)

3. Lightly oil an 8 × 8-inch ovenproof casserole (or one that will accommodate the mixture comfortably) and spoon in the potato mixture. Bake on the middle oven rack until golden and puffed, 40 to 45 minutes. Garnish with the parsley and serve directly from the casserole.

MAKES 4 TO 6 SERVINGS

Picadillo de Pescado a la Cubana

CUBAN SNAPPER HASH

This old Cuban recipe is found in *Manual del Cocinero Cubano* (Manual of Cuban Cuisine), dated 1856. The dish traditionally is served with *Plátanos Maduros Fritos* (Fried Sweet Plantains, see page 265), but I often serve it for a light lunch accompanied by a salad of crisp greens and hot garlic bread. Truly delicious!

4 snapper, grouper, halibut, or cod steaks, 4 to 6 ounces each
6 slices white bread, crusts removed, torn into pieces
½ cup milk
1 medium-size onion, finely chopped

2 tablespoons finely chopped fresh parsley
Salt and freshly ground black pepper to taste
¼ teaspoon ground nutmeg
Juice of 1 lime
½ cup pure Spanish olive oil
3 large eggs, hard-boiled and finely chopped

1. Place the fish steaks in a skillet large enough to accommodate them comfortably, cover with salted water, and bring to a boil, uncovered, over medium-high heat. Reduce the heat to low, cover, and simmer over low heat until the fish flakes easily, 8 to 10 minutes. Transfer the poached fish to a platter and allow it to cool.

2. Place the bread in a small bowl, and cover with the milk. Set aside.

3. When the fish is cool enough to handle, flake it and combine it in a large bowl with the onion and parsley. Squeeze the excess milk from the bread and add the bread to the mixture, stirring well to blend, then add the salt, pepper, nutmeg, and lime juice.

4. In a large skillet over medium heat, heat the oil until it is fragrant, then cook the fish mixture, stirring, until all the oil is absorbed and the onion is tender, 8 to 10 minutes. Add the hard-boiled eggs and cook, stirring, 2 to 3 minutes, and serve. Alternatively, the dish can be assembled ahead of time and cooked, stirring, 10 minutes over medium heat just before serving, adding the hard-boiled eggs at the last moment.

MAKES 4 TO 6 SERVINGS

Zarzuela de Mariscos

SPICY SHELLFISH STEW

A *zarzuela* is a Spanish comic opera, delightful and colorful. That must be why this Catalan dish took its name and went on to become a Spanish favorite. It was also a crowd-pleaser in Cuba, where seafood was abundant and delicious, and I was introduced to it by my Abuela Ina. *Zarzuela* was generally made with crabs, but I like to substitute fresh lump crabmeat, and to add clams and scallops as well.

To economize, you may substitute chunks of your favorite firm-fleshed fish for some of the more expensive shellfish.

¼ cup pure Spanish olive oil

3 cloves garlic, finely chopped

1 medium-size onion, finely chopped

1 medium-size green bell pepper, seeded and finely chopped

¼ cup finely chopped smoked ham

1 cup drained and chopped canned whole tomatoes or prepared tomato sauce

1 bay leaf

¼ cup drained pimientos, finely chopped

¼ teaspoon dried oregano

1 pound swordfish steak, skinned and cut into chunks

¼ cup dry sherry

¼ cup dry white wine

2 cups fish stock (pages 78–80), clam juice, or water

2 teaspoons salt

¼ teaspoon powdered saffron or bijol or 3 to 4 saffron threads, crushed

12 mussels, scrubbed under cold running water, debearded, and soaked 10 minutes in lightly salted water to cover by several inches (if mussels disgorge considerable sand, repeat the soaking process)

12 clams scrubbed under cold, running water and soaked 30 minutes in lightly salted water to cover by several inches (if clams disgorge considerable sand, repeat the soaking process), optional

3 raw lobster tails, shelled and cut into thirds (if frozen, defrost)

12 large raw shrimp, shelled and deveined, with the tails left on

12 raw sea scallops, cut in half, or 24 bay scallops

½ pound fresh lump crabmeat, picked over for cartilage

3 tablespoons finely minced fresh parsley

Lime or lemon wedges for garnish

1. In a large, heavy saucepan, heat the oil until fragrant over low heat, then add the garlic, onion, bell pepper, and ham, and cook, stirring, for several minutes, until the onion is tender. Add the tomatoes, bay leaf, pimientos, and oregano, and cook until the mixture has thickened, 10 to 15 minutes. (Can be made ahead up to this point and refrigerated. Reheat to continue with the recipe.)

2. Add the swordfish, sherry, wine, stock, salt, and saffron, stir to blend, and bring to a boil, uncovered, over high heat. Add the

mussels and clams, reduce the heat to medium, cover, and cook 6 to 8 minutes. Then add the lobster, shrimp, scallops, and crabmeat, and cook, covered, 5 minutes. Remove and discard any mussels or clams that do not open, correct the seasonings, transfer the stew to a serving bowl, and serve hot, garnished with minced parsley and lime wedges and accompanied by *Arroz Amarillo* (Yellow Rice, pages 202–203).

MAKES 6 TO 8 SERVINGS

Langosta a la Catalana

SPANISH LOBSTER

A Cuban adaptation of a classic Catalan recipe, this is the version always prepared in our kitchen. Either lobster tails or shrimp fits the recipe perfectly. Serve lots of hot *Pan Frito* (Fried Bread Rounds, pages 179–80) on the side.

½ cup pure Spanish olive oil
1 large onion, finely chopped
4 cloves garlic, finely chopped
¼ pound finely chopped Serrano ham (available at Hispanic markets, or substitute Westphalian or Black Forest ham or prosciutto)
2 cups drained and finely chopped canned whole tomatoes or prepared tomato sauce
½ cup finely chopped drained pimientos
½ cup dry white wine

½ cup fish stock (see pages 79–80) or clam juice
6 to 8 raw lobster tails (or frozen lobster tails, defrosted), each cut into 3 to 4 slices widthwise or cut in half lengthwise (or substitute 2 pounds large shrimp, peeled and deveined, tails left on)
¼ cup cognac
¼ cup finely chopped fresh parsley
Salt to taste

1. In a large saucepan, heat the oil over low heat until fragrant, then cook the onion and garlic, stirring, until tender, 5 minutes. Add the ham and cook, stirring, 2 minutes. Add the tomatoes, pimientos, wine, and stock, raise the heat to medium-high, and bring to a boil. Immediately reduce the heat to low and simmer, partially covered, until the mixture has thickened, about 10 minutes. Add the lobster pieces and continue cooking until the lobster is cooked, and the shells turn red, 5 to 6 minutes.

2. Remove the lobster from the sauce and transfer it to a heated platter. To the sauce, add the cognac, parsley, and salt, bring the mixture to a boil over medium-high heat, pour over the lobster, and serve immediately.

MAKES 6 TO 8 SERVINGS

Langosta a la Crema
ROSIE'S CREAMY LOBSTER TAILS

Cream sauces such as béchamel, velouté, and mornay are widely used in Cuban cooking, especially with fish and poultry. Creamy Lobster Tails are a childhood favorite of mine, prepared especially for me by my godmother, Rosita Arocha-Ferrán.

4 tablespoons (½ stick) salted butter
¼ cup all-purpose flour
2½ cups milk
2 large egg yolks, well beaten
Salt and freshly ground black pepper to taste
2 tablespoons dry sherry
4 to 6 raw lobster tails (defrosted if frozen), cooked, covered, over medium heat in salted water to cover, 5 to 8 minutes, and cut into 3 to 4 pieces each, or 3½ cups cooked lobster meat
2 small, ripe tomatoes, peeled, seeded, and finely chopped
2 tablespoons finely chopped fresh parsley

1. In a large skillet over low heat, melt the butter. When it begins to foam, add the flour and cook, stirring, 2 minutes, until bubbles form. Do not allow it to turn brown. Add 2 cups of the milk and cook over medium heat, whisking, until it comes to a boil.

2. Remove the skillet from the heat. In a mixing bowl, beat the egg yolks with the remaining milk. Slowly add the mixture to the saucepan, stirring, then stir in the salt, pepper, and sherry. (If the sauce is too thick for your taste, add a bit more milk.) Add the lobster, tomatoes, and parsley, cook over low heat to heat the lobster, 4 to 6 minutes, correct the seasonings, and serve immediately with *Arroz Blanco* (Perfect White Rice, pages 200–202).

MAKES 4 TO 6 SERVINGS

Camarones al Ajillo con Ron

SPICY GARLIC SHRIMP WITH RUM

My father got into the cooking act late in life and mostly by necessity. A true Basque, he now excels in the kitchen, and this is one of his many simple and tasty recipes. I often serve it as an appetizer, baked in small *cazuelitas*—individual glazed pottery casseroles.

2½ to 3 pounds large raw
   shrimp, shelled and deveined,
   with tails left on (3 pounds
   yields about 44 shrimp)
Salt to taste
Tabasco sauce to taste

½ cup light rum
Juice of 1 lime
1 tablespoon Worcestershire sauce
½ teaspoon ground cumin
4 tablespoons (½ stick) salted
   butter

½ cup pure Spanish olive oil
4 to 6 cloves garlic, finely
  chopped

¼ cup cracker meal (see page 7)
  or fine bread crumbs
2 tablespoons finely chopped fresh
  parsley

1. Place the shrimp in a large nonreactive bowl and season liberally with salt and Tabasco. In a small nonreactive bowl, combine the rum, lime juice, Worcestershire, and cumin. Add the mixture to the shrimp, toss to blend, and refrigerate, covered, at least 1 hour or until ready to cook.

2. Preheat the broiler. In a small saucepan over low heat, heat the butter and oil. When the butter begins to foam, add the garlic, cook, stirring, 1 to 2 minutes, and set aside.

3. Remove the shrimp from the marinade (discard the marinade), transfer them to a shallow ovenproof dish that will fit them comfortably in a single layer or to individual ramekins, and spoon the garlic sauce evenly over them. Sprinkle the cracker meal on top.

4. Broil 4 inches from the heat source until golden, 8 to 10 minutes. Sprinkle with the parsley and serve at once.

MAKES 6 TO 8 SERVINGS

Camarones al Ajillo

GARLIC SHRIMP

Spanish in origin, this hearty peasant dish is prepared in all Cuban homes, and each cook does it somewhat differently. This is our family's version, although I have reduced the quantities of garlic and oil somewhat, since, in the original recipe, they may have been too generous for American tastes. You may increase both, if you like.

½ cup pure Spanish olive oil or more to taste

4 to 6 cloves garlic, finely chopped

2½ to 3 pounds prawns or extra-large shrimp, shells and heads left on

Juice of 2 limes

Salt to taste

Pinch of dried oregano

¼ cup finely chopped fresh parsley

Dash of Tabasco sauce, optional

1. In a large skillet over low heat, heat the oil until it is fragrant, then cook the garlic, stirring, 1 to 2 minutes. Raise the heat to medium, add the shrimp, and cook, stirring, until they turn pink, 5 minutes. (If you prefer extra oil, add it along with the shrimp.) Add the lime juice, salt, oregano, and parsley, and stir well. Correct seasonings and add Tabasco.

2. Transfer to a heated serving platter and serve immediately, accompanied by crunchy bread to soak up the garlic-flavored oil.

MAKES 6 TO 8 SERVINGS

Camarones en Crema con Cilantro

SHRIMP IN CREAMY CORIANDER SAUCE

Even though coriander (cilantro) appears in many old Cuban recipes, it was mainly used in Oriente province, not in the west, where we lived, and it never appeared in our house. It is quite popular in Florida-Cuban cooking, because the many South Americans now living in Florida who are familiar with it have added their stamp to the cuisine.

This recipe is my adaptation of my mother's baked shrimp (here prepared on top of the stove), adding coriander, fresh tomatoes, and spices—all giving the dish a sharper, livelier taste than the original.

3 tablespoons salted butter
2 cloves garlic, finely chopped
2 large, ripe tomatoes, peeled, seeded, and finely chopped
1 1/2 teaspoons finely chopped fresh coriander leaves

1/4 cup dry sherry
2 1/2 pounds large raw shrimp, shelled and deveined, with tails left on

FOR THE SAUCE

4 tablespoons (1/2 stick) salted butter
3 tablespoons all-purpose flour
1 cup fish stock (see pages 79–80) or clam juice
1 cup milk

Salt and freshly ground black pepper to taste
Few dashes of Tabasco sauce, optional
1/2 teaspoon Worcestershire sauce

1. In a large skillet over low heat, melt the butter. When it begins to foam, add the garlic, tomatoes, coriander, sherry, and shrimp, and cook, stirring, 4 to 5 minutes.

2. To prepare the sauce, in a saucepan over low heat, melt the butter. When it begins to foam, add the flour and cook, stirring, until well blended but not brown, 2 minutes. Raise the heat to medium, whisk in the stock and milk, and cook, whisking, until the mixture comes to a boil. Add the salt, pepper, Tabasco, and Worcestershire.

3. Add the sauce to the shrimp, stir to blend, and cook over low heat 3 to 4 minutes. Remove to a heated serving platter and serve hot with *Arroz Blanco* (Perfect White Rice, pages 200–202).

MAKES 6 TO 8 SERVINGS

Cangrejos Enchilados

CRAB IN CREOLE SAUCE

Enchilados are among the few sharp and peppery recipes in Cuban cuisine. Rosalie, our cook, was famous for her *cangrejos enchilados*, of which this recipe is a variation. Her original recipe used live land crabs, which she cleaned, dismembered, and swiftly plunged into a simmering *sofrito*. Since these crabs are hard to find in the United States, I have substituted crabmeat, which makes for a somewhat different and quicker preparation that is equally delicious in the spicy tomato sauce.

Rosalie also included some *aji cachucha* (Rocatillo pepper) or *habanero* chilies in this recipe, but you can achieve similar results with a small, hot chili pepper or Tabasco sauce to taste. Feel free to alter the degree of spiciness to suit your palate.

6 tablespoons pure Spanish olive oil

3 large cloves garlic, finely chopped

1 large onion, finely chopped

1½ cups drained and chopped canned whole tomatoes or prepared tomato sauce

1 tablespoon tomato paste

1 bay leaf

½ cup dry sherry

½ cup finely chopped drained pimientos

1 tablespoon Worcestershire sauce

Salt and freshly ground black pepper to taste

1 teaspoon finely chopped seeded Rocatillo pepper (see page 4) or hot chile pepper, or Tabasco sauce to taste

2½ pounds fresh lump crabmeat, picked over for cartilage

Juice of 1 lime

3 tablespoons finely chopped fresh parsley for garnish

1. To prepare the *sofrito*, in a large skillet over low heat, heat the oil until fragrant, then cook the garlic and onions, stirring, until tender, 6 to 8 minutes. Add the tomatoes, tomato paste, bay leaf, sherry, pimientos, Worcestershire, salt, pepper, and Scotch bonnet pepper and cook until the mixture has thickened, another 10 minutes.

2. Five minutes before serving, add the crabmeat and lime juice and cook over low heat until the crabmeat is heated. Transfer to a platter, garnish with parsley, and serve immediately, accompanied by *Arroz Blanco* (Perfect White Rice, pages 200–202).

MAKES 6 SERVINGS

Variations: For *Enchilado de Langosta* (Lobster in Creole Sauce), substitute 4 to 6 lobster tails, in the shell, cut into thirds. For *Camarones Enchilados* (Shrimp in Creole Sauce), substitute 1½ pounds large raw shrimp, shelled and deveined. Cook each in the sauce over low heat 4 to 6 minutes, until heated through.

Congrejos con Harina

CRAB AND CORNMEAL STEW

This gutsy one-dish meal is a favorite in our house, but the votes are split as to whether we incorporate the crabmeat into the cornmeal casserole (the traditional practice) or serve the crabmeat spooned over the top. I prefer the latter, because you can really taste the *sofrito*—which I like highly spiced for this dish. And the eye appeal is undoubtedly greater when the stew is served unmixed.

FOR THE SAUCE:

1/4 cup pure Spanish olive oil

2 cloves garlic, finely chopped

1 medium-size onion, finely chopped

1 large red bell pepper, seeded and finely chopped

1 cup drained and chopped canned whole tomatoes or prepared tomato sauce

1/4 cup chopped drained pimientos

1 bay leaf

1 tablespoon red wine vinegar, optional

1/2 teaspoon Tabasco sauce, optional

1/4 cup dry sherry (I prefer La Ina)

1 teaspoon salt

Freshly ground black pepper to taste

1 1/2 to 2 pounds fresh lump crabmeat, picked over for cartilage (no substitutes)

FOR THE CORNMEAL:

1 cup stone-ground yellow cornmeal

6 cups cold water

3 tablespoons pure Spanish olive or vegetable oil

2 teaspoons salt

Generous grindings of black pepper

1. In a medium-size skillet, heat the oil over low heat until fragrant, then add the garlic, onion, and bell pepper, and cook, stirring, until soft, 6 to 8 minutes. Add the remaining sauce ingredients (except crabmeat) and cook over low heat 10 minutes, then add the crabmeat and cook another 6 to 8 minutes. Taste for seasoning—the sauce should have a sharp flavor. (This can be prepared ahead of time and reheated over low heat while the cornmeal cooks.)

2. In a large, nonstick saucepan over medium-high heat, combine the cornmeal, water, oil, and salt, and mix well. Bring the mixture to a boil, reduce the heat to low, cover, and cook until the mixture thickens, 25 to 30 minutes, raising the lid occasionally to whisk. (Cooking time for cornmeal can vary considerably.)

3. When the cornmeal has thickened, season it with pepper and

remove the bay leaf from the crabmeat sauce. Either combine the crabmeat sauce and the thickened cornmeal and ladle the mixture into a large serving bowl, or ladle the cornmeal alone into individual rimmed soup bowls and and pour the crabmeat sauce over it. Serve immediately.

MAKES 4 TO 6 SERVINGS

A colonial Cuban kitchen in the late 1800s. Rosalie's kitchen had a massive wood-fired stove like this one. Reprinted with permission of the Richter Library of the University of Miami.

Rosalie's Kitchen: Rice, Beans, and Eggs

Puerta de Golpe, the commercial hub of the Vuelta Abajo region, was a charming small town where the owners of nearby plantations lived on comfortable estates. We occupied the only red house in town, a large brick colonial with a center courtyard. It had been built in 1906 for my mother's grandmother, María Cecilia Díaz Tabares, shortly after her marriage, when she had settled in town to be near El Chamizo, her husband's cattle ranch.

When my parents married and my father planned to run for local office, they moved into the house, although by then it had been closed for years. My brothers, sisters, and I spent our early years in this sun-filled home, with its spacious bedrooms, baths, and sitting rooms in one wing, guest rooms in another, and kitchen/pantry/laundry complex at the far end. The back overlooked acres of gardens and woods, and behind them stood my father's family home.

A wide driveway separated the house from the servants' quarters, a large garage, and a vacant slaughterhouse. To this last building my great-grandmother had brought cattle from El Chamizo, and the wide tables and sharp metal hooks remained as eerie memories of their butchering. We children loved to play there—the place was spooky, and ripe for fantasy, as we made up stories appropriately full of blood and gore.

My favorite retreat was the steamy, bustling kitchen, a spacious, high-ceilinged room tiled in white with a floor of terra-cotta. A long wood-burning stove with its immense brick oven stood next to a modern American GE range, and on both giant kettles of stock perpetually simmered. Several refrigerators lined the walls—it seemed to me that we kept buying refrigerators and arranging them along the sides of the room. Marble worktables ran down the center, and pots and pans of all sizes hung from hooks in the ceiling. Adjoining this room was a capacious pantry, where rice, grains, cornmeal, and other foods were stored in bulk.

My kitchen memories center around Rosalie, a large, competent African-Cuban woman who had been my parents' cook since they were first married. Many years before that, she had moved in with my paternal grandmother, Abuela Ina, as cook when my father was born. Rosalie's family had lived in Cuba for generations.

Rosalie was the undisputed queen of the kitchen and perhaps of the entire household. She ruled the staff with an iron hand: cooks worked busily at the stoves and tables, maids, laundresses, and nannies came and went, gardeners and chauffeurs sometimes wandered in, and when Rosalie snapped her fingers, they all obeyed her—immediately. The pantry was accessible to her alone, and only the keys hung from her waist could unlock it.

Since my father and mother had known each other since childhood, Rosalie was especially close with Mom and the two shared recipes and confidences. Whenever I was with Rosalie I felt surrounded by love. I would sit with her for hours at an old marble table near a window and listen to her lively stories and gossip. Even when I was too young to sit in a chair she would prop me up and talk to me. Rosalie kept the radio on and followed the *novelas*—soap operas—keeping me up to date on their characters and plots. The neighbors' comings and goings engaged her even more than these radio intrigues, and she shared them with me in great detail. I found her tales so enchanting that I remembered them word for word and occasionally, to her dismay, I repeated them. Once, when I was about five years old, she told me about the man who delivered our drinking water and his romance with the woman who worked for the family next door. Feeling chatty, I repeated the story to the woman in question, who marched over to our house and almost came to blows with Rosalie for betraying her confidences.

ROSALIE'S SPECIALTIES

The cuisine that had been brought to Cuba by the African slaves was based on filling root vegetables such as yams, okra, and taro; over the years it combined with elements of Spanish cooking such as *sofritos*, as well as fish, vegetables, and spices native to our island, to make an original Cuban-Creole cuisine. Many people felt that African Cubans uniquely understood this cuisine, while Cubans of Spanish descent tended to cook more like Europeans and thus lose the true Creole essence. The novel *Cecilia Valdés*, written by Cirilo Villaverde in the nineteenth century (and later made popular as a play and film), paid warm tribute to this Creole food and culture in telling the story of the slave girl Cecilia.

Rosalie's repertoire included a spicy *enchilado* sauce—a piquant tomato-and-vegetable mixture, and many rice dishes prepared with stock from the ever-simmering pots in the kitchen. She stirred the rice patiently over low heat to prepare *asopaos*, rice dishes with a somewhat runny consistency.

One of our family's favorites was *arroz con comino*. This translates as cumin rice, but it is much more than that. The rice was first cooked with tomatoes, onions, peppers, and saffron, and then perfumed with toasted cumin seeds and tossed with succulent sautéed pork chunks. The dish was rich with meat and vegetables but delicately flavored at the same time.

Rosalie made an outstanding *arroz con pollo*—chicken and yellow rice—a hearty combination of chicken, saffron, rice, onions, peppers, tomatoes, and peas, as well as a mouth-watering *arroz con jamón y quimbombó*, flavored with small bits of savory ham and given texture by chunks of fresh-picked okra.

Rosalie prepared eggs imaginatively, and her *plato Cubano* is my husband's and my favorite weekend breakfast. It consists of Cuban fried eggs over white rice served with fried sweet plantains (or plain sliced yellow bananas if plantains are unavailable). Unlike American fried eggs, Cuban eggs are deep-fried in very hot oil, with which they are basted as they cook, crisp on the outside and soft inside. Another of Rosalie's egg dishes was fried eggs over a yellow cornmeal. Cuban cornmeal is very finely ground, and it cooks into a porridge, so I grew quite fond of mushy cornmeal with eggs on top—a hearty farm dish.

When our parents were out for dinner and we kids were home, omelettes were the usual fare. Rosalie's omelette with sweet plantains was crisp on the outside, soft on the inside, and typically Cuban. Her wonderful baked eggs were simplicity itself: she put two eggs and some warm, fresh milk into a small individual pan and baked it. She sprinkled the dish with chorizo slices and served it with crusty Cuban bread. This was made quickly in our American oven rather than the slower brick oven.

I remember the commotion in the kitchen when Rosalie prepared her magnificent crab Creole, *cangrejos enchilados*. Step one was always the arrival in the courtyard of a man carrying a large burlap sack that seemed to be giving him a lot of trouble. He insisted upon seeing Rosalie and would not release his cargo to anyone else. She bustled out and firmly took it from him, as he explained anxiously that it contained the freshest crabs he could get and she should be very pleased. I hoped for his sake that she would be.

I would follow her into her domain to watch a fantastic preparation. Oblivious to the crabs as they clawed one another and climbed around in the sack, giving it a life of its own, Rosalie set about preparing a *sofrito*, a spicy, slow-cooking sauté of onions, tomatoes, garlic, wine, and olive oil. She never used green peppers for this *sofrito*. Its heady aroma soon filled the entire kitchen.

Once this *sofrito* was assembled, she began to pick up the crabs one by one. With great directness, she scrubbed each down with a stiff brush, pulled off its claws, and tossed it into the simmering sauce. She scrubbed each as if for surgery, with total concentration and never missing a beat. The result of all this was a perfect marriage of ingredients and a flavor so potent that it permeated even the crab shells, which we licked with pleasure after emptying them of their meat. *Cangrejos enchilados* was always served with fluffy white rice, which Rosalie glazed using the back of a large wooden spoon dipped into lard.

Rosalie shared her recipes with Mom, who transcribed them in the original Spanish and took them with her when we left Cuba. She loved Cuba fiercely and refused to move to the United States with us, although we pleaded. We wanted her with the family so we could care for her, but she felt she was too old to leave and, as ever, she won.

RICE, BEANS, AND EGGS ON THE CUBAN TABLE

The rice dishes we love are Spanish in origin, often colored with saffron, flavored with a *sofrito* of tomatoes, bell peppers, onions, and garlic, and mixed with chicken (*Arroz con Pollo*), sausage (*Arroz con Chorizo*), codfish (*Arroz con Bacalao*), pork (*Arroz con Puerco y Comino*), or other ingredients.

Dried beans, soaked and cooked with a spicy *sofrito*, are a Creole staple. Black beans are the most popular, served alone, with white rice, as a soup, or combined with white rice in *Moros y Cristianos* ("Moors and Christians"), while red beans are served the same way—the dish combining them with white rice is called *Congrí*. Chick-peas mixed with rice become *Arroz con Garbanzos*, and lentils, the only dried beans that do not require presoaking, are combined with white rice in *Arroz con Lentejas*. When beans, chick-peas, or lentils are combined with rice, the resulting dish is usually African-inspired. White beans, served least often, are represented here by *Munyetas del Judias*, a torte of Spanish origin. They appear in the chapter on soups and stews in *Caldo Gallego* (Galician Bean Soup) and *Potaje de Judias* (Navy Bean Soup).

Spain inspires our egg dishes, and our Basque-style robust omelettes, bursting with *sofritos* and other hearty fillings, are cut into wedges to serve at least four people. Our fried and baked egg recipes are both Spanish and Creole, the first served with white rice and plantains, the second baked with ham or chorizos or baked over *sofrito* and garnished with shrimp, canned asparagus, and canned peas. But Rosalie's plantain omelette, and some other simpler omelettes, are also made as individual omelettes in the French style.

Baked egg dishes, such as *Huevos al Plato* (Baked Eggs), *Huevos a la Malagueña* (Baked Eggs Malaga), and *Huevos Habaneros* (Eggs Havana Style) are traditionally prepared in individual glazed pottery ramekins called *cazuelitas*, which are available at the Williams-Sonoma shops.

Arroz Blanco

PERFECT WHITE RICE

Whether you cook with the traditional Cuban long-grain white rice or you use converted white rice, a long-grain rice that has been parboiled, your first step should be to ignore the package directions.

Bring the rice, water, oil, and salt to a boil over high heat and boil until all the water has been absorbed and small "craters" form on top. Then and only then, cover the rice and let it finish cooking over low heat. If you have never prepared rice this way, and you are intimidated by Uncle Ben, you will be tempted to lower the heat and cover the pot too early. But follow my directions and you will be rewarded with the fluffiest rice you have ever cooked. Even if you double or quadruple the recipe, you will get the same perfect results.

The amount of liquid differs for the different kinds of rice but the method is the same. Cooking time will increase with the addition of other ingredients.

2 cups raw long-grain white rice or converted long-grain white rice

2 tablespoons pure Spanish olive oil

2 teaspoons salt

4 cups water if using long-grain white rice; 5 cups water if using converted

1. Combine all the ingredients in a large saucepan, bring to a boil over high heat, and cook, uncovered, until most of the water has been absorbed and small craters form on top of the rice, 10 to 15 minutes.

2. Stir the rice with a fork, cover, reduce the heat to low, and cook until the rice is fluffy, 8 to 10 minutes. Fluff the rice with a fork and serve immediately.

MAKES 3 CUPS

Variations: These suggestions are not classically Cuban, but given that caveat, go ahead and try them. They add pleasant variety to ordinary rice. Results are even better in a nonstick pan.

Instead of using water, you may prepare the rice with Cuban

Beef Stock (pages 77–78), fish stock (pages 79–80), or chicken stock (pages 78–79).

When you lower the heat and simmer the rice, add any of the following:

- Fresh parsley, mint, coriander (cilantro), or a combination of fresh herbs to taste.
- Freshly ground black pepper to taste. The peppery taste is a great accompaniment for a roasted or barbecued chicken.
- 1 teaspoon cumin seeds
- ½ cup chopped onion and 10 olives, pitted and chopped, cooked in a little pure Spanish olive oil, stirred, in a skillet over low heat until tender.
- 2 cloves garlic, crushed and removed before serving. This garlic-perfumed rice goes well with grilled steak.
- Grated peel of ½ lemon, with the white pith removed. This is refreshing with roasted lamb.

Arroz Amarillo

YELLOW RICE

For yellow rice, we color white rice with a condiment called bijol (a saffron substitute), or with crushed saffron threads or powdered crushed saffron. The simplest yellow rice is made using only rice and coloring; this enriched recipe has a touch of *sofrito* as well, making it extra delicious as well as colorful. Yellow rice can be used wherever white rice is called for to accompany most Cuban dishes.

FOR THE SOFRITO:

1/4 cup pure Spanish olive oil
2 cloves garlic, finely chopped
1 medium-size onion, finely
    chopped
1 small green bell pepper, seeded
    and finely chopped

1 cup drained and chopped
    canned whole tomatoes or
    prepared tomato sauce
1/4 cup dry sherry
1/4 cup chopped drained pimientos
1 bay leaf

FOR THE RICE:

2 cups raw long-grain white rice
4 cups water
2 teaspoons salt
1/2 teaspoon bijol (see page 5),
    1/4 teaspoon powdered saffron,

or 3 to 4 saffron threads,
    crushed
Freshly ground black pepper to
    taste

In a medium-size saucepan over low heat, heat the oil until fragrant, then cook the garlic, onion, and bell pepper, stirring, until tender, 6 to 8 minutes. Add the tomatoes, sherry, pimientos, and bay leaf and cook 8 to 10 minutes. Raise the heat to high, add the rice, water, salt, and bijol, and cook, uncovered, over high heat, until all the water has been absorbed and small craters appear on top of the rice, 10 to 15 minutes. Reduce the heat to low, stir with a fork, cover, and cook until the rice is dry and fluffy, 10 minutes.

MAKES 6 SERVINGS

Arroz a la Milanesa

CUBAN RISOTTO

This dish is very, very Cuban and you will find it served in every restaurant and cafeteria in Cuban communities. Despite its name, it bears no resemblance to rice Milanese style either in technique or in the kind of rice used, but it does share the same ingredients. It allows for many variations, with additions of chicken, sausage, or ham, according to the whim of the cook. This recipe comes from Tia Mani, my aunt, Carmen Sampedro Mas.

¼ pound (1 stick) salted butter
½ cup finely chopped onion
3 cups chicken stock (see pages 78–79) or canned chicken broth
¼ teaspoon powdered saffron or 3 to 4 saffron threads, crushed

2 cups raw long-grain white rice
1 teaspoon salt
¼ pound freshly grated Parmesan cheese

1. In a large saucepan over medium heat, melt half the butter. When it begins to foam, cook the onions, stirring, until tender, 6 to 8 minutes. Add the stock, saffron, rice, and salt and bring to a boil. Continue cooking until most of the liquid has been absorbed, 10 to 15 minutes, and small craters form on top of the rice.

2. Cover and simmer over low heat without stirring until all the stock has been absorbed, 10 to 15 minutes. Just before serving, add the remaining butter, cut into small pieces, and the Parmesan cheese and stir to blend, using 2 forks.

MAKES 6 SERVINGS

Moros y Cristianos
BLACK BEANS AND RICE

A Cuban classic, this goes perfectly with all pork dishes, as well as poultry and fish. The black beans point to its origin in the western provinces; in the east, rice is combined with red beans to make *Congrí* (recipe follows). Here, I prefer to use converted white rice, which makes the dish moister. The classic recipe calls for long-grain.

4 ounces slab bacon, rind removed and cut into ¼-inch dice, or 5 tablespoons pure Spanish olive oil

1 medium-size onion, finely chopped

1 medium-size green bell pepper, seeded and finely chopped

2 cloves garlic, finely chopped

1 cup dried black beans, rinsed, soaked overnight, and prepared according to directions on package to yield 2 to 2½ cups cooked black beans, or two 16-ounce cans black beans, undrained

2 cups raw converted white rice

4½ cups water

2 teaspoons salt

1 bay leaf

2 tablespoons pure Spanish olive oil

¼ teaspoon ground cumin

Freshly ground black pepper to taste

1. In a large saucepan, cook the bacon 6 to 8 minutes over low heat, or heat the oil until fragrant. Add the onion, bell pepper, and garlic and cook, stirring, until tender, 6 to 8 minutes. Add the remaining ingredients and cook over medium-high heat until all the water has been absorbed and small craters form over the surface of the rice, 10 to 15 minutes.

2. Stir with a fork, cover, and cook over low heat until the rice is tender, 10 to 15 minutes. Discard the bay leaf and serve.

MAKES 8 SERVINGS

Congrí Oriental

RED BEANS AND RICE

Rice cooked with beans is a popular Cuban combination, but the color and type of beans vary according to what part of the island you are from. In the western provinces, black beans are popular and they are combined with rice in *Moros y Cristianos* (preceding recipe). In the eastern provinces the beans of choice are red, and they appear in *congrí*. This recipe comes from Oriente Province, via a friend of my mother's.

½ pound dried red kidney beans, rinsed and soaked overnight in water to cover by several inches, or quick-soaked according to package directions, or 3 cans red kidney beans, undrained, plus 3 cups water

1 large green bell pepper, seeded and cut into strips

1 bay leaf

4 ounces slab bacon, rind removed and cut into ½-inch dice

¼ pound ham steak, cut into ½-inch dice

¼ cup pure Spanish olive oil

1 medium-size onion, finely chopped

1 small green bell pepper, finely chopped

3 to 4 cloves garlic, finely chopped

¼ teaspoon dried oregano

½ teaspoon ground cumin

3 teaspoons salt

Freshly ground black pepper to taste

2 cups raw long-grain white rice

1. If you are using dried beans, the day after soaking, add additional water to the beans to cover by several inches, along with the bell pepper and bay leaf, and bring to a boil over high heat. Reduce the heat to low, cover, and simmer until the beans are tender, 1½ to 2 hours, adding additional water if needed.

2. In a large casserole over medium heat, cook the bacon until crisp and brown, 5 minutes, remove it, and drain on paper towels. In the same casserole over medium heat, cook the ham in the fat rendered from the bacon, stirring, 5 minutes, remove it, and set it aside. Wipe out the casserole with paper towels.

3. To make the *sofrito,* in the same casserole, heat the oil over medium heat until fragrant, reduce the heat to low, and cook the onion, bell pepper, and garlic, stirring, until tender, 5 to 6 minutes. Return the bacon and ham to the casserole and set aside.

4. When the beans are done, drain them and reserve 3 cups of the liquid. Add the beans to the onions and peppers along with the reserved liquid. Place the casserole over high heat, add the oregano, cumin, salt, pepper, and rice, and cook, uncovered, until most of the liquid has been absorbed and small craters appear on the surface of the rice, 15 to 20 minutes. Stir the rice with a fork, reduce the heat to low, cover, and simmer until the rice is tender, 10 to 15 minutes. Discard the bay leaf, adjust the seasonings, and serve.

MAKES 8 SERVINGS

Arroz con Lentejas

RICE WITH LENTILS

My family and friends like this combination so much that I serve it with American meals such as roast beef and lamb chops, as well as with Cuban meals.

Although it is not traditional, I prefer to use converted white rice in this recipe, since it makes the finished dish moister. If you want to use long-grain white rice, prepare with only three cups reserved cooking liquid, rather than five as directed below.

1 cup dried lentils
1 bay leaf
1 medium-size green bell pepper, seeded, cut in half, and one half finely chopped
7 cups water
1/4 cup pure Spanish olive oil
1/2 pound slab bacon, rind removed, or thickly sliced bacon, cut into 1/4-inch dice

1 medium-size onion, finely chopped
2 cloves garlic, finely chopped
2 teaspoons salt or to taste
1/4 teaspoon freshly ground black pepper
1/2 teaspoon dried oregano
1/2 teaspoon ground cumin
2 cups raw converted or long-grain white rice

1. In a large saucepan over medium heat, combine the lentils, bay leaf, the unchopped bell pepper, and water, and bring to a boil, uncovered. Reduce the heat to low, cover, and simmer until the lentils are tender, 45 to 60 minutes. Drain the lentils, reserving 3 to 5 cups cooking liquid, and discard the bay leaf.

2. In the same saucepan over low heat, heat the oil until fragrant, add the bacon, and cook, stirring, until crisp, 8 to 10 minutes. Add the onion, chopped bell pepper, and garlic and cook, stirring, until the onion is tender, 6 to 8 minutes.

3. Add the lentils, the remaining ingredients, and 5 cups of the reserved cooking liquid (3 cups if you are using long-grain white rice), raise the heat to high, and cook, uncovered, until all the liquid has been absorbed and small craters form on the surface of the rice, 15 to 20 minutes. Stir the rice with a fork, reduce the heat to low, cover, and simmer until the rice is dry and fluffy, 10 to 15 minutes. Transfer to a serving platter and serve hot.

MAKES 8 SERVINGS

Arroz con Garbanzos

RICE WITH CHICK-PEAS

This is my mother's recipe, always a family favorite. It makes a delicious addition to any buffet table.

½ pound dried chick-peas, rinsed in cold water, picked over, and left in water to cover overnight, or 4 cups canned chick-peas, drained

2 quarts water

1 bay leaf

One 4-ounce piece salt pork, rind removed

1 large onion, finely chopped

2 cloves garlic, finely chopped

*1 large green bell pepper, seeded
  and finely chopped*
*¼ pound smoked slab bacon,
  rind removed and finely diced*
*1 cup drained and chopped
  canned whole tomatoes or
  prepared tomato sauce*

*1 chorizo or other spicy sausage,
  diced (see pages 6–7)*
1½ teaspoons salt
*Freshly ground black pepper to
  taste*
¼ cup dry sherry
2 cups raw long-grain white rice

1. If using dried chick-peas, place the soaked peas in a large stockpot with the water and bay leaf and simmer, covered, over low heat 2½ hours, or until tender. Drain, reserve the cooking liquid, and discard the bay leaf. There should be 3 cups of liquid; if necessary, add some water to make that amount. If using cooked or canned chick-peas, use 4 cups water in place of the reserved cooking liquid.

2. In a large, heavy casserole, cook the salt pork, stirring, over low heat 4 to 5 minutes. Add the onion, garlic, bell pepper, chorizo, and bacon, and cook over low heat until the onions are tender, 8 to 10 minutes. Add the tomatoes, salt, pepper, sherry, and cook for 5 minutes. Add rice, reserved cooking liquid, and chick-peas, and stir to blend.

3. Cook over medium-high heat until most of the liquid has been absorbed and small craters appear over the top of the rice, 20 to 25 minutes. Reduce the heat to low, stir the rice with a fork, cover, and cook until the rice is tender, 10 to 15 minutes. Remove the salt pork and serve.

MAKES 8 SERVINGS

Arroz con Pollo de Rosalia

ROSALIE'S CHICKEN AND YELLOW RICE

This family favorite, one of our cook Rosalie's most memorable offerings, is an excellent party dish. It is easy to make in large quantities, and it can be prepared in advance, improving in flavor as it waits to be served. The finished rice should be soft and somewhat soupy, in the *asopado* style.

One 3-pound chicken, cut into 8
  pieces and skin removed
2 teaspoons salt
Freshly ground black pepper to
  taste
Juice of 1 lime
1/2 cup pure Spanish olive oil
1 medium-size onion, finely
  chopped
1 medium-size green bell pepper,
  seeded and finely chopped
3 to 4 cloves garlic, minced
1 cup canned crushed tomatoes or
  prepared tomato sauce
1/4 cup finely chopped drained
  pimientos
1 teaspoon ground cumin

1 bay leaf
1/2 cup dry white wine
5 cups chicken stock (pages 78–79)
  or canned chicken broth
One 14-ounce package, or 1 1/2
  cups, short-grain rice
  (Valencia), soaked for 1 hour
  in cold water to cover with 2 to
  3 saffron threads or 1/2
  teaspoon powdered saffron, and
  drained
1/4 teaspoon powdered saffron or 3
  to 4 saffron threads, crushed,
  optional
1 cup drained canned early sweet
  peas (I prefer LeSueur)
2 pimientos, chopped, for garnish

1. Wash the chicken, pat it dry with paper towels, and sprinkle it with the salt, pepper, and lime juice.

2. In a large, heavy casserole over medium heat, heat 1/4 cup of

the oil over low heat until it is fragrant, then brown the chicken 6 to 8 minutes on each side. Remove the chicken and set it aside. Add the remaining oil and cook the onion, bell pepper, and garlic, stirring, until the onion is transparent, 6 to 8 minutes. Add the tomatoes, pimientos, cumin, and bay leaf, and cook, stirring, 5 minutes. Add the chicken, mix well, add the wine, and cook 5 minutes.

3. Add the stock and bring to a boil. Adjust the seasonings—it should be somewhat salty, since the rice will absorb salt later on.

4. Preheat the oven to 350° F. Add the drained rice and, if it is not yet bright yellow, add the additional saffron. Bring it to a boil over high heat and cook, uncovered, until most of the water has been absorbed and small craters form on top of the rice, 20 to 25 minutes.

5. Remove from the heat, add ¾ cup of the peas, cover, and place in the oven until the rice is tender, about 20 minutes. (You can do this step on top of the stove over medium heat, but the rice cooks better and becomes more tender in the even heat of the oven. This is especially true if you double or triple the recipe to serve a large group.)

6. Transfer the chicken and rice to a large platter, garnish with the remaining peas and the chopped pimientos, and serve hot.

MAKES 4 SERVINGS

Arroz con Pollo Milanesa

CHICKEN AND RICE MILANESE

My mother uses short-grain Valencia rice, the kind used in paellas, for this classic Spanish recipe, even though some Cuban cooks prefer converted white rice or long-grain white rice.

4 tablespoons (½ stick) salted
   butter
1 large onion, finely chopped
2 cloves garlic, finely chopped
2 to 3 pounds boneless skinless
   chicken breast, cut into
   bite-size pieces
1 cup ¼-inch-diced ham steak
1 cup drained and chopped
   canned whole tomatoes or
   prepared tomato sauce
¼ cup dry sherry
One 14-ounce package (1½ cups)
   short-grain rice (Valencia or
   Arborio) or converted white rice

1 teaspoon salt
½ teaspoon powdered saffron or 6
   to 8 saffron threads, crushed
5 cups chicken stock (see pages
   78–79) or canned chicken
   broth
½ cup freshly grated Parmesan
   cheese
Freshly ground black pepper to
   taste
½ cup drained canned early
   sweet peas (I prefer LeSueur)
   for garnish

1. In a large, heavy-bottomed casserole over low heat, melt the butter. When it begins to foam, cook the onion and garlic, stirring, until the onion is tender, 4 to 6 minutes. Add the chicken and ham and cook, stirring, until the chicken is opaque, 8 to 10 minutes. Add the tomatoes and sherry and cook 3 to 4 minutes. Raise the heat to high, add the rice, salt, saffron, and stock, and bring to a boil.

2. Reduce the heat to low, cover, and cook until the rice is tender, 18 to 20 minutes, or bake in a preheated 350° F oven, covered, for 20 minutes.

3. Add the Parmesan cheese, mix well, and adjust the seasonings. Transfer to a serving platter and serve hot.

MAKES 6 SERVINGS

Variation: If you prefer to prepare this recipe with long-grain white rice, use 2 cups rice and 3 cups stock.

Arroz con Chorizo

RICE WITH CHORIZO

This easily prepared dish needs only a salad to make a wonderful meal. Use the finest quality chorizo—as much or as little as you like—or, if necessary, substitute any highly spiced garlic sausage.

¼ cup pure Spanish olive oil

4 to 6 medium-size chorizos (5 to 6 inches), cut into ¼-inch rounds (see pages 6–7)

1 medium-size onion, finely chopped

1 medium-size green bell pepper, seeded and finely chopped

2 cloves garlic, finely chopped

1 cup drained and chopped canned whole tomatoes

½ cup dry sherry

1 bay leaf

¼ teaspoon powdered saffron or 3 to 4 saffron threads, crushed

2 teaspoons salt or to taste

¼ teaspoon freshly ground black pepper

2 cups long-grain white rice

3 cups water

1. In a medium-size saucepan over low heat, heat the oil until fragrant, then cook the chorizo, onion, bell pepper, and garlic, stirring, until the vegetables are tender, 6 to 8 minutes. Add the tomatoes, sherry, and bay leaf, and cook 10 minutes.

2. Raise the heat to high, add the saffron, salt, pepper, rice, and water, and cook until all the water has been absorbed and small craters appear over the top of the rice, 15 to 20 minutes. Reduce the heat to low, cover, and simmer, stirring several times with a fork, until the rice is dry and fluffy, 10 to 15 minutes. Transfer to a serving platter and serve hot.

MAKES 6 SERVINGS

Arroz con Jamón y Quimbombó

RICE WITH HAM AND OKRA

This tasty Creole rice can be a main course, along with traditional accompaniment of *Boniatos Fritos* (Fried Sweet Potato Rounds, page 265). It can also be expanded according to your own creativity—or leftovers—by the addition of more ham or chunks of chicken.

1/2 pound fresh small okra, washed, trimmed, and cut into 1/2-inch slices or one 10-ounce package frozen cut okra, thawed and rinsed

3 cups cold water

Juice of 1 lemon

3 tablespoons pure Spanish olive oil

1/2 cup slab bacon, rind removed and finely diced

1 cup boneless smoked ham, rind removed and cut into 1/4-inch dice

1 medium-size onion, finely diced

2 cloves garlic, finely chopped

1 small green bell pepper, seeded and finely chopped

1 cup drained and chopped canned whole tomatoes or prepared tomato sauce

1/3 cup drained finely chopped pimientos

1/2 cup dry sherry

2 teaspoons salt

1/4 teaspoon freshly ground black pepper

2 cups raw converted white rice

4 1/2 cups water

1/2 teaspoon powdered saffron or 6 to 8 saffron threads, crushed

1. If using fresh okra, soak about 30 minutes in the cold water with the lemon juice to remove any gumminess.

2. In a large saucepan, heat the oil until fragrant, then cook, stirring, the bacon, ham, onion, garlic, and bell pepper over low heat until tender, 8 to 10 minutes. Add the tomatoes, pimientos, sherry, salt, and pepper, and cook until thickened, about 10 minutes.

3. Add the rice, water, saffron, and drained okra, stirring well. Cook, uncovered, over medium heat until most of the liquid has been absorbed and small craters appear over the top of the rice, about 15 to 20 minutes. Stir with a fork, cover, and simmer over low heat until the rice is tender, 10 to 15 minutes.

MAKES 6 SERVINGS

Arroz con Puerco y Comino

CUMIN RICE

Every winter Mom's friends would drive in from Havana to choose a Christmas tree from El Chamizo's magnificent pine forest. Each time they requested that our cook Rosalie prepare her famous cumin rice, and it always awaited them when they had finished their walk through the trees.

1½ pounds boneless pork (shoulder or chops), cut into 1-inch cubes
Salt and freshly ground black pepper to taste
Juice of 1 lime
⅓ cup pure Spanish olive oil
1 large onion, finely chopped
1 large green bell pepper, seeded and finely chopped
4 cloves garlic, finely chopped
1 tablespoon cumin seeds
1 cup drained and chopped

canned whole tomatoes or prepared tomato sauce
½ cup drained pimientos, finely chopped
One 8½-ounce can sweet early peas (I prefer LeSueur)
½ cup dry sherry
2 cups raw long-grain white rice
2½ cups water
1 tablespoon salt
¼ teaspoon freshly ground pepper
¼ teaspoon powdered saffron or 3 to 4 saffron threads, crushed

1. Preheat the oven to 300° F. Season the pork cubes with the salt, pepper, and lime juice.

2. In a large Dutch oven, heat the oil over medium heat until fragrant, then cook the pork cubes, stirring, until browned on all sides. Add the onion and bell pepper, and cook, stirring, 2 to 3 minutes.

3. In a mortar, crush the garlic together with the cumin seeds until they make a thick paste, then add to the pork along with the tomatoes, half the pimientos, and half the peas, including their liquid, and the sherry, and bring to a boil.

4. Add the rice, water, salt, pepper, and saffron, stir well to blend, and cook over high heat, uncovered, until all the liquid has been absorbed and small craters appear over the top of the rice, 20 to 25 minutes. Cover and cook in the oven until the rice is fluffy and dry, 10 to 15 minutes.

5. Transfer to a serving bowl or platter, garnish with the remaining pimientos and peas, and serve immediately.

MAKES 6 SERVINGS

Arroz Amarillo con Pescado

YELLOW RICE WITH FISH

This impressive company dish can be assembled in steps and finished in the oven.

4 grouper, snapper, or swordfish steaks, 6 ounces each

Salt and freshly ground black pepper to taste
Juice of 2 limes

FOR THE SOFRITO:

½ cup pure Spanish olive oil

1 medium-size onion, finely
   chopped

1 medium-size green bell pepper,
   seeded and finely chopped

3 cloves garlic, finely chopped

1 cup drained and chopped
   canned whole tomatoes or
   prepared tomato sauce

½ cup chopped drained pimientos

1 teaspoon ground cumin

1 bay leaf

½ cup dry sherry

TO COMPLETE THE DISH:

Flour for dredging fish

5 cups fish stock (see pages
   79–80) or clam juice

One 14-ounce package (1½ cups)
   short-grain rice (Valencia or
   Arborio), soaked for 1 hour in
   cold water to cover with 2 to 3
   saffron threads or ¼ teaspoon
   powdered saffron

¼ teaspoon powdered saffron or 3
   to 4 saffron threads, crushed,
   optional

½ cup drained canned early
   sweet peas (I prefer LeSueur)

2 pimientos, chopped, for garnish

1. On a nonreactive platter, sprinkle the fish steaks liberally with salt, pepper, and the lime juice, cover, and refrigerate at least 1 hour.

2. While the fish is marinating, prepare the *sofrito*. In a medium-size skillet, over low heat, heat ¼ cup of the oil until fragrant, then cook the onion, bell pepper, and garlic, stirring, until tender, 6 to 8 minutes. Add the tomatoes, pimientos, cumin, bay leaf, and sherry, and cook, uncovered, 8 to 10 minutes. Set aside.

3. Remove the fish from the marinade, pat dry, and roll in the flour. In a large skillet over medium heat, heat the remaining oil until fragrant, then brown the fish lightly, 3 to 4 minutes on each side, and set aside.

4. Forty-five minutes before serving, preheat the oven to 300° F. Place the *sofrito* in a large Dutch oven and return it to the stove, add the fish stock, and bring to a boil over medium-high heat. Add the

drained rice and, if it is not yet bright yellow, add the additional saffron. Reduce the heat to low, cover, and simmer until all the liquid has been absorbed and small craters form on top of the rice, stirring occasionally with a fork to prevent sticking, 15 to 20 minutes. Mix in the peas and place the fried fish on top. Cover and bake until the rice is dry and tender, 20 minutes. Garnish with the pimientos and serve immediately.

MAKES 4 SERVINGS

Arroz con Bacalao

RICE WITH CODFISH

Cuba and the other Caribbean islands have always been great consumers of codfish. It was usually served at home on Fridays, and it still can be found on many Miami-Cuban menus on that day. This one-dish meal, based on reconstituted dried codfish, comes from my paternal grandmother, Abuela Ina.

¼ cup pure Spanish olive oil

2 leeks, the white bulb and tender part of the green shoot, cleaned thoroughly and thinly sliced

2 cloves garlic, finely chopped

½ cup drained and chopped canned whole tomatoes or prepared tomato sauce

¼ cup finely chopped drained pimientos

1 bay leaf

1 tablespoon red wine vinegar

¼ teaspoon powdered saffron or 3 to 4 saffron threads, crushed

¼ cup dry sherry

Freshly ground black pepper to taste

2 cups (1 pound) dried codfish, desalted, cooked, and flaked (see pages 4–5)

2 cups raw converted white rice

4 cups water

2 tablespoons minced fresh parsley for garnish

1. In a large, heavy saucepan, heat the oil over low heat until fragrant, then add the leeks and cook, stirring, until tender, 6 to 8 minutes. Add the garlic and cook, stirring, 1 minute. Add the remaining ingredients, except the parsley, and stir to blend.

2. Cook, uncovered, over high heat until all the water has been absorbed and small craters appear over the top of the rice, 15 to 20 minutes. Stir with a fork, cover, and simmer over low heat until the rice is tender, 10 to 15 minutes. Place in a serving bowl and garnish with the parsley.

MAKES 6 SERVINGS

Arroz Imperial

IMPERIAL RICE

This yellow rice and chicken casserole has begun to appear on the menus of many Cuban restaurants in Florida. A version of *arroz relleno* (stuffed rice), it was served to me at my sister-in-law Lily's baby shower, and I promptly requested the recipe from her caterer and prepared it at home. I found it truly delicious.

FOR THE CHICKEN-TOMATO FILLING:

One 3-pound chicken, cut into serving pieces and skin removed

Salt and freshly ground black pepper to taste

2 tablespoons fresh lime juice

3 tablespoons pure Spanish olive oil

1 small onion, finely chopped

1 small green bell pepper, seeded and finely chopped

4 large cloves garlic, finely chopped

1 cup canned crushed tomatoes or prepared tomato sauce

¼ cup chopped drained pimientos

½ cup dry sherry

FOR THE RICE:

2 cups raw converted white rice

¼ teaspoon powdered saffron or 3
   to 4 saffron threads, crushed

4 cups chicken stock (see pages
   78–79) or canned chicken
   broth

TO COMPLETE THE DISH:

½ cup drained canned early
   sweet peas (I prefer LeSueur)

½ cup mayonnaise

¼ cup freshly grated Parmesan
   cheese

1. Wash the chicken, pat it dry with paper towels, and season it liberally with salt, pepper, and the lime juice. In a large, heavy-bottomed casserole, heat the oil over medium-high heat until fragrant, then cook the chicken pieces until golden brown on all sides, and transfer them to a platter.

2. Using the same casserole (add more oil if necessary) over low heat, cook the onion, bell pepper, and garlic, stirring, until tender, 6 to 8 minutes. Add the tomatoes and cook another 10 to 15 minutes. Add the pimientos, sherry, and chicken pieces, cover, and simmer 35 minutes. Transfer the chicken pieces to a plate and allow them to cool.

3. Remove the tomato mixture from the heat, reserve half, and set aside. To the remaining half in the casserole, add the rice, saffron, and stock, and cook, uncovered, over high heat until most of the liquid has been absorbed and small craters appear over the top of the rice, 20 to 25 minutes. Reduce the heat to low, cover, and cook, stirring frequently, until the rice is tender, 10 to 15 minutes.

4. Meanwhile, cut the cooled chicken into bite-size pieces, remove the bones, and combine the chicken with the reserved tomato sauce and the peas.

5. Preheat the oven to 350° F. In a 4-quart ovenproof glass casserole, spread the yellow rice mixture to about a ½-inch thickness. Pour all the chicken mixture over it, spreading evenly. Cover with a thin layer of rice, then a thin layer of mayonnaise, another thin layer of rice, and a second thin layer of mayonnaise. Finally, cover with the Parmesan cheese.

6. Bake 10 to 15 minutes, just long enough to heat through and allow the cheese to melt. Serve hot from the casserole.

MAKES 8 SERVINGS

Arroz con Maíz, Jamón, y Col

RICE WITH CORN, HAM, AND CABBAGE

Although the ingredients in this recipe are found in many Cuban rice dishes, this rendering is the inspiration of Rosalie, our family cook. When we were children, she often served it to us topped by a fried egg, Cuban style (*Huevos Fritos a la Cubana*, page 237).

1/4 pound slab bacon, rind removed and cut into 1/4-inch dice

1/4 cup pure Spanish olive oil

1/2 pound ham steak, cut into 1/2-inch dice

1 medium-size onion, finely chopped

1 small green bell pepper, seeded and finely chopped

2 cloves garlic, finely chopped

1 cup drained and chopped canned whole tomatoes or prepared tomato sauce

1/2 cup dry sherry

1/4 cup finely chopped drained pimientos

2 teaspoons salt

1/4 teaspoon freshly ground black pepper

1/4 teaspoon powdered saffron or 3 to 4 saffron threads, crushed

2 cups raw long-grain white rice

3 cups water

1 1/2 cups fresh or frozen corn kernels

1 1/2 cups coarsely chopped green cabbage

1. In a large saucepan over medium-high heat, cook the bacon, stirring, until some of the fat is rendered, 2 to 3 minutes, then add the oil and ham and cook 2 to 3 minutes, stirring. Reduce the heat to low, add the onion, bell pepper, and garlic, and cook, stirring, until the onion is tender, 6 to 8 minutes. Add the tomatoes, sherry, and pimientos and cook, stirring, 10 minutes.

2. Raise the heat to high, add the remaining ingredients except the corn and cabbage, and cook, uncovered, until all the liquid has been absorbed and small craters appear over the top of the rice, 15 to 20 minutes. Add the corn and cabbage, mix well, cover, and simmer over low heat, stirring several times with a fork to prevent sticking, until the rice is dry and fluffy, 10 to 15 minutes. Serve hot.

MAKES 8 SERVINGS

Frijoles Negros

MOM'S BLACK BEANS

My mother's black beans are rich and thick, with a smooth, opaque broth. My family judges Cuban restaurants by their beans—in other words, are the *frijoles negros* as good as Mom's? Very few have even come close.

1 pound dried black beans, rinsed in cold water, picked over, and soaked overnight in cold water to cover by 1½ inches (remove

any beans that float to the top)
1 bay leaf
1 medium-size green bell pepper, seeded and cut into quarters

FOR THE SOFRITO:

⅔ cup pure Spanish olive oil

3 to 4 cloves garlic, finely chopped

1 large onion, finely chopped

1 medium-size green bell pepper, seeded and finely chopped

2 to 3 teaspoons ground cumin

2 tablespoons cider vinegar, optional

1 teaspoon finely chopped seeded aji cachucha (Rocatillo pepper, see page 4) or green chile, optional

Salt and freshly ground pepper to taste

1. The next day, check that the water is still covering the beans by 1½ to 2 inches, and add more water if needed. Pour into a large saucepan, add the bay leaf and green pepper, bring to a boil over high heat, reduce the heat to low, and cook uncovered, until the beans are tender and they have almost cracked open, about 2 hours. Check the beans while they are cooking and if they need more liquid, add some hot water.

2. To prepare the *sofrito,* in a skillet heat the oil over low heat until it is fragrant, then add the garlic, onion, and bell pepper and cook, stirring, until the onion is transparent, 8 to 10 minutes. Add the cumin, vinegar, and Rocatillo pepper, and mix well.

3. Add the *sofrito* to the beans, mix well, and cook over low heat, covered, until the beans crack open, 30 to 40 minutes. Season to taste and serve.

MAKES 8 SERVINGS

Note: Depending on their quality and freshness, beans will vary in the amount of cooking time needed and the amount of liquid they will absorb.

Frijoles de Lata

QUICK AND EASY BLACK BEANS

"Is there a shortcut to making black beans?" my American friends ask me. Yes, and here it is, too good to be considered merely second-best. The tomatoes and herbs give the dish freshness and flavor.

If you are Cuban, you may consider this an "Americanized" version of a classic, but I urge you to try it anyway.

½ cup pure Spanish olive oil
2 cloves garlic, finely chopped
½ small red onion, finely chopped
1 medium-size green bell pepper, seeded and finely chopped
1 large, ripe tomato, chopped, or ½ cup chopped and drained canned whole tomatoes
Two 16-ounce cans black beans, with their liquid
½ cup Cuban Beef Stock (see pages 77–78), canned beef broth, or water

1 teaspoon ground cumin
Few dashes of Tabasco sauce, optional
1 tablespoon red wine vinegar, optional
Salt and freshly ground black pepper to taste
Chopped onion, minced fresh parsley, or minced fresh coriander (cilantro) for garnish

In a medium-size saucepan over low heat, heat the oil until it is fragrant, then cook the garlic, onion, and bell pepper, stirring, until tender, 10 minutes. Add the tomatoes and cook another 10 minutes. Add the beans, stock, cumin, Tabasco, and vinegar, stir to blend, correct the seasonings, and simmer, covered, until heated through, 20 minutes. Garnish and serve the beans hot over *Arroz Blanco* (Perfect White Rice, pages 200–202).

MAKES 6 SERVINGS

Variation: To turn the beans into a soup, cook as above. Puree the beans and broth in a food processor fitted with a steel blade, return to the saucepan, and simmer over low heat to heat through, 5 to 10 minutes. Serve in warmed bowls, garnished to taste. For a lighter puree, add an additional cup of stock.

Frijoles Colorados

RED BEANS

These beans are the basic ingredient of *congrí*, the popular Cuban dish of red beans and rice that is similar to *moros y cristianos*, the Cuban combination of black beans and rice.

1 pound dried red kidney beans or pink beans, rinsed in cold water, picked over, and soaked in water to cover overnight with

1 large green bell pepper, seeded and diced
3 quarts water
1 bay leaf

FOR THE SOFRITO:
1/4 cup pure Spanish olive oil
1/4 pound slab bacon, rind removed, and cut into 1/4-inch dice
1/2 pound boneless pork, cut into small dice, optional
4 cloves garlic, finely chopped
1 large onion, finely chopped

1 medium-size green bell pepper, seeded and finely chopped
1 cup prepared tomato sauce
1 tablespoon red wine vinegar, optional
1/2 cup dry sherry
1/4 teaspoon dried oregano
Salt and freshly ground black pepper to taste

1. To the beans and their soaking water, add the additional water and bay leaf, bring to a boil over high heat, reduce the heat to low, and simmer, covered, until the beans are tender, 1½ to 2 hours. Add more water if needed.

2. To prepare the *sofrito*, heat the oil until fragrant in a medium-size skillet over low heat, then add the bacon, pork, garlic, onion, and bell pepper, reduce the heat to low, and cook, stirring, until the vegetables are tender, 10 to 15 minutes. Add the tomato sauce, vinegar, sherry, oregano, salt, and pepper, and cook, stirring, until thickened, 10 to 15 minutes.

3. When the beans are tender, add the *sofrito*, stir to blend, and cook over medium heat an additional 30 minutes. The consistency should be thick and rich. Discard the bay leaf and serve the beans with white rice.

MAKES 6 TO 8 SERVINGS

Munyetas de Judias

BEAN TORTE

When I moved to New York City, the first neighbor I became friendly with was Guillermo Fernandez, a wonderful man and a great Cuban cook. This traditional recipe came from his Spanish-born mother, Adela Mesa-Padilla, another outstanding cook. In this torte the beans cook down to something like a bean pancake. Garlicky and delicious, it goes well with everything from hamburgers to a barbecued butterflied leg of lamb.

½ cup cubed boneless smoked ham
6 cloves garlic, peeled
¼ cup pure Spanish olive oil, plus extra

Two 16-ounce cans great northern beans, undrained
Salt and freshly ground black pepper to taste
1 tablespoon finely minced fresh parsley

1. In a food processor fitted with a steel blade, process the ham and garlic until finely chopped.

2. In a 9-inch nonstick frying pan, heat the oil over high heat until fragrant. Add the ham and garlic and cook, stirring, 5 minutes.

3. Add the beans in their broth, add the salt and pepper, and cook, stirring frequently with a spatula and pushing down on the beans until they have cooked into a thick, dry paste, 25 minutes.

4. Once all the liquid has been absorbed, the beans should come away from the sides of the pan. Drizzle a bit of olive oil along the edges of the beans and shake the pan back and forth several times to loosen them. Continue cooking until the bottom of the torte is dry and crisp, 8 to 10 minutes.

5. To turn the torte, place a large plate over the pan and invert quickly. Slide the other side of the torte back into the pan and cook another 3 to 5 minutes. If the pan is dry, drizzle additional oil around the edges of the torte.

6. Once again, invert the torte onto a plate, allow it to rest a few minutes, and cut it into wedges. Serve hot or at room temperature garnished with the minced parsley.

MAKES 6 TO 8 SERVINGS

Garbanzos con Chorizo

CHICK-PEAS WITH CHORIZO

My youngest brother, Cali, loves this fragrant combination of sausage and chick-peas. Try to use chorizo, which has a unique flavor, but if it is not available, any highly spiced garlic sausage is a good substitute. Since this recipe calls for canned chick-peas, it is quick and easy to prepare.

½ cup pure Spanish olive oil
1 large onion, finely chopped
1 small green bell pepper, seeded and finely chopped
2 to 3 cloves garlic, finely chopped
½ cup drained and chopped canned whole tomatoes or prepared tomato sauce

3 cups (two 19-ounce cans) canned chick-peas, drained
3 to 4 medium-size chorizos, finely chopped (see pages 6–7)
¼ pound boiled or baked ham, finely chopped
2 tablespoons finely chopped fresh parsley

1. In a large skillet over low heat, heat the oil until fragrant, then cook the onion, bell pepper, and garlic, stirring, until tender, 6 to 8 minutes. Add the tomatoes and cook until heated through, 2 to 3 minutes.

2. Add the chick-peas, chorizo, and ham, reduce the heat to low, cover, and cook until heated through, 20 to 25 minutes. (If you want to serve the dish later, cool at room temperature, refrigerate, and reheat, covered, in a preheated 300° F oven 20 to 25 minutes.) Garnish with the parsley and serve hot.

MAKES 6 SERVINGS

Tortilla Vasca

BASQUE OMELETTE

When we visited relatives in Bermeo in the Basque region of Spain, they carefully taught my brother Ralph to make a perfect *tortilla vasca*—Basque omelette. The Basques like their omelettes thick, filled with many kinds of meats, fish, or vegetables, cooked in olive oil, and large enough to serve several people. An omelette is cooked until it appears set to the eye, then it is inverted onto a plate, slipped back into the skillet, and cooked on the other side. Basque omelettes are puffier and drier than French-style omelettes, and somewhat resemble Italian fritattas.

3 tablespoons pure Spanish olive oil

2 medium-size all-purpose potatoes, peeled and cut into ½-inch dice

1 medium-size onion, finely chopped

½ medium-size green bell pepper, seeded and finely chopped

1 medium-size chorizo or other spicy sausage, cut into ¼-inch dice (see pages 6–7)

2 cloves garlic, finely chopped

¼ pound ham steak, cut into ¼-inch dice

12 medium-size raw shrimp, peeled, deveined, and cut into thirds

6 large eggs

Salt and freshly ground black pepper to taste

¼ cup drained pimientos cut into strips, for garnish

4 canned asparagus spears, at room temperature, for garnish

2 tablespoons finely chopped fresh parsley for garnish

1. In a 10-inch nonstick skillet over medium heat, heat the oil until fragrant, then cook the potatoes, stirring, until browned on all sides, 5 to 6 minutes. Reduce the heat to low, add the onion, bell pepper, and chorizo, and cook, stirring, until the vegetables are tender, 8 to 10 minutes. Add the garlic, ham, and shrimp and cook, stirring, 2 to 3 minutes.

2. In a mixing bowl, whisk the eggs, salt, and pepper together until frothy. Raise the heat in the skillet to medium-high, pour the eggs over the potato mixture, stir, and cook, moving the eggs from the sides to the center of the pan and back with a spatula and allowing the uncooked eggs to run under the cooked, so they can set, 5 to 6 minutes.

3. When the omelette looks set, place a plate over the skillet and quickly invert the omelette onto it. Add more oil to the pan if necessary, slide the omelette back into the skillet, uncooked-side down, and cook 1 minute. Invert the omelette onto a serving platter, garnish with the pimiento and asparagus, and sprinkle with the parsley. Allow to stand at room temperature 5 minutes, cut into wedges, and serve.

MAKES 4 SERVINGS

Tortilla de Cangrejos

CRAB OMELETTE

For an informal lunch or brunch, try a wedge of this elegant omelette accompanied by ripe avocado slices.

3 tablespoons pure Spanish olive oil
3 tablespoons salted butter
1 small onion, finely chopped
1 small green bell pepper, seeded and finely chopped
2 cloves garlic, finely chopped
½ cup prepared tomato sauce
2 tablespoons dry sherry

1½ cups fresh crabmeat, picked over for cartilage
8 large eggs
1 teaspoon salt
1 teaspoon freshly ground black pepper
1 tablespoon water
2 tablespoons finely chopped fresh parsley for garnish

1. In a 10-inch nonstick skillet, heat the oil and butter over low heat until fragrant, then cook the onion, bell pepper, and garlic, stirring, until tender, 6 to 8 minutes. Add the tomato sauce and sherry, reduce the heat to low, and cook 5 minutes, stirring. Add the crabmeat and cook until the crab has absorbed the sauce, 8 to 10 minutes.

2. In a mixing bowl, whisk the eggs, salt, pepper, and water together until frothy. Pour over the crabmeat mixture, raise the

heat to medium-high, and keep moving the eggs from the sides to the center of the pan, and back, allowing the uncooked eggs to run under the cooked, until the omelette is firmly set all over, but not dry, and a crust forms on the bottom.

3. Place a plate over the skillet and quickly invert the omelette onto the plate. Add more oil to the skillet if necessary, slide the omelette back onto the skillet, uncooked-side down, and cook 1 to 2 minutes, just to brown. Invert the omelette onto a serving platter, sprinkle with the parsley, cut into wedges, and serve.

MAKES 6 TO 8 SERVINGS

Tortilla de Plátanos Maduros

PLANTAIN OMELETTE

Here is a truly Cuban omelette. I often enjoyed it as a child for a light dinner, and it makes a delicious lunch, paired with a crisp salad.

1 recipe Plátanos Maduros Fritos (Fried Sweet Plantains, see page 265)
2 tablespoons pure Spanish olive oil

6 large eggs
Salt and freshly ground black pepper to taste
1 tablespoon finely chopped fresh parsley for garnish

1. In an 10-inch nonstick skillet, heat the oil over medium heat until fragrant, then add the fried plantain, raise the heat to medium-high, and cook just until warm, 2 to 3 minutes.

2. In a mixing bowl, whisk together the eggs, salt, and pepper until frothy. Pour the eggs over the plantain in the skillet, and with a spatula, keep moving the eggs from the sides to the center of the pan, and back, allowing the uncooked eggs to run under the cooked, so they can set. Cook until the omelette is set.

3. Place a plate over the skillet and quickly invert the omelette onto the plate. Add more oil to the skillet if necessary, slide the omelette back onto the skillet, uncooked-side down, and let cook for 1 to 2 minutes.

4. Invert the omelette onto a serving platter, sprinkle with the parsley, cut into wedges, and serve.

MAKES 4 TO 6 SERVINGS

Huevos al Plato

BAKED EGGS

I often serve this favorite childhood dish to weekend guests on Sunday morning. It couldn't be simpler, and everyone loves it. At home we baked the eggs in *cazuelitas,* individual glazed pottery casseroles.

6 thin slices boiled or baked ham or 2 medium-size chorizos, finely chopped (see pages 6–7)
12 large eggs

6 tablespoons (¾ stick) salted butter, melted
¾ cup milk or half-and-half
Salt and freshly ground black pepper to taste

1. Preheat the oven to 350° F. Lightly butter 6 individual *cazuelitas* or au gratin dishes. For each dish place a slice of ham or ⅙ of the chopped chorizo on the bottom, break two eggs into a saucer, slide them on top of the ham or chorizo, and drizzle with 1 table-spoon melted butter and 2 tablespoons milk.

2. Bake 10 to 12 minutes, until the whites are set and the yolks are still soft. Sprinkle with salt and pepper, and serve immediately from the baking dishes. (Place each on a serving plate, to protect the table.)

MAKES 6 SERVINGS

Huevos Habaneros

EGGS HAVANA STYLE

Like the other baked egg dishes, this one traditionally is served in *cazuelitas* (glazed pottery ramekins), but you can also use au gratin dishes. For a spectacular brunch dish for a crowd, bake in large nonstick muffin tins, carefully invert the hot molded eggs onto a serving platter, and spoon the *sofrito* over them.

FOR THE SOFRITO:

¼ cup pure Spanish olive oil
1 small onion, finely chopped
1 small green bell pepper, finely chopped
2 cloves garlic, finely chopped
1 cup drained and chopped canned whole tomatoes or prepared tomato sauce

½ cup finely chopped drained pimientos
2 tablespoons dry sherry
Salt and freshly ground black pepper to taste

TO COMPLETE THE DISH:

8 large eggs
4 tablespoons (½ stick) salted butter, melted

Salt and freshly ground black pepper to taste
1 tablespoon finely chopped fresh parsley for garnish

1. Preheat the oven to 350° F. In a medium-size skillet over low heat, heat the oil until it is fragrant, then cook the onion, bell pepper, and garlic, stirring, until tender, 8 to 10 minutes. Add the tomatoes, pimientos, and sherry, cook until thickened, 15 minutes, and season with salt and pepper.

2. Lightly oil 4 *cazuelitas* or au gratin dishes and divide the *sofrito* among them. For each dish, break two eggs into a saucer, slide them on top of the tomato mixture, and drizzle with 1 tablespoon melted butter.

3. Bake until the whites are set and the yolks are still soft, 10 to 12 minutes. Sprinkle with salt, pepper, and parsley, and serve immediately from the baking dishes. (Place each on a serving plate, to protect the table.)

MAKES 4 SERVINGS

Huevos a la Malagueña

BAKED EGGS MÁLAGA

If you prepare the *sofrito* ahead of time, this attractive dish can be an easy luncheon main course, served with garlic bread and *Ensalada de Aguacate* (Avocado Salad, page 244). We Cubans make it with canned asparagus and canned peas, but you certainly can substitute fresh, if you prefer.

FOR THE SOFRITO:

¼ cup pure Spanish olive oil
1 small onion, finely chopped
1 small green bell pepper, seeded and finely chopped
2 cloves garlic, finely chopped

1 cup drained and chopped canned whole tomatoes or prepared tomato sauce
½ cup finely chopped drained pimientos
2 tablespoons dry sherry

TO COMPLETE THE DISH:

8 large eggs

4 tablespoons (½ stick) salted butter, melted

2 slices boiled or baked ham, finely chopped

8 small shrimp, shelled, deveined, and cooked in boiling salted water over medium heat for 2 minutes

8 canned asparagus tips, at room temperature

½ cup drained canned early sweet peas (I prefer LeSueur), at room temperature

Salt and freshly ground black pepper to taste

1 pimiento, finely chopped, for garnish

1. In an 8-inch skillet over low heat, heat the oil until fragrant, then cook the onion, bell pepper, and garlic, stirring, until tender, 8 to 10 minutes. Add the tomatoes, pimientos, and sherry and cook until thickened, 10 to 15 minutes. The sauce should be thick; reduce over medium heat, if necessary.

2. Preheat the oven to 350° F. Lightly oil 4 *cazuelitas* or au gratin dishes and divide the tomato sauce evenly among them. For each dish, break two eggs into a saucer and slide them on top of the tomato mixture, drizzle with 1 tablespoon melted butter, sprinkle with ham, and top with 2 shrimps, 2 asparagus tips, and 2 tablespoons peas.

3. Bake until the whites are set and the yolks are still soft, 10 to 12 minutes. Sprinkle with salt, pepper, and pimientos, and serve immediately from the baking dishes. (Place each on a serving plate, to protect the table.)

MAKES 4 SERVINGS

Pisto Manchego

SCRAMBLED EGGS SPANISH STYLE

Spanish in origin, these eggs are very popular in Cuban cuisine. Unlike American scrambled eggs, they are filled generously with meat, vegetables, and seafood. Each mouthful of *pisto* is mostly vegetables and shrimp with just a light coating of egg.

½ cup pure Spanish olive oil

1 medium-size onion, finely chopped

1 medium-size green bell pepper, seeded and finely chopped

2 to 3 cloves garlic, finely chopped

2 medium-size all-purpose potatoes, peeled, cut into ¼-inch dice, and fried over medium heat in 3 tablespoons vegetable oil until crisp, 6 to 8 minutes

1 chorizo, cut into ¼-inch dice (see pages 6–7)

¼ pound ham steak, cut into ¼-inch dice

½ cup prepared tomato sauce

3 tablespoons dry sherry

1 pound shelled, deveined large shrimp, cut into thirds

8 large eggs

Salt and freshly ground black pepper to taste

1 cup drained canned asparagus tips

½ cup drained canned early sweet peas (I prefer LeSueur)

¼ cup finely chopped drained pimientos for garnish

2 tablespoons finely chopped fresh parsley for garnish

1. In a 10-inch skillet over low heat, heat the oil until fragrant, then cook the onion, bell pepper, and garlic, stirring, until tender, 5 to 6 minutes. Add the potatoes, chorizo, and ham, mix thoroughly, and cook 2 to 3 minutes. Add the tomato sauce and sherry and cook 8 to 10 minutes. Add the shrimp, mix thoroughly, and cook 2 to 3 minutes.

2. In a large bowl, whisk together the eggs, salt, and pepper until frothy. Raise the heat under the skillet to medium, add the eggs, and cook, stirring with a folding motion, until the eggs are almost set, 5 to 6 minutes. Add the asparagus and peas, mix gently, and cook until set to taste. Transfer to a large, heated serving platter, garnish with the pimientos and parsley, and serve immediately.

MAKES 6 TO 8 SERVINGS

Huevos Fritos a la Cubana

FRIED EGGS CUBAN STYLE

Fried eggs Cuban style traditionally are served over rice and accompanied by *picadillo* and fried sweet plantain. This is one of the many recipes Rosalie, our family cook, prepared for us, and is now a favorite of my stepson Craig.

1 cup vegetable oil or pure Spanish olive oil

1 clove garlic, unpeeled and crushed

6 large eggs

1. In an 8-inch skillet over medium-high heat, heat the oil until it is sizzling hot, with ripples on the surface, then add the garlic. When the garlic has turned brown, discard it.

2. Break an egg into a saucer, slide it into the hot oil, and immediately spoon the oil over it, basting with oil until the egg is done, 1 to 2 minutes. The egg should be crisp on the outside and soft inside. Lift out the egg with a slotted spoon, drain on paper towels, and repeat with all the other eggs, cooking no more than 2 at a time. Serve on *Arroz Blanco* (Perfect White Rice, pages 200–202), accompanied by *Picadillo* (pages 122–23) and *Plátanos Maduros Fritos* (Fried Sweet Plantains, page 265).

MAKES 6 SERVINGS

Our family and friends at the Spa at San Diego de los Baños, circa 1912. My maternal great-grandmother is the young woman in the black skirt, my maternal grandmother the little girl with the bow in her hair.

The Spa at San Diego de los Baños: Salads and Vegetables

If you followed Río Hondo northward from El Chamizo cattle ranch, through the province of Pinar del Río, you would arrive at the town of San Diego de los Baños, where deep underground sulfur springs, and the hotels built around them, attracted visitors from all over the island.

The spa at San Diego de los Baños had been in operation since 1793, and it was revered as a cure for digestive problems, arthritis and rheumatism, and skin ailments. Sulfurous waters, heated far below the earth's surface, bubbled up to provide baths ranging in intensity from *El Tigre* (The Tiger) at 100° F (38° C) through *Templado* (Temperate) at 97° F (36° C) to *La Gallina* (The Chicken), obviously a lot cooler. All three were housed in a cavernous, echoing building where the smell of sulfur was inescapable, as steaming water gushed from elephant-trunk-shaped spouts.

My maternal grandmother visited the Spa at San Diego de los Baños twice a year, along with my great-grandmother, and she always came home excited about her well-being and the foods grown locally and brought by the farmers to San Diego. Salads and vegetables were her foods of choice on these vacations, but they were only part of a large, often heavy menu. Unlike modern spas, San Diego was not a haven for dieters or exercisers—quite the opposite. Eating generous meals of many courses took up a large part of the day, and much of the rest was spent drinking the mineral water or bathing in it.

My grandmother started visiting the spa with her mother when she was only about six years old. She and her mother traveled by train from Havana to a town near the spa, where they were met by a *volanta*, a carriage drawn by four horses, which was accompanied by a man on horseback riding alongside. In those early years there was only one hotel in San Diego, the Cabarrouy, owned by Dr. Cabarrouy, a great advocate of the waters. They visited the hotel twice each year for thirty consecutive years, and this despite the fact that they had no particular physical complaints. The same chambermaid, Maria Lau, always cared for them.

Much later, when grandmother was grown and married to Dr. Ildefonso Mas, she and her mother rented a private house where we visited them during the spring and autumn seasons. By then the Miramar Hotel had been built high on a mountaintop. We loved to sit on its breezy porches in the evening, drinking in the fragrance of night jasmine and oleander, and finally free from the odor of sulfur permeating everything below. As usual, there were lots of children playing, giggling, and conspiring while the adults relaxed after dinner.

Of course we children didn't take the waters. Our days at San Diego were spent roller skating, playing in the park, or visiting Finca de Cortina, a beautiful farm with exquisite, tranquil Japanese gardens. I usually arrived at the farm early in the morning and I stayed until the sun went down because it had wonderful ponies and horses—I made something of a nuisance of myself. But the owner, who also owned the baths, was like extended family and didn't mind; he was a senator from the province of Pinar del Río, a friend of Dr. Mas, my grandfather.

Grandmother and great-grandmother hired Pelayo, the Cabar-rouy hotel chef to work at great-grandmother's home during the off-seasons. He was a salad virtuoso, producing magnificent bouquets of fresh vegetables, chicken salads, Russian salad, and stuffed avocados, as well as luscious compotes of fresh fruits. These colorful dishes, bursting with flavor and garden-fresh aromas, were always accompanied by a glass of sulfur water, smelling so foul that you had to hold your nose while drinking it.

CUBAN SALADS AND VEGETABLES

Grandmother and Pelayo to the contrary, green salads and vegetables were not a common part of classic Cuban cuisine. In the Cuba of my childhood, 1950s' popular American cooking, leaning heavily toward canned fruits and vegetables, mayonnaise, and cream cheese, set the standard. "Salad" meant chicken, fish, or ham salad dressed with mayonnaise and molded. "Fruit salad" meant canned fruit cocktail, perhaps mixed with fresh fruits and cream cheese and mayonnaise and decoratively molded.

Except for Basque Tossed Salad, combinations of tossed greens were unusual, and lettuce leaves were more often found lining a serving platter containing rich chicken or seafood molds. Tomatoes were served quartered over watercress or iceberg lettuce, and bell peppers usually appeared in sauces. But radishes were plentiful around Christmastime, and could be found in salads accompanying our *Noche Buena* (Christmas Eve) dinner.

Avocado was and is the most popular salad vegetable (though it is technically a fruit) in Cuba, and some kind of avocado salad accompanies many meat, chicken, and fish main dishes. Avocado's classic presentation is simply with onions, oil, and vinegar, and it is also combined with pineapple or seafood.

In our vegetable cookery, the African influence is strong, obvious in the many uses of *boniato* (white sweet potato), *ñame* (tropical yam), bland but versatile yuca, and *calabaza* (West-Indian pump-kin). *Plátano* (plantain), the banana-as-vegetable, also appears on the Cuban table in many different preparations. *Malanga* or *yautía* (taro), a potatolike root, is often prepared as fritters, and in the abundant summer season, I cook fresh corn the same way. Corn also is used in soups and stews and ground into cornmeal. Eggplant is prepared in sauces or soufflés, very much in the Italian and French style.

Aside from okra, fresh green vegetables were rare when I was growing up. American canned asparagus, peas, and green beans were readily available, although these were used mainly for salads and garnishes, rather than on their own. Somehow these canned vegetables worked well in our recipes, and they still do today.

Ensalada Vasca

BASQUE TOSSED SALAD

This simple, healthful salad comes from my paternal grandfather, a Basque from the town of Bermeo. He taught his wife, Abuela Ina, how to prepare it, and she passed on the recipe to our cook, Rosalie. Our family enjoyed it so much that it became a staple of Rosalie's kitchen. Rosalie used lime juice in the dressing, but you may sub-stitute lemon.

4 ripe tomatoes, coarsely chopped
1 medium-size red bell pepper, diced
2 medium-size cucumbers, peeled, seeded, and coarsely chopped
½ medium-size Spanish or red onion, chopped

¼ teaspoon dried oregano
½ cup drained pimiento-stuffed green olives, chopped
Salt and freshly ground black pepper to taste
¾ cup pure Spanish olive oil
Juice of 2 lemons

2 large eggs, hard-boiled and
   chopped
6 large red radishes, quartered

2 tablespoons minced fresh
   parsley

1. In a large bowl, combine the tomatoes, bell pepper, cucumbers, onion, oregano, olives, salt, and pepper. Toss with the oil and lemon juice (whisked together if you choose).

2. Serve on a large platter, garnished with the eggs, radishes, and parsley.

MAKES 4 TO 6 SERVINGS

Habichuelas al Escabeche

PICKLED GREEN BEANS

For this tart, refreshing salad, warm fresh green beans are tossed in vinaigrette and allowed to marinate at room temperature for an hour. It is a perfect partner for most rice dishes.

2 pounds fresh green beans, tips
   snapped off
1/2 cup red wine vinegar
1/3 cup pure Spanish olive oil
1 clove garlic, crushed
1 tablespoon sugar
1 tablespoon salt

2 tablespoons finely chopped fresh
   parsley
1 small yellow onion, thinly
   sliced and separated into rings
Freshly ground black pepper to
   taste

1. Bring a pot of salted water to a boil over medium heat, add the beans, and cook, uncovered, until they are medium-soft, 7 to 10 minutes. Check frequently to prevent overcooking. In a mixing bowl, combine the remaining ingredients.

2. Drain the beans, and while they are still warm, toss them with the vinaigrette. Marinate at room temperature at least 1 hour. Serve cold or at room temperature.

MAKES 8 SERVINGS

Ensalada de Aguacate

AVOCADO SALAD

This is the most popular Cuban salad of all, and it is served with almost any Cuban dish you can imagine. Like so many other Cubans, I never tire of it.

Watercress or lettuce leaves for lining the platter, optional
2 large, ripe Florida avocados, or 4 smaller Haas avocados, peeled, pitted, halved lengthwise, and thinly sliced
1 small onion, cut in half and halves thinly sliced

Salt and freshly ground black pepper to taste
½ cup pure Spanish olive oil or to taste
3 tablespoons white vinegar or fresh lemon juice
1 teaspoon finely chopped fresh parsley

On a large platter lined with the greens, arrange the avocado slices, place the onions on top, and sprinkle with salt and pepper. Whisk together the oil and vinegar and drizzle over the salad. Sprinkle with the parsley and serve.

MAKES 8 SERVINGS

Ensalada de Aguacate y Mango

AVOCADO AND MANGO SALAD

This composed salad is my own creation, combining two Cuban classics. Although the avocado and mango have similar textures, each stands on its own. If mangoes are not available, the salad is equally good made with papaya.

1 bunch watercress, stems removed, optional

1 large, ripe Florida avocado or 2 smaller Haas avocados, peeled, pitted, and thinly sliced

1 large, ripe mango, peeled, pitted, and thinly sliced (see page 8)

½ medium-size red onion, cut in half lengthwise and each half cut into thin slices

Pure Spanish olive oil to taste

Fresh lime or lemon juice to taste

Salt and freshly ground black pepper to taste

Line a large platter with the watercress and arrange over it alternating slices of avocado, mango, and onion. Drizzle with the oil and juice (whisked together if you choose), and season with salt and pepper.

MAKES 4 SERVINGS

Ensalada de Aguacate y Piña

AVOCADO AND PINEAPPLE SALAD

Another avocado salad, this time combining avocado with fresh pineapple, offers the flavors of the Caribbean.

2 large, ripe Florida avocados or 4 smaller Haas avocados, peeled, pitted, halved lengthwise, and cut into bite-size cubes

2 cups fresh or canned pineapple, cut into bite-size cubes

Juice of 1 lemon or lime

1/2 cup pure Spanish olive oil or to taste

Salt and freshly ground black pepper to taste

Watercress or lettuce leaves for lining the platter, optional

In a large bowl, combine the avocado and pineapple cubes, sprinkle with the lemon juice, and drizzle with the olive oil. Toss lightly to mix and season with salt and pepper. Transfer to a large platter lined with greens, and serve.

MAKES 8 SERVINGS

Ensalada de Aguacate y Salmón

AVOCADO AND SALMON SALAD

Cuba in the 1950s was flooded with American canned foods, and canned salmon was one of the most popular. In a favorite salad of the day, the canned fish was mixed with avocado and chopped cooked vegetables, dressed with mayonnaise, and served on a bed of iceberg lettuce.

I have updated and simplified this salad, substituting broiled fresh salmon for canned and eliminating the mayonnaise. It is at its best when the salmon is on the warm side and the avocado is cool. If you are pressed for time, broil the fish early in the day and warm it in the microwave at the last minute.

½ cup pure Spanish olive oil
1 clove garlic, finely chopped
Juice of 1 lime
2 salmon steaks, each about 8
    ounces and 1 inch thick
Salt and freshly ground black
    pepper to taste

1 large, ripe Florida avocado or 2
    smaller Haas avocados, peeled,
    pitted, and cut into thin
    crosswise slices
2 tablespoons finely chopped fresh
    parsley
Lime wedges for garnish

1. In a small bowl, combine 3 tablespoons of the oil with the garlic and lime juice, and set aside.

2. Place the salmon steaks in a glass dish that will fit them comfortably in a single layer, season liberally with salt and pepper, and pour the oil mixture over them. Cover and refrigerate at least 1 hour, turning once.

3. Preheat the broiler. Line a broiler pan with aluminum foil and transfer the steaks to the pan, reserving the marinade. Broil 4 inches from the heat source for 5 minutes on each side, basting with the reserved marinade.

4. Transfer the steaks to a platter. When cool enough to handle, flake the salmon into bite-size pieces and arrange the avocado slices alongside the fish. Sprinkle with salt and pepper, drizzle with the remaining olive oil, and garnish with the chopped parsley and lime wedges.

MAKES 2 TO 4 SERVINGS

Aguacate Relleno

STUFFED AVOCADO

Next to a banana split, this was my favorite luncheon treat when I went shopping in Havana with Mom. This is a 1950s' dish—in Cuba and in the United States—that still works well today.

1 pound shelled, deveined, medium-size shrimp, cooked over medium-high heat in boiling water barely to cover until pink, 3 minutes, drained well, cooled, and cut into thirds

2 tablespoons finely chopped onion

2 large eggs, hard-boiled and finely chopped

2 tablespoons drained brine-packed Spanish capers, optional

2/3 cup mayonnaise

2 tablespoons tomato paste or ketchup

1/4 teaspoon Spanish paprika or mild paprika

1 tablespoon chopped fresh parsley

Salt and freshly ground black pepper to taste

3 medium-size ripe avocados, sliced in half with skin left on, pit removed, and a small slice cut off the bottom of each half to allow the fruit to sit steadily on the plate

Salad greens to line the plates

1 pimiento, finely chopped, for garnish

1. In a large bowl, combine the shrimp, onion, eggs, and capers. In a small bowl, mix together the mayonnaise, tomato paste, paprika, and parsley, pour the mixture over the shrimp, and toss lightly to mix. Season with salt and pepper, and refrigerate until ready to serve.

2. Place each avocado half on a plate lined with salad greens, mound with the shrimp salad, garnish with the pimiento, and serve.

MAKES 6 SERVINGS

Ensalada Rusa

MIXED VEGETABLE SALAD

Although Russian Salad also can include string beans, olives, and beets, in my grandmother's house it was made simply with potatoes, carrots, peas, and eggs. She served this for lunch with *entremeses* (cold meats).

4 medium-size all-purpose potatoes, boiled over medium heat in salted water to cover until tender, 20 to 25 minutes, drained, and allowed to cool

4 large carrots, scraped, cut into thirds, boiled over medium heat in salted water to cover until tender, 20 to 25 minutes, drained, and allowed to cool

1 cup drained canned early sweet peas (I prefer LeSueur)

4 large eggs, hard-boiled and chopped

1 cup mayonnaise

1/2 teaspoon Spanish paprika or mild paprika

Salt and freshly ground black pepper to taste

Peel the potatoes, then cut them and the carrots into ¼-inch cubes, and place in a deep bowl with the peas and eggs. Combine the mayonnaise and paprika and toss lightly with the vegetables. Season with the salt and pepper, cover, and refrigerate until ready to serve. You can serve from the bowl or invert the salad onto a round platter, and reshape it with a spatula.

MAKES 6 TO 8 SERVINGS

Ensalada de Frutas Tropicales

TROPICAL FRUIT SALAD

Quite possibly, Columbus discovered these same tropical fruits when he discovered the New World, but I don't know if he bothered to combine them, as we do here. The delicious dressing is modern; it comes from my American friend Nancy Axthelm.

FOR THE DRESSING:

¾ cup mayonnaise or to taste
Juice of 1 lime
2 tablespoons honey or to taste

1 tablespoon curry powder or to taste

FOR THE SALAD:

4 ripe Red Cuban or Ladyfinger bananas or 2 large, ripe yellow bananas, sliced (see page 5)
1 cup fresh pineapple, cut into bite-size cubes
2 cups watermelon balls (cut with a melon baller)

1 medium-size, ripe mango, peeled and cut into bite-size cubes (see page 8)
1 orange, peeled, membranes removed, and divided into segments
¼ cup shredded sweetened coconut

1. To make the dressing, whisk together all the ingredients and refrigerate until ready to use.

2. In a large bowl, combine the fruits, toss lightly with the dressing, or serve with a dollop of dressing on top of the fruit, and sprinkle with the coconut. Serve cold.

MAKES 6 TO 8 SERVINGS

Ensalada de Frijoles Negros

BLACK BEAN SALAD

The late Donald Sacks was one of my dearest friends, a great cook, and the proprietor of a well-known food shop in New York City's SoHo. This is my version of one of his favorite salads.

1 pound dried black beans, rinsed in cold water, picked over, and soaked overnight in cold water to cover by 1½ inches, or four 16-ounce cans black beans, drained

1 bay leaf

1 large red onion, finely chopped

1 large red bell pepper, seeded and finely chopped

1 large yellow bell pepper, seeded and finely chopped

1 bunch fresh parsley, stems removed and finely chopped

3 tablespoons finely chopped fresh coriander (cilantro)

3 teaspoons ground cumin

¼ cup fresh lemon juice or to taste

½ cup pure Spanish olive oil or to taste

½ teaspoon Tabasco sauce

Salt and freshly ground pepper to taste

1. The next day, check that the water is still covering the beans by 1½ to 2 inches, and add more water if needed. Pour into a large saucepan, add the bay leaf, and bring to a boil over high heat. Reduce the heat to low and cook, uncovered, until the beans are tender, but have not cracked open, 1 to 1½ hours. Check the beans while they are cooking and if they need more liquid, add some water. When the beans are done, drain, and cool at room temperature.

2. Remove the bay leaf, toss the cooled beans with the remaining ingredients, and correct the seasonings. Transfer to a serving bowl and refrigerate until shortly before serving time. Serve at room temperature.

MAKES 8 TO 10 SERVINGS

Ensalada de Moros y Cristianos

BLACK BEANS AND RICE SALAD

When my brother Tony worked for *House & Garden* magazine, he noticed a recipe for a rice salad that intrigued us both, and we decided it cried out for some black beans. Following James Beard's rule, we dressed the combined rice and beans with vinaigrette while they were still warm, so they could fully absorb its flavor. We both agree that this is an inspired recipe.

2 cups raw converted white rice

5½ cups water

2 teaspoons salt

2 tablespoons pure Spanish olive oil

1 clove garlic, crushed

2 cups cooked (see page 5) or one 16-ounce can black beans, drained

½ small red bell pepper, seeded and finely chopped

½ small green bell pepper, seeded and finely chopped

½ small yellow bell pepper, seeded and finely chopped

3 scallions, white bulb and tender part of the green stem, thinly sliced

½ cup drained pimiento-stuffed green olives, chopped

2 tablespoons drained brine-packed Spanish capers

2 tablespoons finely chopped fresh parsley

1 tablespoon finely chopped fresh coriander (cilantro)

Lettuce leaves for lining the platter

¾ cup pure Spanish olive oil

2 tablespoons fresh lime juice

2 tablespoons red wine vinegar

½ teaspoon ground cumin

Salt and freshly ground black
*   pepper to taste*

1. In a medium-size saucepan over high heat, combine the rice, water, salt, oil, and garlic, bring to a boil over high heat, and cook, uncovered, until most of the water has been absorbed and small craters form on top of the rice, 15 to 20 minutes. Stir the rice with a fork, cover, reduce the heat to low, and cook until dry and fluffy, 10 to 15 minutes. Remove the garlic and transfer the rice to a large bowl.

2. Add the beans, bell peppers, scallions, olives, capers, parsley, and coriander to the hot rice. Combine the vinaigrette ingredients and add to the rice and vegetables, stirring to blend well. Cool to room temperature and serve on a platter lined with lettuce leaves.

MAKES 6 TO 8 SERVINGS

Ensalada de Garbanzos y Pulpo

CHICK-PEA AND OCTOPUS SALAD

My sister Annie created this wonderful "pantry-shelf" salad one day while searching through the kitchen for something to eat in a hurry. It is quick and tasty and makes an interesting first course. *Pulpo* (octopus) is available in many supermarkets and gourmet shops.

Two 4-ounce cans octopus in oil (I prefer Goya), drained, oil reserved, and cut into small pieces

One 16-ounce can chick-peas, rinsed and well drained (I prefer Goya)

Juice of 1 lemon

2 tablespoons chopped fresh parsley

Freshly ground black pepper to taste

Watercress, red leaf lettuce, or endive to line the plates

1. Combine all the ingredients, except the greens, add the reserved oil, and mix well.

2. Serve the salad on individual plates over mixed greens, or arrange endive spears on each plate in a sunburst pattern and spoon the octopus salad in the center.

MAKES 4 APPETIZER SERVINGS

Ensalada de Papa

CUBAN POTATO SALAD

Here is another variation on a timeless theme, the homemade potato salad—this one very Cuban. It's really a Cuban chicken salad—without the chicken and the apples.

6 medium-size all-purpose potatoes, boiled over medium heat in salted water to cover until tender, 20 to 25 minutes, drained, and allowed to cool

1/4 cup finely sliced scallions, the white bulb and tender part of the green stem

1/4 cup finely chopped celery

1/2 cup finely chopped drained pimiento-stuffed green olives

1/4 cup finely chopped drained pimientos

1 cup mayonnaise

3 large eggs, hard-boiled and finely chopped

1 cup drained canned early sweet
   peas (I prefer LeSueur)
Salt and freshly ground black
   pepper to taste

2 tablespoons finely chopped fresh
   parsley

Peel the potatoes, cut into ½-inch cubes, and place in a bowl with the scallions, celery, olives, and pimientos. Add the mayonnaise, toss to mix, add the eggs, peas, salt, and pepper, and toss lightly. Cover and refrigerate until ready to serve, and garnish with the parsley just before serving.

MAKES 6 SERVINGS

Papas en Escabeche

PICKLED POTATOES

This excellent potato salad, enhanced by a warm vinaigrette, is a great companion to grilled hamburgers or roasted chicken.

4 medium-size all-purpose
   potatoes, boiled over medium
   heat in salted water to cover
   until tender, 20 to 25 minutes,
   drained, and allowed to cool
Salt and freshly ground black
   pepper to taste

2/3 cup pure Spanish olive oil
1 large onion, cut in half and the
   halves thinly sliced
1 medium-size green bell pepper,
   seeded and cut into thin strips
3 cloves garlic, finely chopped
1/3 cup cider vinegar

1. Once the potatoes have cooled, peel them, cut into ¼-inch rounds, and place them in a shallow glass bowl. Sprinkle liberally with salt and pepper.

2. In a medium-size skillet over high heat, heat the oil until fragrant, reduce the heat to low, and cook the onion and pepper, stirring, until tender, 6 to 8 minutes. Add the garlic and cook, stirring, 2 minutes. Add the vinegar, raise the heat to medium, bring to a boil, and remove the skillet from the heat.

3. Pour the vinaigrette over the potatoes and allow to marinate, refrigerated, overnight. Serve at room temperature.

MAKES 4 TO 6 SERVINGS

Ensalada de Pollo de Titi

TITI'S CHICKEN SALAD

It would be unthinkable to buy prepared chicken salad for our family gatherings, when we can commission Aunt Titi to make her spectacular creation. Titi is absolutely disrespectful of anyone who makes a chunky chicken salad, and she painstakingly chops every ingredient into fine dice to ensure a silken texture. She arranges the salad in a large serving bowl lined with greens, outlines the perimeter with chopped hard-boiled egg, and decorates the top with 4 spears of asparagus radiating from a center of chopped pimiento. Finally, she sprinkles tiny green peas in the four sections marked off by the asparagus. As the centerpiece of a buffet or on its own, this is a special salad.

One 3-pound roasting chicken, roasted at 375° F 1 to 1½ hours and allowed to cool, then skinned, boned, and the meat cut into ¼-inch dice

2 medium-size celery stalks, finely chopped

1 large apple, peeled, cored, and finely chopped

⅔ cup mayonnaise or to taste

2 medium-size all-purpose potatoes, boiled over medium heat in salted water to cover until tender, 20 to 25 minutes, drained, and allowed to cool, then peeled and cut into ¼-inch dice

3 large eggs, hard-boiled and finely chopped

1 cup drained canned early sweet peas (I prefer LeSueur), plus ¼ cup for garnish

1 cup finely chopped drained canned asparagus tips

¼ cup finely chopped drained pimientos

Salt and freshly ground black pepper to taste

Red leaf lettuce to line the bowl

2 pimientos, cut into thin strips, for garnish

4 canned asparagus spears for garnish

1. In a large bowl, combine the chicken, celery, apple, and mayonnaise, and mix thoroughly. Add the potatoes, two-thirds of the eggs, 1 cup of the peas, the asparagus tips, and chopped pimientos, toss gently to combine, and season with the salt and pepper.

2. Line a deep serving bowl with the lettuce, choosing the best leaves for the sides, and place the chicken salad over the lettuce, smoothing the top with a spatula. Garnish with the remaining hard-boiled egg, the pimiento strips, asparagus spears, and the remaining peas as described at the beginning of the recipe, or garnish to taste. Serve cold.

MAKES 6 TO 8 SERVINGS

Ensalada de Arroz con Pollo

CHICKEN AND YELLOW RICE SALAD

During one of our family visits to Sanibel Island, Florida, I decided to make a salad from some leftover yellow rice and chicken. My mother grimaced with disapproval at my unorthodox concoction, but she enjoyed two helpings for lunch! The salad is so good, it is worth creating leftovers for.

2 cups raw converted white rice

5 cups water

3/4 cup pure Spanish olive oil, plus 2 tablespoons

2 teaspoons salt

1/2 teaspoon powdered saffron or 6 to 8 saffron threads, crushed

1 clove garlic, crushed

1/4 cup white wine vinegar

2 cups cooked skinless, boneless chicken, cut into bite-size pieces

1/4 cup seeded and finely chopped green bell pepper

3 medium-size, ripe tomatoes, seeded and chopped

1/2 cup finely chopped drained pimiento-stuffed green olives

1/4 cup finely chopped drained pimientos

1/4 cup finely chopped scallions, the white bulb and tender green stem

1/4 cup finely chopped fresh parsley

1 tablespoon drained brine-packed Spanish capers

Freshly ground black pepper to taste

1. In a medium-size saucepan over high heat, cook the rice, water, 2 tablespoons of the oil, the salt, saffron, and garlic, uncovered, until all the liquid is absorbed and small craters appear on the surface of the rice, 20 to 25 minutes. Reduce the heat to low, cover, and simmer until the rice is dry and fluffy, 10 to 15 minutes.

2. Transfer the hot rice to a large bowl, allow it to rest 5 minutes,

and remove the garlic. Add the remaining olive oil and the vinegar, and mix well. Allow the rice to cool to room temperature.

3. When the rice has cooled, add the remaining ingredients, correct the seasonings, and serve at room temperature.

MAKES 6 TO 8 SERVINGS

Ensalada de Mariscos

SEAFOOD SALAD

Tia Luisa, my grandmother's sister, would serve us this salad of sparkling fresh shellfish at her seaside home, where the seafood was plentiful and delicious.

1 pound shelled and deveined medium-size shrimp, cooked over medium-high heat in boiling, salted water to cover until pink, 3 minutes, and drained well

1 pound cooked lobster meat, from 4 lobster tails simmered over medium heat in salted water to cover 5 minutes, meat taken from the shells and cut into thin slices or bite-size pieces

1 pound cooked lump crabmeat, picked over for cartilage (purchased cooked from the fish market)

3 tablespoons finely chopped onion

3 tablespoons seeded and finely chopped green bell pepper

3 tablespoons finely chopped fresh parsley

2 tablespoons drained brine-packed Spanish capers

1/2 cup chopped, drained pimiento-stuffed green olives

1/3 cup fresh lemon or lime juice

2/3 cup pure Spanish olive oil or to taste

Salt and freshly ground black pepper to taste

1 bunch watercress to line platter

2 large eggs, hard-boiled and quartered, for garnish

2 pimientos, finely chopped, for garnish

1. In a large bowl, lightly toss together the shrimp, lobster, crab-meat, onion, bell pepper, parsley, capers, and olives.

2. In a small mixing bowl, whisk together the lemon juice and oil and pour it over the seafood. Add the salt and pepper, toss to mix, cover, and refrigerate until ready to serve.

3. Line a large platter with the watercress, arrange the seafood salad on top, and garnish with the eggs and pimientos.

MAKES 8 SERVINGS

Ensalada de Camarones, Fruta Bomba, y Aguacate

SHRIMP, PAPAYA, AND AVOCADO SALAD

This beautiful composed salad is not traditionally Cuban, although all the ingredients are. Searching for a light first course to serve with Cuban dinners, I came up with this delightful combination.

FOR THE DRESSING:
3/4 cup pure Spanish olive oil
1/4 cup fresh lemon juice
Salt to taste
1/4 teaspoon freshly ground black
   pepper

1/4 teaspoon ground cumin
1 tablespoon finely chopped fresh
   parsley

FOR THE SALAD:

*Salad greens for lining platter,
    optional*
*1 pound shelled and deveined
    medium shrimp cooked over
    medium-high heat in boiling,
    salted water barely to cover
    until pink, 3 minutes, and
    drained well*

*1 large ripe papaya, peeled,
    seeded, and thinly sliced*
*1 large, ripe Florida avocado or 2
    smaller Haas avocados, peeled,
    pitted, and thinly sliced*
*½ small red onion, finely
    chopped*
*Salt and freshly ground black
    pepper to taste*

1. In a small bowl, whisk together all the dressing ingredients, cover, and refrigerate until ready to serve.

2. On a large platter lined with salad greens, arrange the shrimp in the center and the avocado and papaya along the sides. Sprinkle with the onion, salt, and pepper, drizzle the dressing over, and serve.

MAKES 4 SERVINGS

Ensalada de Pargo

TONY'S RED SNAPPER SALAD

My brother Tony can raid a refrigerator and come up with incredible dishes prepared from leftovers, and this salad is one of his best. Surely most refrigerators aren't stocked with a pound and a half of freshly cooked snapper, as ours was when two dinner guests cancelled. But you can prepare this dish if you cook a fish especially for it, and you will find it worth the effort.

One 2½- to 3-pound snapper, sea
  bass, or porgy, cleaned and
  prepared for baking, with the
  head and tail left on (this
  makes for a moister fish)
Salt and freshly ground black
  pepper to taste
Juice of 1 lemon
3 tablespoons pure Spanish
  olive oil
½ small onion, finely chopped
2 scallions, white bulb and tender
  green part, thinly sliced
1 celery stalk, finely chopped
½ medium-size red bell pepper,
  seeded and finely chopped

½ cup chopped, drained
  pimiento-stuffed green olives or
  pitted black olives
¼ teaspoon hot paprika
¾ cup mayonnaise
2 tablespoons finely chopped fresh
  parsley
1 tablespoon finely chopped
  coriander (cilantro)
Salt and freshly ground black
  pepper to taste
Lettuce leaves and avocado slices,
  or Pan Frito (see pages
  179–80) for garnish

1. Rinse the fish with cold water, dry with paper towels, season
with salt and pepper, and sprinkle with the lemon juice.

2. Preheat the oven to 375° F. Place the fish in a lightly oiled
baking pan, drizzle with the rest of the oil, cover with aluminum
foil, and bake on the upper oven rack, until it flakes easily, 30 to 40
minutes

3. Remove the fish from the oven and allow it to cool at room
temperature. Once it is cool enough to handle, remove the skin and
break the flesh into chunks.

4. In a mixing bowl, toss the cooled fish chunks with the remaining ingredients, except the garnishes, correct the seasonings,
and refrigerate. Serve individual portions on a bed of lettuce garnished with avocado slices, or *pan frito.*

MAKES 4 SERVINGS

Salteado de Quimbombó

OKRA SAUTÉ

The Hotel Cabarrouy in San Diego de los Baños got all its produce from nearby farms, and the chef prepared this okra sauté with fresh, young pods that had been picked hours earlier. My grandmother never tired of it, and would request it for dinner every night of her stay.

2 pounds small fresh okra, ends
    trimmed and cut ½-inch thick
Fresh lemon or lime juice,
    optional
6 tablespoons pure Spanish
    olive oil

3 cloves garlic, crushed
Salt and freshly ground black
    pepper to taste
Juice of 1 lime

1. Place the okra in a bowl of cold water to cover, adding a few drops lemon or lime juice, if desired, soak 30 minutes to remove gumminess, drain, and pat dry with paper towels.

2. In a large skillet over high heat, heat the oil until fragrant, then cook the garlic cloves, stirring, 1 minute. Add the okra, sprinkle with salt, pepper, and the lime juice, reduce the heat to low, cover, and simmer until tender, 25 minutes, stirring several times. Transfer to a serving bowl or platter, remove the garlic, and serve immediately.

MAKES 6 SERVINGS

Plátanos a la Tentación

BAKED SWEET PLANTAINS

For this recipe, select very ripe plantains that are soft to the touch, with skins that are almost black. Don't be misled by the cinnamon and brown sugar—this is not a dessert. It is a wonderful accompaniment to spicy Creole dishes.

4 medium-size, very ripe plantains (the skins should be black), peeled (see pages 9–10)

1/2 cup dry white wine or light rum

1/4 cup dry sherry

1/4 cup firmly packed brown sugar

4 tablespoons (1/2 stick) salted butter, cut into cubes

Ground cinnamon or nutmeg to taste

1. Preheat the oven to 350° F. Arrange the plantains in an ovenproof casserole, pour the wine, sherry, and sugar over them, and sprinkle with butter and cinnamon.

2. Cover the plantains and bake 20 to 25 minutes. Uncover, turn the plantains over, baste, and bake, uncovered, until golden brown on top, another 15 minutes. Serve hot.

MAKES 6 TO 8 SERVINGS

Maduros

LANTAINS

outside, these sweet morsels are my
s. Try them with any highly seasoned

black), peeled (see pages 9–10)
and sliced ¼ inch thick
diagonally

heat, heat 1 inch of oil to 375° F, or
when it touches the oil. Fry as many
e layer, until golden brown, 2 to 3
g with a slotted spoon. Drain on a
serve immediately. (If you are frying
eep them warm in a 200° F oven until

ERS

ocha-Ferrán, gave me the recipe for
heat beautifully, making them easy to
plantains create delicate, spidery
e spiders."

*4 medium-size green plantains,
    peeled (see pages 9–10) and
    grated*

*Salt and freshly ground black
    pepper to taste
Peanut or vegetable oil for frying*

1. Combine the plantains and a generous amount of salt and pepper in a large bowl.

2. Take a handful of grated plantain and squeeze it very tightly, forming a patty about the size of a silver dollar. (Don't worry about shaping it neatly.) Form patties with the remaining plantain.

3. In a medium-size saucepan over medium heat, heat 2 inches of oil to 375° F, or until a drop of plantain sizzles upon touching the oil. Fry several patties at a time, turning frequently with a spatula and pushing down on them until crisp, and drain on a paper-towel-lined platter. Do not fry too many at once, or the oil temperature will fall and they will be soggy rather than crisp. Transfer to a serving bowl and sprinkle with additional salt, if desired. *Aranitas* may be prepared ahead and reheated in a preheated 350° F oven for 20 to 25 minutes.

MAKES 24 ARANITAS

Tostones

TWICE-FRIED GREEN PLANTAINS

These crisp rounds, which also can be called *plátanos al puñetazo, chatinos,* or *aplastados,* are fried twice for extra crispness. My friend Guillermo Fernandez adds peeled cloves of garlic to the second frying, which gives them a light fragrance.

Tostones are a favorite side dish—they go with everything!

Vegetable or peanut oil for frying
3 medium-size green plantains,
  peeled (see pages 9–10) and
  sliced ¾ inch thick

4 cloves garlic, peeled and
  crushed
Salt to taste

1. In a large skillet over medium-high heat, heat 1 inch of oil to 375° F, or until a plantain round sizzles when it touches the oil. Fry as many rounds as will fit in a single layer until light brown, about 2 minutes for each side, turning with a slotted spoon, and drain on a paper-towel-lined platter. Set aside the skillet and the oil.

2. Fold a brown paper bag in half, place several plantain rounds between the halves, and using the heel of your hand or a soup can, press down hard on the plantains until they are about ⅛-inch thick. If you are refrying later, store the plantains, covered, at room temperature until ready to complete the recipe.

3. Several minutes before you are ready to serve the *tostones*, return the skillet to the stove and reheat the oil over medium heat, adding the garlic. Remove the garlic when it starts to brown. When the oil is 375° F, fry as many rounds as will fit in a single layer until golden, 3 to 4 minutes on each side, turning with a slotted spoon. Drain on a paper-towel-lined platter, sprinkle with salt, and serve immediately. (If you are frying a large number of plantains, keep them warm in a 200° F oven until ready to serve.)

MAKES 6 SERVINGS

Boniatos Fritos

FRIED SWEET POTATO ROUNDS

*B*oniatos—Cuban sweet potatoes—are white rather than orange, and have a nuttier flavor and a mealier texture than American sweet potatoes, but the orange potatoes can be used in this recipe.

For this dish, some Cuban cooks fry the potatoes twice, but I prefer to regulate the heat carefully and fry them over very high heat first, and then lower the temperature. This way, they will be crisp on the outside and cooked through inside.

Vegetable or peanut oil for frying
4 medium-size boniatos or
   American sweet potatoes or

yams, peeled and cut into
   ¼-inch rounds (see pages 5–6)
Salt to taste

1. In a large skillet over medium-high heat, heat ½ inch of oil to 375° F, or until a piece of potato sizzles when it touches the oil. Add as many potato rounds as will fit in a single layer, reduce the heat to medium, and fry until golden on both sides, 4 to 5 minutes, turning with a slotted spoon.

2. Drain on a paper-towel-lined platter, sprinkle with salt, and serve hot. If you are frying large quantities, keep them warm in a 200° F oven until all are done.

MAKES 4 TO 6 SERVINGS

Boniatos Asados

OLD-FASHIONED SWEET POTATOES

Only *boniatos* (white sweet potatoes) should be used in this preparation. In the old days, this dish was slowly cooked over a wood fire, and the steaming potatoes perfumed the entire kitchen. This old-fashioned recipe is purposely vague about cooking time—that is entirely up to the potatoes.

6 medium-size boniatos (see
   pages 5–6)

Salt and freshly ground black
   pepper to taste
Salted butter to taste

1. Place the sweet potatoes in a large saucepan with salted water to half cover. Place half a large brown-paper bag under cold running water and squeeze it until softened. Cover the potatoes with the paper, arranging it to conform to the pan size, and cover the pan tightly with a lid.

2. Cook over low heat until the potatoes are soft, 45 to 60 minutes. The time will depend upon the size and age of the potatoes. If the water boils away, add a bit more as needed.

3. Transfer the potatoes to a serving platter, cut in half, season with salt and pepper, and toss with butter.

MAKES 6 SERVINGS

Puré de Boniatos

SWEET POTATO PUREE

*B*oniatos are wonderful simply baked or steamed, but I like them best pureed with butter and sprinkled with nutmeg.

Boniatos usually accompany *tasajo* (salt-dried beef) and are used in *Tambor de Tasajo* (Salt-dried Beef Pie); see the variation following this recipe.

2 pounds medium-size boniatos or American sweet potatoes or yams, peeled and cut in half
6 tablespoons (3/4 stick) salted butter

1/2 cup milk
Salt and freshly ground black pepper to taste
Ground nutmeg to taste, optional

1. In a large saucepan over medium heat, cook the potatoes in salted water to cover until tender, 30 to 35 minutes. Drain and put back over low heat for 2 minutes, shaking the pan to evaporate any remaining moisture.

2. Using an electric or hand mixer, potato masher, or fork, mash the potatoes with the butter and milk until smooth. Sprinkle with salt, pepper, and nutmeg, transfer to a serving bowl, and serve immediately.

MAKES 6 SERVINGS

Variation: This recipe is used for *Tambor de Tasajo* (Salt-dried Beef Pie). Prepare either *Tasajo a la Cubana* (Stir-fried Dried Beef, pages 127–28) or *Aporreado de Tasajo* (Salt-dried Beef Stew, pages 128–29). Spread the meat mixture in a lightly oiled casserole, top with the sweet potato puree made without the milk, and bake in a preheated 350° F oven until heated through, 30 minutes, to make 6 to 8 servings.

Puré de Calabaza

PUMPKIN PUREE

We grew up with this puree, and I now serve it to accompany *Puerco Asado* (Roast Pork Loin, pages 133–34) or any baked chicken dishes.

3 pounds calabaza (see page 6) or Hubbard or butternut squash, peeled, seeded, and cut into 2-inch chunks
6 tablespoons (¾ stick) salted butter

1 small onion, finely chopped
2 cloves garlic, finely chopped
Salt and freshly ground black pepper to taste
¼ cup milk or to taste

1. In a large saucepan over medium heat, simmer the pumpkin, covered, in salted water barely to cover, until very tender, 20 to 25 minutes.

2. In a small skillet over low heat, melt the butter. When it begins to foam, cook the onion and garlic, stirring, until tender, 6 to 8 minutes. Set aside.

3. Drain the pumpkin, return it to the saucepan over low heat, and mash it, using a fork or potato masher. Add the onion and garlic, mixing well with a wooden spoon, then add the salt, pepper, and milk, and continue mixing until smooth, adding additional milk if necessary. Correct the seasonings, transfer to a serving bowl, and serve immediately. (To make ahead, place the prepared puree in a lightly oiled ovenproof glass casserole, cover, and refrigerate.) Bring to room temperature and bake, covered, in a preheated 300° F oven until heated through, 30 to 40 minutes.

MAKES 6 SERVINGS

Calabaza con Ajo

PUMPKIN WITH GARLIC

*C*alabaza—what Cubans call pumpkin, West Indian pumpkin, or green pumpkin—is actually a squash bearing no resemblance to the American Halloween version. If you cannot find *calabaza,* a good substitute is Hubbard or butternut squash.

3 pounds calabaza (see page 6) or Hubbard or butternut squash, peeled, seeded, and cut into 2-inch chunks

⅓ cup pure Spanish olive oil or to taste
3 cloves garlic, finely chopped
1 tablespoon finely chopped fresh parsley for garnish

1. In a large saucepan over medium heat, simmer the pumpkin, covered, in salted water barely to cover until very tender, 20 to 25 minutes.

2. In a small skillet over high heat, heat the oil until fragrant, then add the garlic, immediately remove from the heat, and set aside.

3. Drain the pumpkin, shake off any excess moisture, and place in a serving bowl or on a serving platter. Drizzle the oil and garlic over it, sprinkle with the parsley, and serve immediately.

MAKES 6 SERVINGS

Yuca con Mojo

YUCA WITH GARLIC SAUCE

Our prized tuber, boiled and tossed with *Mojo Criollo*—Creole Garlic Sauce—is the traditional accompaniment to *Lechón Asado* (Roast Suckling Pig, pages 131–33) on *Noche Buena* (Christmas Eve), and it is the usual companion to most pork dishes.

4 medium-size yucas, peeled and cut 1 to 1½ inches thick (see page 11)

1 recipe Mojo Criollo (see page 26)

2 tablespoons finely chopped fresh parsley, optional

1. In a large saucepan over medium heat, simmer the yuca, covered, in salted water to cover, until very tender, 25 to 30 minutes, and drain.

2. Transfer the yuca to a serving bowl or platter, toss with the garlic sauce, and sprinkle with the parsley. Serve immediately.

MAKES 6 SERVINGS

Yuca Frita

FRIED YUCA

I usually prepare this dish with leftover yuca, cutting it into rounds, quarters, or sticks, depending upon my whim. Serve this as you would french fries, to accompany steak, chicken, or pork.

Vegetable or peanut oil for frying
3 medium-size yuca, cooked, covered, over medium heat in salted water to cover until very tender, 25 to 30 minutes, and *cut into ½-inch pieces (see page 11)*
Salt to taste
1 recipe Mojo Criollo (see page 26)

1. In a large skillet over medium heat, heat 1 inch of oil to 375° F, or until a piece of yuca sizzles when it touches the oil, and fry the yuca until crisp on all sides, 5 to 6 minutes, turning with a slotted spoon. Fry only 5 or 6 pieces at a time so the oil temperature does not go down. Drain on a paper-towel-lined platter and keep warm in a 200° F oven.

2. Transfer to a serving platter, sprinkle with salt, and serve with the *mojo criollo* on the side.

MAKES 4 TO 6 SERVINGS

Frituras de Maíz Tierno

CORN FRITTERS

These lightly sweetened, crunchy fritters are delicious served with any poultry or meat dish.

2 cups fresh corn kernels, or frozen kernels thawed and drained
½ small onion, coarsely chopped
2 large eggs, lightly beaten
2 tablespoons sugar
1 teaspoon salt

½ teaspoon freshly ground black pepper or to taste
3 to 4 tablespoons all-purpose flour as needed to thicken the batter
½ teaspoon baking powder
Vegetable or peanut oil for frying

1. In a blender or food processor fitted with a steel blade, process the corn and onion together until smooth. Add the eggs, sugar, salt, pepper, flour as needed, and baking powder and pulse until blended and smooth (batter should be thick).

2. In a large skillet over medium heat, heat 1 inch of oil to 375° F, or until a drop of corn mixture sizzles when it touches the oil. Fry the mixture by tablespoonfuls, turning with a slotted spoon, until brown on all sides, 4 to 5 minutes. Do not fry more than 5 to 6 fritters at a time, or the oil temperature will go down and they will be soggy. Drain on a paper-towel-lined platter, and serve immediately.

MAKES 8 SERVINGS

Frituras de Malanga

TARO FRITTERS

In the Caribbean and in Hispanic markets, as well, *malanga* may be called *taro*, *yautía*, or *dasheen* and may be available both fresh and frozen. This is my mother's recipe for creamy fritters made with this tuber, which she served with steaks and roasts.

3 medium-size taros, peeled and thinly sliced (see page 8)	*Salt and freshly ground black pepper to taste*
3 cloves garlic, crushed	*1 tablespoon flour*
1 large egg	*Vegetable or peanut oil for frying*

1. In a food processor fitted with a steel blade, process all the ingredients, except the oil, together into a smooth, thick paste. Transfer to a bowl and let stand, covered, at room temperature for 30 minutes.

2. In a large, heavy-bottomed saucepan over medium heat, heat 2 inches of oil to 375° F, or until a drop of taro mixture sizzles when it touches the oil. Drop the mixture by tablespoonfuls into the hot oil and cook, turning with a slotted spoon, until golden brown on all sides, 4 to 5 minutes. Cook no more than 5 to 6 fritters at once, so the oil does not cool and the fritters become soggy. Drain the fritters on a paper-towel-lined platter, sprinkle with salt, and serve at once.

MAKES 6 SERVINGS

Papas Pelayo

CRUSHED POTATOES

Potatoes boiled and then flattened, and later fried in the manner of *Tostones* (Twice-fried Green Plantains, pages 266–67), were the inspiration of Pelayo, my great-grandmother's chef. The process may sound odd, but it produces a delicious potato. If you would rather not fry them, you may broil the cooked potatoes just before serving. The onion and parsley garnish must be chopped by hand to achieve the proper crunch.

8 medium-size new potatoes, unpeeled

¼ cup pure Spanish olive oil, if frying, or 2 tablespoons for brushing, if broiling, plus extra for garnish

Coarse salt and freshly ground black pepper to taste

½ medium-size onion, finely chopped by hand

6 tablespoons finely chopped fresh parsley

1. In a medium-size saucepan over medium heat, boil the potatoes in salted water to cover, until tender, about 15 minutes.

2. Drain the potatoes and let cool a bit. Place one in a folded, clean kitchen towel and, with the palm of your hand, gently press down until you feel the potato crush. Repeat with all the potatoes. Place the potatoes on a plate and set aside at room temperature.

3. If frying, heat the oil in a medium-size skillet over medium heat until fragrant, and cook the potatoes until crisp, 4 to 5 minutes on each side. If broiling, preheat the broiler 10 minutes before serving. Brush the tops of the potatoes with the 2 tablespoons olive oil, place on a lightly oiled cookie sheet on the middle broiler rack, and broil until golden brown, 2 to 4 minutes on each side.

4. Sprinkle the potatoes with pepper, salt, onions, and parsley, and, if you like, a few drops of olive oil. Serve hot.

MAKES 4 SERVINGS

Papas con Chorizo

POTATOES WITH CHORIZO

Of all the dishes in Mom's repertoire, my sister María Elena most often requests this simple, savory mix of chorizo and potatoes steamed together. Because the chorizos are salty, it is a good idea to correct the seasonings at the last minute.

3 medium-size chorizos or other spicy sausage, cut in 1-inch rounds (see pages 6–7)
12 medium-size new potatoes, peeled and cut in half
1 large onion, cut in half and the halves thickly sliced

1 large green bell pepper, seeded and cut into thin strips
3 tablespoons pure Spanish olive oil, plus extra for garnish
Salt and freshly ground black pepper to taste

1. Place the chorizos, potatoes, onion, bell pepper, and oil in a large saucepan with a tight-fitting lid, add a small amount of cold water to barely cover, and bring to a simmer over very low heat. Simmer, covered, until the potatoes are tender, 20 to 25 minutes. Drain, then shake the pan over low heat for 2 minutes to evaporate any remaining moisture. Transfer to a serving platter, drizzle with olive oil, if desired, correct the seasonings, and serve hot.

MAKES 6 SERVINGS

This was the style of my grandfather's Las Canas home. Inside, however, it was the perfect English cottage. Reprinted with permission of the Richter Library of the University of Miami.

Las Canas Orange Groves: Desserts

The remarkably beautiful Las Canas orange groves in the province of Pinar del Río were owned by my maternal grandfather, Dr. Ildefonso Mas. They comprised 150 acres of gently rolling hills that were covered with row after row of orange trees, astounding in their symmetry. From a distance, the perfect lines of trees looked like they were drawn on graph paper.

Visitors entered Las Canas through gates in a high stone wall covered with flowering yellow allamanda and then followed a steep downhill road running through an arbor of bamboo trees that formed a long, shady tunnel. My brothers and I would coast our bikes down the hill, with the sunlight casting checkered patterns through the darkness of the trees and the rustling bamboo giving off high-pitched, crackling sounds.

On another hill sat the white farmhouse, a single-story colonial surrounded on all sides by wide porches. The side facing the orange groves was screened, and it was furnished with soft string hammocks hung up between the pillars, comfortable rattan chairs and sofas, and tables set up for backgammon, checkers, and chess. This breezy space was designated for lunch, cocktails, games, and tea-time—*merienda*. If you wandered inside the house you were likely to see Dr. Mas reading contentedly, surrounded by his travel books, his Audubon Society bulletins, and his *National Geographic* magazines, all arranged in majestic floor-to-ceiling mahogany bookcases. He decorated the house in the style of an English cottage, with overstuffed club chairs and sofas covered in faded printed linen. The pale tiled floors were covered by a soft, worn rug, and sunlight filtered in through ceiling-high shutters. The look was one of total comfort and serenity.

MEMORIES OF DR. MAS

My grandfather was a cardiologist, scholar, philanthropist, world traveler, and self-made man. He had been orphaned at an early age and, living with older sisters, had worked as a pharmacist's delivery boy and paid for his own medical education. The groves, producing plentiful crops of oranges, sour oranges, mandarins, and white and pink grapefruit, were his hobby and gave him pleasure throughout his life. He had hoped to establish a frozen orange juice plant in the area, using juice from his groves, but he never achieved this goal.

Dr. Mas was a serious, diligent man, yet he understood children perfectly and he was a wonderful grandfather. I remember his impromptu visits to my boarding school, when he brought me boxes of Milky Way bars and sacks of nickels for the Coke machine. Then he would go off to discuss my nutrition with the sisters!

Our frequent visits to Las Canas were memorable. The aroma of good food wafted out to meet us as we entered the porch, and we knew we would find laughter and comfort. For us children, there was a special delight in the freedom to roam the hills and follow the animals without supervision. Most important, there was my grand-

In an orange grove like Las Canas, newly planted seedlings and some older trees, from the early part of the century. Reprinted with permission of the Richter Library of the University of Miami.

father, who was elegant, handsome, funny, and erudite. From him we learned to be true to ourselves, to be open and honest, and to accept others who might seem different.

But our warm memories end sadly. Doctors were not allowed to leave Cuba after the revolution, so when we emigrated to the United States he stayed behind. We always hoped for the reunion that was not to be, and he died in his homeland, old and sick, cared for by neighbors.

THE KITCHEN AT LAS CANAS

Since dinnertime was Dr. Mas's quiet hour to be alone, we usually visited him for lunch and then spent the afternoon. The plump white rabbits and iridescent peacocks that scampered through the groves provided hours of play for us children, while our parents lingered on the comfortable porch sipping banana or pineapple daiquiris and nibbling on spicy meat brochettes, chorizo rounds, fried plantain chips, and all sorts of savory meat and fish croquettes.

Luis was grandfather's excellent cook, who kept us eating and drinking from the moment we arrived at the house. He made delectable black beans and the best fried green plantain chips any of us had ever tasted.

Luis picked the small, bitter fruits called *Guayavitas del Pinar,* which were native to Pinar del Río. Bushes thick with their diminutive flowers sprouted wild all over the groves but none seemed to grow across the highway in Puerta de Golpe. *Guayavitas* were transformed by Luis into a delectable liqueur, as were the sweet, brightly colored mandarin oranges that grew in abundance. My grandfather used the potent orange liqueur as flavoring for the daiquiris he served to guests.

During harvest season, Luis outdid himself, coming up with new and delicious ways to use the copious crop: we were treated to delicate *Flan de Naranjas* (Orange Flan), *Naranjas en Ron* (Coral

My aunts and uncles on the front porch at Las Canas, 1949.

Oranges), and *Dulce de Toronja* (Sweetened Grapefruit Shells), as well as relishes, soufflés, and ice cream. When my Aunt Titi came to visit, she took over in the kitchen for a while and produced our favorite cake, *Titi's Cake de Naranja* (Titi's Orange Cake), light, orange-flavored layers filled with a delicate lime and orange cream.

Talented chef he may have been, but to the children, Luis was nothing more than a devil. During one of our visits he offered a savory cocktail brochette of dark-colored meat, with a tangy overtone and woodsy aroma. Sour orange was the secret ingredient, he announced. It always tenderized rabbit. Rabbit! All the young cousins began weeping and shouting. Luis was butchering our beloved rabbits and serving them with daiquiris! Yet another time he prepared what we thought was turkey, although it seemed somewhat chewy and sweet, and then he proudly announced that it was peacock. We hated this murderer. We never again trusted him or ate any meat he offered.

A beautiful river wound through the groves, so perfectly clear that we could count the colored pebbles at the bottom. Here Luis fished for the abundant silvery trout that he simply sautéed or grilled over a wood fire, and seasoned with salt, pepper, and lime juice. We grudgingly accompanied Luis to the banks and helped him fish for our lunch, but the instant we returned to the house, we staked out the kitchen and watched his every move.

CUBAN DESSERTS

Luis regaled us with creations based on tangy fresh oranges and grapefruits, and our family cook, Rosalie, specialized in fritters and crisps filled with fragrant, ripe bananas, but these fruit delicacies were only accessories at the Cuban dessert table.

Sugar was the star of our island, and most Cubans were brought up on intoxicatingly sweet flans, custards, and bread puddings. Our *torrejas* (French toast) calls for sugar in the milk that softens

Fragrant, ripe oranges grew in profusion at Las Canas. Reprinted with permission of the Richter Library of the University of Miami.

the bread and sugar in the syrup that flavors the finished toast. On the farms and in the small towns a popular dessert was *boniatillo* (sweet potato paste), a sweet and filling combination of the earthy white sweet potatoes, egg yolks, sherry, cinnamon, and a lot of sugar.

Sugar was always cheap, available, and even patriotic—it supported our economy, after all. So Cuban cuisine is known for desserts like *natilla* (sweet custard), *leche frita* (fried milk squares), and *coco quemado* (crispy coconut). These dishes may not have been elegant, like the French desserts available in Havana's patisseries, but they were rich, sweet, and satisfying. And when we were in the mood for more worldly fare, and we found ourselves in Havana, we trooped into El Carmelo and ordered the famous *helado tostado El Carmelo* (molded baked ice cream).

Flan de Naranjas

ORANGE FLAN

My grandfather owned extensive orange groves, and during harvest time the oranges made their appearance in delicious relishes, salads, cake, puddings, and as beautifully caramelized sections. We loved this flan, a variation of a traditional Cuban dessert, enlivened with the juice and zest of fresh oranges.

1 cup sugar	1 tablespoon finely grated orange
2 cups light cream or	peel
half-and-half	Pinch of salt
½ teaspoon vanilla extract	Canned mandarin orange
6 large eggs	sections, drained, or fresh
¼ cup fresh orange juice	raspberries for garnish

1. Preheat the oven to 350° F. In a small, heavy skillet over medium heat, cook ½ cup of the sugar, stirring frequently after it begins to bubble, until golden brown, 6 to 8 minutes. Be careful that it does not burn. Remove from the heat, divide the syrup among 6 to 8 custard cups (depending upon their size), or pour into a 2-quart ovenproof mold, and swirl to coat the bottom.

2. In a small, heavy saucepan over medium heat, combine the cream, the remaining sugar, and vanilla, heat until bubbles begin to form around the sides, and remove from the heat. In a mixing bowl, combine the eggs, orange juice, peel, and salt, and whisk until smooth and light. Add the cream mixture and mix well.

3. Strain the mixture through a fine sieve into the caramelized custard cups or mold, place in a large pan, and fill the outer pan with lukewarm water two thirds the height of the cups or mold.

4. Bake 1 hour for a large mold or slightly less for custard cups, or until a cake tester inserted in the flan comes out clean, then

remove from the water bath, cool to room temperature, cover, and refrigerate.

5. To unmold, run a knife along the edge of the mold and invert it onto a serving platter. Spoon the caramel over the flan and serve at once, garnished with the oranges.

MAKES 6 TO 8 SERVINGS

Flan de Mama Nena
TRADITIONAL FLAN

Flan is our most popular dessert, and this is a very simple, classic recipe from my great-grandmother.

1½ cups sugar	2 large eggs
4 cups milk	10 large egg yolks
Pinch of salt	1 teaspoon vanilla extract
1 cinnamon stick	

1. In a small, heavy saucepan over medium heat, cook ½ cup of the sugar, stirring after it starts to bubble, until it caramelizes, 6 to 8 minutes. Pour it into a 2-quart ovenproof mold, swirl to coat the bottom, and set aside. Preheat the oven to 350° F.

2. In a heavy saucepan over low heat, simmer the milk, salt, the remaining sugar, and the cinnamon until the sugar dissolves. Remove from heat and let cool to room temperature.

3. In a bowl, mix the whole eggs and egg yolks until lemon-colored. Strain the egg mixture into the cooled milk, stir, add the vanilla, and mix well.

4. Pour the mixture into the caramelized pan, set it into a larger pan on the middle oven rack, and pour lukewarm water into the outer pan, reaching two thirds of the way up the side of the custard.

5. Bake 1 hour, uncover, and insert a cake tester in the center to see if it is set. (Or use Mama Nena's method: shake the pan, and if the custard is wobbly, it is not done.) If not set, cook the custard, uncovered, another 15 minutes. Remove from the oven and the water bath, let cool to room temperature, cover, and refrigerate 2 to 3 hours.

6. To serve, run a knife around the inside edges of the pan, invert the custard onto a serving plate, and spoon the caramel over it.

MAKES 6 TO 8 SERVINGS

Natilla

SWEET CUSTARD

This rich, velvety dessert is pure comfort food. My mother remembers that when she was a small child, the crisp sugar crust was achieved by pouring sugar over the custard and then pressing it down with an iron (the kind used to iron clothing) that had been heated over coals.

10 large egg yolks
4 cups milk
¼ cup cornstarch
1 cup sugar

1 teaspoon vanilla extract
Cinnamon for dusting or 1 cup
  sugar for the crust

1. In a bowl, mix the egg yolks with 1 cup of the milk. In another bowl, mix the cornstarch with another cup of milk, then add the sugar and the remaining milk. Strain the egg-yolk mixture through a fine strainer into the cornstarch mixture and stir to combine well.

2. In a heavy, medium-size saucepan over medium heat, cook the mixture, stirring constantly, until thickened, 20 minutes. Remove from heat, add the vanilla, and stir to blend.

3. Pour into a serving bowl, let cool to room temperature, cover, and refrigerate 2 hours or overnight. Before serving, dust with cinnamon. If you are caramelizing the custard, cook the sugar in a small, heavy saucepan over medium heat, stirring constantly after it starts to bubble, until it is golden brown, 6 to 8 minutes. Drizzle it over the custard and refrigerate until the caramel sets. If you want a crisp sugar crust, pour the custard into an ovenproof mold, and refrigerate as directed above. Before serving, sprinkle the sugar over the top, and place under a preheated broiler just until the sugar melts. Watch closely, as the sugar burns quickly. Serve within 10 to 15 minutes.

MAKES 6 TO 8 SERVINGS

Flan de Coco

COCONUT FLAN

This light and airy flan was often served by my aunt, Tia Yeya. The original recipe is tedious, as it requires the aggressive maceration of a coconut. Packaged shredded coconut delivers the cook from all that work, and is very successful in this dish.

1 cup sugar
2 cups half-and-half or light
  cream
4 large eggs, lightly beaten
2 large egg yolks

½ cup tightly packed finely
  chopped shredded sweetened
  coconut
½ teaspoon vanilla extract
Fresh berries for garnish

1. Preheat the oven to 350° F. In a small, heavy saucepan over medium heat, cook ½ cup of the sugar, stirring constantly after it starts to bubble, until it caramelizes, 6 to 8 minutes. Divide the syrup among 8 custard cups, or pour into a 2-quart ovenproof mold, and swirl to coat the bottom. Set aside.

2. In a medium-size, heavy saucepan over medium heat, heat the half-and-half and sugar almost to scalding, and set aside.

3. In a large bowl, whisk the eggs and yolks together until blended. Gradually add the cooled half-and-half, coconut, and vanilla, and mix well.

4. Pour the mixture into the prepared custard cups or mold, place in a large pan, and fill the outer pan with lukewarm water two thirds the height of the cups or mold. Bake 1 hour for a large mold and slightly less for custard cups, or until a cake tester inserted in the flan comes out clean. Remove from the water bath, allow to cool to room temperature, cover, and refrigerate.

5. To unmold, run a knife along the inner edge of the mold or cups and invert the custard onto a plate. Spoon the caramel over the top and garnish with fresh berries.

MAKES 8 SERVINGS

Variation: Combine 1 pint of berries with sugar to taste, puree in a food processor fitted with a steel blade or blender, and spoon around the flan.

Arroz con Leche de Carmen María

CARMEN'S RICE PUDDING

My cousin Carmen María has been cooking and baking since she was barely tall enough to reach the kitchen counter. Now the mother of two and a busy career woman, she relaxes by making confections from the recipes of the great French pastry chefs. This deceptively humble treat is a bit more Cuban.

1½ cups water
½ cup raw short-grain white rice
   (Valencia or Arborio)
1 quart milk
Peel of ¼ lime, bitter white pith
   removed, and 1 cinnamon stick

Pinch of salt
1 cup sugar
Ground cinnamon for garnish

1. In a heavy, medium-size saucepan over medium heat, cook the rice with water until the rice is softened, 15 to 20 minutes. Pour off any excess water.

2. Reduce the heat to low, add the milk, lime peel and cinnamon, salt, and sugar, and cook, stirring frequently to avoid sticking, until the pudding has thickened, about 45 minutes to an hour. Remove the lime rind, transfer the pudding to a serving bowl, garnish with cinnamon, cover, and refrigerate until ready to serve.

MAKES 6 SERVINGS

Pudín de Pan de Mama Nena

GREAT-GRANDMOTHER'S BREAD PUDDING

Going against tradition, my mother insists that this pudding be made with French or Italian bread rather than Cuban. She finds Cuban bread too coarse, while the others are finer-textured and make a better pudding.

1 loaf stale French or Italian
   bread
2 cups milk
4 large egg yolks
1 cup sugar
¼ pound (1 stick) salted butter
   plus 1 to 2 tablespoons for
   greasing the pan, at room
   temperature

1 tablespoon vanilla extract
¼ cup dry sherry
½ cup golden raisins
½ cup sliced blanched almonds
Flour for coating raisins and
   nuts
¼ to ½ cup fine bread crumbs
   for thickening, if needed

1. Preheat the oven to 325° F. In a large mixing bowl, crumble the loaf of bread, pour the milk over it, and let it stand 1 hour. Pour off any milk not absorbed.

2. In another bowl, beat together the egg yolks, sugar, softened butter, vanilla, and sherry. Stir the egg-yolk mixture into the bread mixture, coat the raisins and almonds with flour (so they will not sink to the bottom of the pudding), and add them to the mixture. If the mixture is runny, add the bread crumbs to thicken it. (Some breads absorb more liquid than others.)

3. Butter a 9 × 13 × 2-inch baking dish, pour the pudding into it, place on the middle oven rack, and bake until browned, about 1 hour and 10 minutes. Cool to room temperature before serving.

MAKES 8 TO 10 PORTIONS

Torrejas

FRENCH TOAST

My aunt, Carmen Sampedro Mas — Tia Mani — effortlessly whips up tempting desserts like this one. Cubans consider this sweet version of French toast definitely a dessert, not a breakfast or brunch dish.

FOR THE SUGAR SYRUP (almibar):

2 cups sugar

1 cup water

2-inch piece lime peel, white pith
  removed

FOR THE FRENCH TOAST:

4 cups milk

4 large egg yolks

¾ cup sugar

1 tablespoon vanilla extract

Eight to ten 1-inch-thick slices
  stale French bread, crusts
  removed

1 tablespoon dry sherry for each
  slice of bread

Ground cinnamon for sprinkling

2 large eggs, lightly beaten

4 tablespoons (½ stick) salted
  butter or vegetable oil

1. To prepare the sugar syrup, in a small, heavy saucepan over high heat, stir together all the syrup ingredients until thickened 8 to 10 minutes, then remove from the heat, and allow to cool at room temperature. Remove the lime peel.

2. In a large, deep bowl that will fit the bread comfortably, mix together the milk, egg yolks, sugar, and vanilla, and soak the bread slices 1 hour. Remove the bread from the milk bath and sprinkle both sides of each slice with the sherry and cinnamon. Dip each slice into the beaten whole eggs and set aside.

3. In a large, heavy-bottomed skillet, melt the butter over medium heat. When it begins to foam, fry the bread until golden brown, 2 to 3 minutes on each side, then drain on paper towels.

4. Place the French toast slices on a platter, pour the sugar syrup over them, and serve.

MAKES 8 TO 10 SERVINGS

Leche Frita

FRIED MILK SQUARES

This traditional Spanish dessert evokes happy memories of Abuela Ina, my paternal grandmother. She was my favorite person in the world when I was a small child, and her kitchen was a magic place, from which glorious treats—like *leche frita*—emerged.

5 tablespoons cornstarch
3 cups cold milk
Peel of 1 lime, white pith removed
5 tablespoons sugar
4 tablespoons (½ stick) salted butter
3 large eggs, lightly beaten

¼ cup fine bread crumbs or all-purpose flour
Vegetable or peanut oil for frying
1 tablespoon ground cinnamon mixed with ½ cup sugar for dusting

1. Dissolve the cornstarch in 1 cup of the milk. Set aside.
2. In a medium-size saucepan over medium heat, heat the remaining milk, the lime peel, sugar, and butter until it almost reaches a boil. Reduce the heat to low and gradually add the cornstarch mixture, stirring constantly. Continue cooking and stirring with a wooden spoon until the custard comes to a boil and has thickened.
3. Remove the lime peel and pour the custard into an 8 × 8-inch Pyrex dish, spreading it evenly. Cover and refrigerate at least 4 hours, or until firm.
4. Cut the custard into 2-inch squares, dip the squares into the beaten eggs, and then into the crumbs, covering all sides. In a large, heavy skillet over medium heat, heat the oil until very hot but not smoking, and cook the squares until brown, 2 minutes on each side, turning carefully with a spatula. Drain on a paper-towel-lined plate, transfer to a serving platter, sprinkle with the cinnamon and sugar to taste, and serve hot.

MAKES 16 2-INCH SQUARES, SERVING 8

Naranjas en Ron

CORAL ORANGES

My grandfather's chef, Luis, created this recipe, but my sister Maria Elena named it.

She described these exquisite oranges perfectly. Not only do they look beautiful, they taste heavenly with ice cream.

4 large navel or Valencia oranges, peeled and pith removed, thinly sliced
3 tablespoons light rum
3 tablespoons grenadine syrup

2 tablespoons fresh orange juice or water
Grated orange peel or fresh mint leaves for garnish

1. Place the orange slices in a large, shallow bowl. Combine the rum, grenadine, and juice, pour over the oranges, cover, and refrigerate at least 2 hours.

2. Divide the oranges among 6 individual plates, spoon the sauce over them, and garnish with orange peel. If desired, top with a scoop of vanilla ice cream.

MAKES 6 SERVINGS

Helado Tostado El Carmelo

BAKED ICE CREAM

Everyone in Havana frequented the trendy El Carmelo restaurant, which was famous for its baked ice cream mold, a Cuban version of

Baked Alaska. Ladies visited the restaurant for lunch, children for ice cream, teenagers after the movies, and adults for dinner and late-night snacks. Some Cubans recall this dish with pound cake, others swear it was sans cake—both ways are delicious.

1 quart best-quality chocolate ice cream	*⅛ teaspoon cream of tartar*
2 large egg whites	*Pinch of salt*
	½ cup sugar

1. The day before serving, fill four 8-ounce ovenproof ramekins with ice cream to about ½ inch from the top and, using your fingers or a spoon, press down so that the ice cream conforms to the shape of the ramekin. Cover and place in the freezer.

2. Using an electric mixer at moderate speed, beat the egg whites until foamy, then add the cream of tartar and salt, and increase the mixer speed to high. When soft peaks form, add the sugar gradually, beating until stiff peaks form and the sugar is dissolved. The whites should have a glossy appearance.

3. Cover the ramekins with the meringue, smoothing the tops with a spatula and making sure the entire border is well sealed and no ice cream shows through. Cover with aluminum foil and return to the freezer to harden, at least 2 hours or overnight.

4. Minutes before serving, place the cold ramekins under a preheated broiler, 4 to 5 inches from the heat source until the meringues brown lightly (watch closely, as they burn quickly), about 1 minute. Serve immediately from the ramekins, placed on serving plates to avoid burning the table.

MAKES 4 SERVINGS

Variation: Place small pieces of pound cake in the bottom of each ramekin, pressing down gently, to form a bottom crust. Add the ice cream and proceed with the recipe.

Coco Quemado

CRISPY COCONUT

Ana Rosa Besu, whose family owned La Majagua tobacco ranch, was famous for her desserts, and as a child I used to love watching her create them in her own private corner of Majagua's large kitchen. This is her recipe for a traditional Cuban dish, a rich confection of coconut. My mother has streamlined the recipe somewhat, substituting canned coconut in heavy syrup for the original coconut-from-scratch that Ana Rosa used. This is an extremely sweet dessert.

One 16-ounce can coconut in
    heavy syrup, undrained
    (available at Hispanic
    markets)
¼ cup sugar
1 stick cinnamon
Pinch of salt

4 large egg yolks
2 large eggs
4 tablespoons salted butter at
    room temperature
½ cup slivered blanched almonds
Whipped cream or ice cream,
    optional

1. In a heavy, medium-size saucepan over low heat, heat the coconut and its syrup, the sugar, cinnamon stick, and salt, stirring, until it comes to a boil and the sugar is dissolved. Remove the cinnamon stick and allow the mixture to cool at room temperature.

2. Preheat the oven to 325° F. In a large bowl, beat together the egg yolks and the whole egg. Add the eggs and butter to the cooled coconut mixture and mix well. Pour the mixture into an 8 × 8-inch Pyrex baking dish, sprinkle the almonds on top, and bake until browned and crisp on top, 30 to 40 minutes. Allow to cool, cut into squares, and serve with whipped cream.

MAKES 8 TO 10 SERVINGS

Boniatillo

SWEET POTATO PASTE

If you love sweet desserts, this one's for you! *Boniatillo*, a rich confection made with our white Cuban sweet potato, the *boniato*, dates as far back into our culinary heritage as sugar itself, combining the earthy sweetness of the root vegetable with the extra kick of pure sugar. At Cuban parties, this sweet is served in tiny fluted foil cups—just a little goes a long way.

For this recipe, no other type of potato can be substituted for the *boniato*.

1½ pounds Cuban white sweet
*   potatoes, peeled and cut into*
*   large chunks (see pages 5–6)*
2 cups water
2 cups sugar

1 cinnamon stick
Peel of 1 lime, white pith removed
3 large egg yolks, lightly beaten
¼ cup dry sherry
Ground cinnamon for garnish

1. In a large saucepan over medium heat, boil the potatoes in lightly salted water to cover until tender, about 20 minutes. Drain the potatoes and puree them in a blender or food processor fitted with a steel blade.

2. In a large saucepan over medium heat, heat the water, sugar, cinnamon, and lime peel, stirring constantly, until the syrup reaches the soft-ball stage (250° F), on a candy thermometer, about 15 minutes. Reduce the heat to low, carefully remove the cinnamon and lime peel, add the pureed potatoes, and cook 6 to 8 minutes, stirring constantly, until the paste is thoroughly blended.

3. Remove from the heat, add the egg yolks, and mix well. Return to low heat for 2 to 3 minutes, stirring constantly. Remove from the heat, mix in the sherry, and allow the paste to cool at room temperature 10 to 15 minutes.

4. Transfer the mixture to a serving bowl or individual dessert dishes, cover, and refrigerate at least 2 hours. Sprinkle with cinnamon and serve cold.

MAKES 6 TO 8 SERVINGS

Mango con Crema Batida

MANGO FOOL

Hispanic markets sell canned mango *mermelada*, fruit puree in a heavy syrup, which I serve Cuban style, with a white cheese such as *queso blanco*, Gouda, or Edam. My husband's taste is more American, however, and for him I prepare a fruit "fool" with heavy whipped cream. When fresh mangoes are in season, I puree them with sugar and put together this mango fool that even my Cuban family adores.

This recipe can be prepared with fresh guavas, as well.

*2 large, ripe mangoes, peeled and
    cubed (see page 8)*
½ cup sugar or to taste

2 cups heavy cream
*Fresh berries and mint leaves for
    garnish*

1. In a blender or a food processor fitted with a steel blade, puree the mangoes. Transfer to a large bowl, mix in the sugar, and set aside.

2. In a large bowl, using an electric mixer, beat the cream to soft peaks. Fold the cream into the mango puree, pour into a deep bowl or individual dessert glasses, cover, and chill at least 2 hours, or until set. Garnish with the fresh berries of your choice.

MAKES 6 SERVINGS

Variation: To make this with canned mango (or guava) puree, use 1 cup mango to 2 cups unwhipped cream. You can vary the proportions somewhat, adding more fruit for a sweeter taste.

Dulce de Toronja

SWEETENED GRAPEFRUIT SHELLS

Grapefruits, sweet oranges, and sour oranges were abundant in Cuba, and sugar was our cheapest commodity, available everywhere to everyone. Thrifty farmers were able to consume even the rinds of the fruit by cooking them in a sweet sugar syrup and serving them as a confection. This peasant dessert has no class boundaries—it was enjoyed by farmer and landowner alike, and it graced our luncheon table at Majagua.

3 large, ripe grapefruits   *4 cups water*
2 cups sugar

1. Quarter and peel the grapefruits, removing as much of the bitter white pith as possible (save the pulp for another use). Place the shell quarters in cold salted water to cover for 24 hours, changing the water every 3 hours, to remove bitterness.

2. The next day, drain the shells and discard the soaking water. Place the shells in a large saucepan with fresh cold water to cover and bring to a boil over medium-high heat. Discard the water and repeat the procedure. Drain the shells and pat them dry with paper

towels to remove all the moisture. The shells are now ready to be cooked.

3. Place the shells in a large saucepan with the sugar and water. Cook over low heat, uncovered, until the shells are soft and transparent and the syrup has thickened, 1½ to 2 hours.

4. Allow the shells and syrup to cool at room temperature. Transfer to a large bowl and refrigerate, covered, until ready to serve. The shells are very sweet, so serve only one or two per person, accompanied by Edam or Gouda cheese.

MAKES 10 TO 12 SERVINGS

Platánitos Horneados

BANANA CRISP

Rosalie, our cook, often made this crisp dessert for us, but she never made it the same way twice. My recipe is more precise than hers, although it has changed over the years, benefiting especially from my step-daughter Nicole's additions. When she was a little girl, Nicole added the peanut-brittle topping, and lately she has sprinkled on some crumbled Hershey chocolate almond bars, too. I haven't tried the chocolate, but you are welcome to use it, or any other topping you desire.

6 medium-size, ripe bananas, peeled and cut ½-inch thick
¼ cup firmly packed brown sugar
1 tablespoon fresh lemon or lime juice

2 tablespoons light rum
½ teaspoon vanilla extract
¼ teaspoon freshly ground nutmeg
4 tablespoons (½ stick) salted butter

1¼ cup crumbled savoiardi
   (toasted ladyfingers) available
   at Hispanic markets, or
   amaretti (Italian cookies)

¼ cup finely ground walnuts
Crumbled peanut brittle to taste,
   optional

1. Lightly butter an 8-inch square Pyrex baking dish or mold that fits the bananas comfortably. In a large bowl, combine the bananas with the sugar, lemon juice, rum, vanilla, and nutmeg, toss to coat well, and transfer to the prepared baking dish. (You can prepare the recipe ahead up to this point, and refrigerate.)

2. Preheat the oven to 350° F. In a small saucepan over low heat, melt the butter, then remove from the heat and stir in the crumbled cookies and walnuts. Sprinkle the crumbs over the bananas and bake until golden brown, 20 to 25 minutes. If you add the peanut brittle, sprinkle it over the dish during the last 5 minutes of baking. Serve hot.

MAKES 6 SERVINGS

Frituras de Plátano

BANANA FRITTERS

Bananas were brought to our kitchen on large stems, just as they grew on the tree, and there were always more than we could eat. Rosalie, our cook, was able to rescue the last, overripe fruits from spoiling by transforming them into fritters perfumed with cinnamon and nutmeg and offering them to us with *mantecado*, sweet vanilla ice cream.

The batter must be made in advance. Then the fritters can be prepared in minutes, while coffee is brewing, and served steaming hot.

FOR THE BATTER:

1 cup all-purpose flour

1/2 teaspoon baking powder

1/2 teaspoon salt

2 tablespoons sugar

Few grindings of nutmeg

Pinch of ground cinnamon

2 large eggs, lightly beaten

1/2 cup milk

1 tablespoon butter, melted

1/2 teaspoon vanilla extract

FOR THE FRITTERS:

Vegetable or peanut oil for frying

4 medium-size, ripe bananas, or
   8 ladyfinger or Red Cuban

bananas, peeled and sliced
   1/2-inch thick (see page 5)

Confectioners' sugar for dusting

1. At least an hour in advance of serving, combine the dry ingredients in a large bowl, then whisk together with the eggs, milk, butter, and vanilla. Allow the batter to rest 1 hour at room temperature.

2. In a large frying pan over medium heat, heat 1 inch of oil to 375° F, or until a drop of batter sizzles immediately when it touches the oil. Dip the banana slices into the batter, coating them well, and cook until golden brown, turning with a slotted spoon. Cook only 5 to 6 slices at a time, so the oil does not cool. Drain the fritters on paper towels, transfer them to a platter, dust with confectioners' sugar, and serve hot.

MAKES 6 TO 8 SERVINGS

Titi's Cake de Naranja

TITI'S ORANGE CAKE

My Aunt Titi is justly proud of the special cake that bears her name. Flavored with fresh orange juice and grated orange peel, it is frosted with a light, fluffy, lime-and-orange butter cream.

FOR THE CAKE:

3 large eggs

12 tablespoons (1½ sticks) salted butter, at room temperature

1½ cups sugar

1 teaspoon grated orange peel

3 cups all-purpose flour

2½ teaspoons baking powder

½ teaspoon salt

¼ teaspoon baking soda

1 cup fresh orange juice

FOR THE FROSTING AND FILLING:

¼ pound (1 stick) salted butter, at room temperature

1 tablespoon grated orange peel

3 cups confectioners' sugar

1 large egg yolk, optional

½ cup fresh orange juice

1 teaspoon fresh lime juice

1 large strawberry and drained, canned mandarin orange sections for decorating the cake

1. Preheat the oven to 350° F. To prepare the cake, using an electric mixer, beat the eggs at high speed 5 minutes in a small bowl and set aside. In a large bowl, using an electric mixer, cream the butter, then gradually add the sugar and orange peel. Add the eggs, beat 2 minutes to combine well, and add the dry ingredients, alternating with the orange juice, until smooth and well blended.

2. Pour the batter into two buttered 9-inch round cake pans and bake until a cake tester inserted in the cake comes out dry, about 35 minutes. Allow to cool at room temperature, then remove the pans.

3. To prepare the frosting, using an electric mixer, cream the butter, then add the orange peel, a small amount of the sugar, and the egg yolk, and continue beating. Add the remaining sugar, al-

ternating with the orange and lime juices, until the frosting is a spreading consistency.

4. When the layers are cool, place one layer on a serving plate and gently spread about a third of the frosting over it. Cover it with the second layer, and frost the sides and top with the remaining frosting. Center the strawberry, and outline the cake with the mandarin orange sections. Refrigerate until ready to serve.

MAKES 8 TO 10 SERVINGS

Torticas de Morón

CUBAN COOKIES

Morón is a town in the province of Camagüey, famous for originating these tasty morsels. At La Majagua tobacco ranch, there were always jarfuls, made according to the recipe of my great aunt, Tia Luisa, whose grandfather founded the ranch.

1 cup sugar	*1½ teaspoons grated lime peel*
1 cup vegetable shortening	*1 teaspoon salt*
4 cups all-purpose flour	*1 teaspoon baking powder*

1. In a large bowl, mix the sugar and shortening thoroughly, using a wooden spoon. Gradually add the remaining ingredients, blending with your hands. Form the dough into a roll about 2 inches in diameter, wrap in plastic wrap, and chill for 1 hour.

2. Preheat the oven to 350° F. With a sharp knife, cut the dough into ¼-inch slices and place them on a nonstick or a lightly buttered regular cookie sheet. With your finger, make a small depression in the center of each cookie, and bake until lightly browned, 20 to 25 minutes. Store in a tightly covered tin. The cookies will keep for one week.

MAKES ABOUT 48 COOKIES

Masa Real de Guayaba

GUAVA TART

This luscious tropical tart is much easier to prepare than anyone would think because it is based on two Cuban shortcuts. First, the super easy pastry requires no chilling or rolling — simply mix it with your hands and place it in the baking pan. Second, the filling consists of slices of guava loaf, a delicious fruit confection available in Hispanic markets. Combine the two, bake, and you have an easy, impressive dessert.

¾ cup vegetable shortening
4 tablespoons (½ stick) salted butter
2 cups all-purpose flour
1 cup sugar
3 large eggs

1 large egg yolk
3 teaspoons baking powder
1 teaspoon salt
3 tablespoons dry sherry
1½ pounds guava paste, cut into ¼-inch slices (see note below)

1. Preheat the oven to 350° F. In a medium-size saucepan over medium heat, melt the shortening and butter together.

2. In a large bowl, combine the remaining ingredients, except the sherry and guava paste. Add the shortening and butter and, using your hands, mix well. Add the sherry and mix until well blended.

3. Divide the dough into 2 equal parts, and place one in a 9 × 12-inch baking pan, patting down evenly to form a bottom crust. Cover with the guava slices, and place the remaining dough on top, patting down evenly to form a top crust. Bake until lightly browned, 40 minutes, allow to cool at room temperature, and cut into 2-inch squares.

MAKES 12 SERVINGS

Note: Guava paste is available in 13-, 16-, and 18-ounce loaves at Hispanic grocery stores.

The Hotel Nacional, designed by McKim, Meade, and White. Reprinted with permission of the Richter Library of the University of Miami.

An American in Havana: Drinks

Havana was a true evening city, radiant, luminous, and mysterious. As dusk arrived, the bright signs on the Malecon lit up, and the larger-than-life neon woman, poised on a rooftop platform in her neon Jantzen bathing suit, dived down the side of a skyscraper. Multicolored stars popped from a huge neon Philco television set, shooting over the dark evening skyline like fireworks. The scene was magical.

The tourists' Havana was a city of pleasure, with a balmy sensuality that affected visitors and natives alike. In the grand hotels like the Nacional, designed by McKim, Meade, and White, every whim was catered to. At the Tropicana nightclub designed by Max Borges Recio, people dined and danced outdoors under the stars and palm trees in the Salon Bajo las Estrellas, while indoors, they dined in Los Arcos de Cristal, an arched salon with walls of glass panels. The Montmartre, an amusing nightclub, was a replica of the Moulin Rouge in Paris. Elegant casinos (under dubious management) lured the high rollers of the international set who gambled until dawn.

Exotic tropical drinks were a part of the tourists' fantasy of Havana, promising glamour and fun. Although some drinks were given American names, like the "Miami Beach" and the "Floridita Bronx," the cocktails enjoyed at bars like Sloppy Joe's and Floridita were typically Cuban, based on rum, sugar, and Caribbean fruits. They may seem overly sweet to our sophisticated tastes, but they were a true reflection of the sweet life that lured so many travelers to Cuba.

My father-in-law, Milton Randelman, had real-estate interests in Cuba, and during the 1940s and 1950s, he and his family often traveled to Havana from New York or Miami, sometimes flying down for the weekend on a moment's notice to see friends or attend a party. On these visits, my mother-in-law, Roslyn, spent time with a group of Cuban women, and although she spoke no Spanish and they spoke no English, they laughed and gestured and had lots of fun. They began the day at the dressmaker, being fitted for beaded dresses (which American women brought back home by the dozens) and then proceeded to the country club for lunch. The evenings were spent at formal dinners in friends' homes, where the hostess often had her private rumba teacher available to teach guests the latest steps.

The women, dressed in long gowns, and the men in tuxedos then moyed on to nightclubs like the Tropicana, where they danced under the stars and watched performers in ruffled midriffs and colorful rumba skirts shake and sway to wild tropical drumbeats. After the last daiquiri was consumed, they moved to the gambling casinos, then to the Riviera, and finally to a small gambling club that was owned by George Raft.

The following morning they recuperated around the pool at the Hotel Nacional, mingling with celebrities and planning their next activities. In my mother-in-law's words: "Once you landed in Havana it was as if a magic spell fell over you. You got silly—it was wonderful and glamorous and fun, like being in Paris. Life consisted of good friends, good food, and glorious weather."

Cocktail hour at Sloppy Joe's. The beautiful lady in white is my mother-in-law.

SLOPPY JOE'S

I never set foot inside Sloppy Joe's bar, made famous by Ernest Hemingway, but my husband went there as a young boy, accompanying his parents. Hal thought it an exotic and grown-up place, as he sat beside his mother at the long, dark mahogany bar and sampled her sweet tropical drink. Large ceiling fans turned slowly overhead, the aroma of Cuban cigars filled the air, and the phonograph blared the Andrews Sisters' "Rum and Coca-Cola." Shelf upon shelf of champagne bottles stored behind the bar awaited regulars and tourists alike, all prepared to celebrate in grand island style.

A young Hal Randelman, my husband, with his mother and a friend at Sloppy Joe's.

LA FLORIDITA

La Floridita, the bar nestled at the foot of the walled city of Old Havana, was another of Ernest Hemingway's haunts, one with a long history. About 1918, according to a Havana newspaper account, it was known as La Piña de Plata—the Silver Pine—and by the 1930s it had become a popular stop for foreign visitors and upper-middle-class Cubans. In the 1930s young Hemingway lived and wrote in the Hotel Ambos Mundos, only eight blocks from La Floridita, and he often spent his evenings at this neighborhood bar, drinking and talking with other Americans.

Hemingway's affection for the Floridita continued all his life, and many years later, when he was living on La Finca Vigia, an estate about fifteen miles outside Havana, he still socialized there. In her autobiography, *Slim: Memories of a Rich and Imperfect Life,* Lady Slim Keith calls La Floridita "the world's greatest bar." She tells of having dinner there with Papa and his wife Mary and enthusiastically downing "Papa Dobles," Hemingway's sugarless version of the daiquiri. These giant drinks were made only of rum and freshly squeezed lime juice, whirled in an electric blender and served in huge glasses.

The daiquiri, a frothy concoction of Cuban rum, fresh lime juice, and sugar, is not Cuba's only contribution to the cocktail hour, but it surely is the most famous. Variations abound—many people take credit for perfecting this essentially simple drink, and many more for inventing it. I especially like the apocryphal story about its creation I found in an old Havana newspaper.

According to this account, early in the history of La Floridita, a young black man entered the bar bringing a bottle of rum. The proprietors insisted that the man leave, because he was carrying in liquor that they, as an ale-house, did not sell, but the patrons insisted that he be allowed to stay and to keep his bottle. In a gesture of appreciation, he introduced them to a special drink. Requesting a lime and some sugar from the waiter, he emptied his bottle of rum into a pitcher, squeezed in the lime's juice, and followed it with the sugar. He added ice cubes, stirred the potion, and served drinks all around. "What do you call this drink?" he was asked. "Call it whatever you like," he shrugged. "I just invented it this minute."

The cover of the Floridita bar book.

Now the story gets even more muddled than the drink. The lime-and-rum concoction was not named that evening, but it soon grew very popular. One night a passerby asked the elderly black gentleman who sold newspapers outside the bar if "that drink" was served inside. Using a phrase once common among African slaves, the old man replied, *"Ah, ∂a kirie"*—simply, "Yes, sir." And so, as an afterthought, the daiquiri was christened.

CUBAN COCKTAILS

I was most fortunate to find a buried treasure at the University of Miami Special Collections: a copy of the Floridita bar's book of recipes. La Floridita was the most famous bar in Cuba and its recipe book captures the style of a vanished time. Most of the drinks in this chapter are drawn from this valuable source, as well as from *La Enciclopedia de Cuba,* and *Cuban Cookery,* a 1950s book by Blanche Z. de Baralt, all part of the Special Collections. The books call for Bacardi rum and use the old classifications, like Carta Oro and Carta Blanca. Rum labeling has changed since these books were written, but I have followed the intent of the recipes, using modern rum classifications. Each recipe will specify light rum, which is clear in color and aged one year; dark rum, which is amber in color and aged up to two years; or añejo, which is dark amber and blended from spirits aged from one to six years.

DAIQUIRI — FLORIDITA SPECIAL

2 ounces rum
1 tablespoon sugar
1 teaspoon grapefruit juice

Juice of ½ lime
1 teaspoon maraschino liqueur
½ cup crushed ice

In a blender or food processor, blend all the ingredients 10 to 20 seconds, and serve in a chilled cocktail glass.

MAKES 1 DRINK

Daiquiri de Embajador D'Arce

AMBASSADOR D'ARCE'S DAIQUIRI

My friend Aurora Lopez-Muñoz, now of Madrid, lived in Havana in the 1950s when her father, Dr. D'Arce, was the Cuban ambassador to Spain. Following his recipe, she makes the world's best daiquiris.

2 ounces Bacardi light rum
1 ounce fresh lime juice
1 teaspoon sugar

½ cup crushed ice
Lime slice for garnish

In a blender or food processor, blend all ingredients (except the garnish) until frosty. Pour into a chilled cocktail glass, and garnish with the lime slice.

MAKES 1 DRINK

Daiquiri de Abuelo Mas

DR. MAS'S DAIQUIRI

At Las Cañas, my grandfather's orange groves, daiquiris were spiked with orange liqueur made from his home-grown fruit.

2 ounces Bacardi light rum
1 tablespoon orange liqueur
2 tablespoons fresh lime juice

½ cup crushed ice
Lime slice for garnish

In a blender or food processor, blend all the ingredients (except the garnish) 10 to 20 seconds. Pour into a chilled cocktail glass, and garnish with the lime slice.

MAKES 1 DRINK

ERNEST HEMINGWAY SPECIAL

This is yet another spin on a daiquiri recipe, memorialized in *La Enciclopedia de Cuba*.

2 ounces light rum
1 teaspoon grapefruit juice
1 teaspoon maraschino liqueur

Juice of 1/2 lime
1/2 cup crushed ice

In a blender or food processor, mix all the ingredients 30 seconds, and pour into a chilled cocktail glass.

MAKES 1 DRINK

FLORIDITA SPECIAL

1 ounce rye
1 1/2 ounces red vermouth
1 1/2 teaspoons curaçao
1/2 tablespoon sugar

Dash of Angostura bitters
One-inch strip lemon peel,
  without the white pith
1/2 cup crushed ice

In a cocktail shaker, mix all the ingredients and shake vigorously 10 seconds. Strain into a chilled cocktail glass.

MAKES 1 DRINK

FLORIDITA BRONX

1 ounce white vermouth
1 ounce red vermouth
1 ounce gin
½ teaspoon curaçao

½ cup crushed ice
Twist of lemon peel for garnish
Maraschino cherry for garnish

Combine all the ingredients in a cocktail shaker and stir to blend (do not shake). Strain into a chilled cocktail glass and garnish with the lemon peel and cherry.

MAKES 1 DRINK

MIAMI BEACH

2 ounces pineapple juice
2 ounces gin

1 teaspoon sugar
½ cup crushed ice

Pour all the ingredients into a cocktail shaker, shake vigorously 10 seconds, and strain into a chilled cocktail glass.

MAKES 1 DRINK

HAVANA BEACH

2 ounces pineapple juice
2 ounces Bacardi light rum

1 teaspoon sugar
½ cup crushed ice

Pour all the ingredients into a cocktail shaker, shake vigorously 10 seconds, and strain into a chilled cocktail glass.

MAKES 1 DRINK

Mojito

In Cuban street slang, *mojo* means "soul"; *mojito* is the diminutive.

2 ice cubes
Juice of 1 lime
2 drops Angostura bitters
2 ounces Bacardi light rum

Splash of sparkling mineral
  water
1 fresh mint leaf for garnish

Place the ice in a chilled cocktail glass, add the remaining ingredients, except the mint leaf, stir, and garnish with the mint leaf.

MAKES 1 DRINK

Mojito "Criollo"

Several sprigs fresh mint
Peel of 1 small lemon, without
  the white pith
Juice of 1 small lime

1 teaspoon sugar
½ cup crushed ice
2 ounces Bacardi light rum
Sparkling mineral water to taste

In a mortar, crush the mint leaves. Combine the leaves and the remaining ingredients, except the mineral water, in a cocktail shaker, stir well to release the mint aroma, pour without straining into a tall glass, and top with sparkling mineral water.

MAKES 1 DRINK

Variation: *Mojito 2*, "a favorite of Americans," according to La Floridita's recipe book, substitutes gin for the rum.

Fuego Liquido

LIQUID FIRE

1 teaspoon sugar
1 ounce pineapple juice
Juice of 1 lime
1½ ounces Bacardi dark rum

½ cup crushed ice
Splash of beer
Pineapple slice and lime wedge
   for garnish

Pour the sugar, pineapple juice, lime juice, rum, and crushed ice into a cocktail shaker, shake vigorously for 10 seconds, pour into a cocktail glass, top with a splash of beer, and garnish with the pineapple and lime.

MAKES 1 DRINK

Monjita

THE NUN

2 ounces Anis del Mono, or other
   anisette

3 ounces sparkling mineral water
½ cup crushed ice

In a cocktail shaker, combine all the ingredients, shake vigorously for 10 seconds, and pour into a chilled 10-ounce glass.

MAKES 1 DRINK

CHIC

2 tablespoons grapefruit juice
1 ounce red vermouth
1 ounce gin

1 teaspoon sugar
½ cup crushed ice

Pour all the ingredients into a cocktail shaker, shake vigorously for 10 seconds, and strain into a chilled cocktail glass.

MAKES 1 DRINK

PRESIDENTE MENOCAL SPECIAL

Crushed ice
2 sprigs fresh mint, crushed
2 ounces Bacardi light rum

1 teaspoon sugar
1 teaspoon fresh lime juice
1 fresh mint leaf for garnish

Fill a 6- to 8-ounce glass with crushed ice, add the remaining ingredients except the garnish, and stir. Garnish with a mint leaf.

MAKES 1 DRINK

Tigre Volador

FLYING TIGER

1 ounce Bacardi dark rum
1 ounce gin
1 teaspoon grapefruit juice

1 teaspoon grenadine
Juice of ½ lemon
1 teaspoon apricot brandy

Pour all the ingredients into a cocktail shaker, shake several times to mix well, and strain into a chilled cocktail glass over ice cubes.

MAKES 1 DRINK

Bacardi Centenario
BACARDI CENTENARIAN

1 ounce Bacardi light rum
1 ounce Bacardi Añejo
1 teaspoon curaçao
1 teaspoon sugar

1 teaspoon grapefruit juice
Juice of ½ lime
½ cup crushed ice

In a blender or food processor, mix all the ingredients for 30 seconds, and serve in a chilled cocktail glass.

MAKES 1 DRINK

HAVANA YACHT CLUB COCKTAIL

2 ounces Bacardi dark rum
1 ounce sweet vermouth

Dash of apricot brandy
½ cup crushed ice

In a cocktail shaker, shake all the ingredients vigorously for 10 seconds, and pour into a chilled cocktail glass.

MAKES 1 DRINK

HAVANA COOLER

Several sprigs fresh mint, crushed   *Ice cubes*
2 ounces Bacardi dark rum   *Ginger ale to taste*

Place the mint leaves and rum in a tall glass, add the ice cubes, and top off with ginger ale.

MAKES 1 DRINK

Bul

The recipe for this thirst-quenching drink was given to me by my godmother, Rosita Arocha-Ferran. Her family served it on hot evenings at their summer house in beautiful Varadaro.

Two 12-ounce bottles beer   *2 cups crushed ice*
½ cup sugar   *Lime slices for garnish*
Juice of 4 limes

In a small pitcher, mix all the ingredients, except the garnish, together well. Serve in chilled tall glasses garnished with the lime slices.

MAKES 4 DRINKS

Cocktail del Country Club

COUNTRY CLUB COCKTAIL

El Country was an affluent suburb of Havana, and its neighborhood club was El Country Club. Generic as the name may sound, it was one of the best clubs in Havana, and this was its house drink.

2 ounces gin
1 ounce sweet vermouth
1/4 teaspoon orange liqueur

Dash of Angostura bitters
1/4 teaspoon sugar
1/2 cup crushed ice

In a cocktail shaker, vigorously shake all the ingredients for 10 seconds, and pour into a chilled cocktail glass.

MAKES 1 DRINK

Batido de Plátano y Ron

BANANA AND RUM MILKSHAKE

This exciting frappe was my first encounter with an alcoholic beverage. As Sara Brown said to Sky Masterson when she tasted a sweet rum cocktail in a Havana café: "You know—this would be a wonderful way to get children to drink milk."

1 small banana
1 cup vanilla ice cream, softened

4 ounces Bacardi Añejo
1/4 cup milk

In a blender or food processor, blend all the ingredients for 30 seconds, and pour into two tall chilled glasses.

MAKES 2 DRINKS

Flamingo Rosado

PINK FLAMINGO

When our youngest brother, Cali, got married, my brother Tony and I wanted to make a special cocktail to suit the ambience of his beautiful garden wedding. We decided to use the juice of the succulent guava, one of the most glorious fruits of the Caribbean, and, of course, champagne. After much measuring and tasting, we got the proportions right for this lovely pink drink.

4 ounces Goya guava nectar　　*Ice cubes*
Split (7 ounces) dry champagne　*Thin slices of lime for garnish*
Splash of fresh lime juice

Combine the nectar, champagne, and lime juice, pour into two tall glasses over ice, and garnish with the lime slices.

MAKES 2 DRINKS

Puesta del Sol

HAVANA SUNSET

Tropical fruit juices make refreshing drinks that evoke memories of Cuba. Experimenting with my favorites, I came up with this tangy vodka cocktail.

2 to 3 drops grenadine
1 ounce Goya guava nectar
3 ounces pineapple juice

2 ounces vodka
½ cup ice cubes
Lime slice for garnish

In a blender or food processor, blend all the ingredients (except garnish) for 10 to 20 seconds, pour into a chilled cocktail glass, and garnish with the lime slice.

MAKES 1 DRINK

Naranjada

NONALCOHOLIC ORANGE COCKTAIL

Luis, my grandfather's chef, made this drink for the children whenever we visited Las Canas orange groves. It resembles the commercial drinks Orangina and Aranciata, but it is homemade and, therefore, I like to think it is better.

Juice of 4 oranges
¼ cup sugar

1½ cups sparkling mineral water
2 cups crushed ice

Pour the juice into a 2-quart pitcher. Add the sugar and stir to mix well. Add the mineral water and crushed ice and stir to combine. Serve immediately.

MAKES 4 DRINKS

Index

Photographs on pages 13, 70, 196, 280, 283, 286, 308, and 314 are reprinted
with the permission of the University of Miami Library, Archives and Special
Collections Department.

The recipe for Cuban Bread, on page 44, is reprinted from *Beard on Bread* by
James Beard, copyright © 1973, with the permission of Alfred A. Knopf, Inc.

The material in the Drinks chapter is reprinted by permission of the
University of Miami Library, Archives and Special Collections Department.

From La Floridita bar book: Floridita Special, Floridita Bronx, Miami
Beach, Havana Beach, *Monjita, Mojito "Criollo,"* The Nun, Chic, and Presidente
Menocal Special.

From *La Enciclopedia de Cuba:* Daiquiri—Floridita Special, Ernest Hemingway
Special, *Fuego Líquido, Mojito, Tigre Volador,* and *Bacardi Centenario.*

From *Cuban Cookery,* by Blanche Z. de Baralt: Havana Yacht Club Cocktail,
Havana Cooler.

Color photography credits: #1 *Platanote* ceramic dish by Carlos Alvez, from Second Hand
Rose; #2 Plantain chip bowl and yellow bowl from Zona; #3 Italian fireside bowl from Zona;
#5 Blue plate and Philippine coconut shell spoons from Zona; #7 Yellow dish from Zona;
#8 Three-tier fruit stand from Zona.
Food stylist: Rebecca Adams